THE DIFFICULTY OF TOLERANCE

T0328772

These essays in political philosophy by T. M. Scanlon, written between 1969 and 1999, examine the standards by which social and political institutions should be justified and appraised. Scanlon explains how the powers of just institutions are limited by rights such as freedom of expression, and considers why these limits should be respected even when it seems that better results could be achieved by violating them. Other topics which are explored include voluntariness and consent, freedom of expression, tolerance, punishment, and human rights. The collection includes the classic essays "Preference and Urgency," "A Theory of Freedom of Expression," and "Contractualism and Utilitarianism," as well as a number of other essays that have hitherto not been easily accessible. It will be essential reading for all those studying these topics from the perspective of political philosophy, politics, and law.

T. M. SCANLON is Alford Professor of Natural Religion, Moral Philosophy, and Civil Polity at Harvard University. He is the author of *What We Owe to Each Other* (Harvard University Press, 1998) and numerous articles on moral and political philosophy.

THE DIFFICULTY OF TOLERANCE

Essays in Political Philosophy

T. M. SCANLON

Harvard University

CAMBRIDGE
UNIVERSITY PRESS

CAMBRIDGE UNIVERSITY PRESS
Cambridge, New York, Melbourne, Madrid, Cape Town, Singapore, São Paulo, Delhi

Cambridge University Press
The Edinburgh Building, Cambridge CB2 8RU, UK

Published in the United States of America by Cambridge University Press, New York

www.cambridge.org
Information on this title: www.cambridge.org/9780521533980

First published 2003
Reprinted 2006

A catalogue record for this publication is available from the British Library

ISBN 978-0-521-82661-7 hardback
ISBN 978-0-521-53398-0 paperback

Transferred to digital printing 2009

For Lucy

Contents

Acknowledgments

I am grateful to Mary Sullivan for preparing the index. The many intellectual debts I acquired in the process of writing these essays are acknowledged in footnotes below. What is not mentioned there is my enormous debt to my wife Lucy for her understanding and support. This volume is dedicated to her.

The essays in this volume appeared in the following publications:

"A Theory of Freedom of Expression," *Philosophy and Public Affairs* 1, no. 2 (1972), 204–26.

"Rights, Goals, and Fairness," in Stuart Hampshire, ed., *Public and Private Morality* (Cambridge: Cambridge University Press, 1978), pp. 93–125.

"Due Process," in J. R. Pennock and J. W. Chapman, eds., *Nomos XVIII: Due Process* (New York: New York University Press, 1977), pp. 93–125.

"Preference and Urgency," *Journal of Philosophy* 72 (1975), 655–69.

"Freedom of Expression and Categories of Expression," *University of Pittsburgh Law Review* 40, no. 4 (1979), 519–50.

"Human Rights as a Neutral Concern," in Peter Brown and Douglas Maclean, eds., *Human Rights and U.S. Foreign Policy* (Lexington: Lexington Books, 1979), pp. 83–92.

"Contractualism and Utilitarianism," in Amartya Sen and Bernard Williams, eds., *Utilitarianism and Beyond* (Cambridge: Cambridge University Press, 1982), pp. 103–28.

"Content Regulation Reconsidered," in Judith Lichtenberg, ed., *Democracy and the Mass Media* (Cambridge: Cambridge University Press, 1990), pp. 331–54.

"Value, Desire, and Quality of Life," in Martha Nussbaum and Amartya Sen, eds., *The Quality of Life* (Oxford: Clarendon Press, 1993), pp. 185–207.

"The Difficulty of Tolerance," in David Heyd, ed., *Toleration: An Elusive Virtue* (Princeton: Princeton University Press, 1996), pp. 226–39.

"The Diversity of Objections to Inequality," The Lindley Lecture, University of Kansas, 1996.

"Punishment and the Rule of Law," in Harold Hongju Koh and Ronald Slye, eds., *Deliberative Democracy and Human Rights* (New Haven: Yale University Press, 1999), pp. 257–71.

"Promises and Contracts," in Peter Benson, ed., *The Theory of Contract Law* (Cambridge: Cambridge University Press, 2001), pp. 86–117.

Introduction

The essays collected here are concerned with the standards by which political, legal, and economic institutions should be assessed. One obvious standard is the degree to which these institutions promote human well-being. But it is also relevant to ask whether institutions are just and whether they respect the rights of individuals. The tension between these two forms of assessment is a central theme in these essays. In order to understand this tension, and decide how to respond to it, several things are required. The first is a better understanding of the idea of well-being and of the ways in which it comes to have moral significance. The second is a deeper understanding of notions such as rights, justice, liberty, and equality, which seem to be, at least potentially, in conflict with the goal of well-being. To what degree are these notions themselves best understood and justified in terms of well-being? Insofar as they are not to be understood in this way, how is their moral force to be explained? The following essays are devoted to these tasks. My aim is not to eliminate this tension – that would be impossible – but to make it less puzzling by placing the notions it involves within a common moral framework. In the case of rights, I believe that the tension is best understood not as arising between rights and well-being, seen as entirely independent and potentially conflicting moral ideas, but rather as a tension that arises within our understanding of rights themselves.

Freedom of expression provides a good example of this tension. The right of free expression would be easy to defend, but pointless, if it applied only to expression that has no serious consequences. It does its work, and our commitment to it is put to the test, by expression that threatens to cause serious harm by, for example, fomenting political unrest or by revealing information that is deemed crucial to national security. So some explanation needs to be given of how it can be wrong for governments to prevent these harms by barring the expression that will lead to them. In "A Theory of Freedom of Expression" (essay 1), I attempted to respond to this challenge. The central component of that article is what I called the

Millian Principle, which limits the consequences that can be appealed to in justifying governmental restrictions on expression. According to that principle, justifications for restricting a form of expression cannot not be based on the fact that, if unrestricted, it would lead people to form false beliefs, or on the harmful consequences of the actions that it would lead people to see as worth performing. I argued that citizens who view themselves as autonomous cannot not accept justifications that violate this principle.

After completing that article I intended to write a book on freedom of expression, and in 1975 I set to work on this project. My plan was to develop more fully the theory outlined in the article and then to discuss its implications for traditional issues of freedom of expression, such as the permissibility of laws against incitement, libel, and expression that threatens national security. I thought that this would not be difficult, but things did not work out as I had expected. The theory I had developed failed to give plausible answers in several of the cases I wanted to discuss. So, following the method of reflective equilibrium, I set out to revise the theory. But the changes required were fundamental. The problem was that the Millian Principle, the centerpiece of the theory, placed too tight a constraint on possible justifications for restricting expression.[1] Looking for a new foundation for my account, I began thinking about what it meant to say that freedom of expression was a right. This led me in turn to the more wide-ranging questions of how rights in general should be understood and how rights limit what can be done in the service of desirable goals.

Questions about rights were also on my mind for other reasons. Robert Nozick's *Anarchy, State, and Utopia* had just appeared and was the subject of much discussion, as was the work of Judith Thomson, in which rights also played a central role. I was attracted by the idea of rights as constraints on the pursuit of good consequences, although I disagreed somewhat with Thomson, and more strongly with Nozick, about what rights people have. I was also concerned with more general questions about rights, such as how we determine what rights people have and how claims about rights are to be justified. It seemed to me that rights must be justified by the interests they serve, but I was not sure in what way this is so. I was also being pressed in my seminars by Peter Railton and Samuel Scheffler, then graduate students at Princeton, who maintained that consequentialism provided the best account of the problems I was concerned with.

The result of this process of thought was "Rights, Goals, and Fairness" (essay 2), the central thesis of which is what I thought of at the time as an

---

[1] For a fuller discussion of the problem, see essay 5, section III.

"instrumental" account of rights. On this account, rights are constraints on the discretion of individuals or institutions to act, which are justified on the grounds that they are necessary and feasible means to prevent unacceptable results that would flow from unlimited discretion. With this view of rights in hand, I returned to the topic of freedom of expression in "Freedom of Expression and Categories of Expression" (essay 5) and, later, in "Content Regulation Reconsidered" (essay 8).

"The Difficulty of Tolerance" (essay 10) deals not only with expression, but also with other forms of activity that affect the nature of a society by influencing what others believe and how they act. This essay develops the idea of "informal politics" that is introduced in the latter parts of essay 5. More than most of the other essays on rights in this collection, "The Difficulty of Tolerance" is concerned with the costs of having certain rights generally recognized, and with the problems posed by their open-ended character. Its particular concern is with the risks involved in having one's society be always open to being altered by the activities of individuals and groups whose values one does not share. I argue that one must bear this risk as the price of recognizing one's fellow citizens as equal members of society – and thus equally entitled to play a role in determining how that society evolves.

The account of rights set forth in "Rights, Goals, and Fairness" also provides the framework for "Human Rights as a Neutral Concern" (essay 6). This account of rights still seems to me broadly correct, but I do not believe that it is as close to consequentialism as I suggested in "Rights, Goals, and Fairness." The fact that this account appeals to the protection of individual interests as a source of justification does not suffice to make it a consequentialist view, and I do not believe that the other values appealed to in that article, such as equality, are best understood as properties of states of affairs that are to be promoted.[2]

It now seems to me that the view of rights set forth in "Rights, Goals, and Fairness," rather than being consequentialist, in fact fits best within the contractualist moral theory I outlined later in "Contractualism and Utilitarianism" (essay 7), according to which the rightness of actions and policies depends on their justifiability to individuals rather than on the value of their consequences. On this view, defensible institutions must promote the well-being of their citizens in certain ways because this is something citizens can reasonably demand, not because doing so will yield a more valuable state of affairs. But direct promotion of their well-being is not the

---

[2] My views on equality are set out more fully in "The Diversity of Objections to Inequality" (essay 11).

only thing that individuals can reasonably demand from their institutions. They also have reason to insist on being treated fairly, and on basic rights, which give them important forms of protection and control over their own lives. Contractualism thus provides a common framework within which these diverse moral claims can be understood.

I am thus no longer inclined, as I once was, to describe my view of rights as an "instrumental" account. This label suggests that the benefits that are promoted by rights are morally fundamental, while the rights, the observance of which promotes these results, are of only derivative significance. It also may suggest that rights differ from duties and other moral requirements in having this derivative status. Both of these suggestions seem to me misleading. Claims about rights, like other claims about what we owe to each other, are claims about the constraints on individual action, and on social institutions, that people can reasonably insist on. In order to decide what rights people have, we need to consider both the costs of being constrained in certain ways and what things would be like in the absence of such constraints, and we need to ask what objections people could reasonably raise on either of these grounds. But the fact that claims about rights, like other moral claims, need to be justified in this way, does not make rights morally derivative, or mere instruments for the production of morally valuable states of affairs.

If claims about what individuals have reason to want are to play an important role in the justification of rights and of institutions, this raises the question of how such claims are themselves to be understood and defended. This question has seemed closely related to the problem of giving an account of well-being, since it is natural to suppose that what a person has a morally significant interest in are just those things that contribute importantly to his or her well-being. When I first began working in this area, preferences were widely thought to provide the answers to both of these questions. The most widely held views of individual well-being identified a person's level of well-being with the degree to which his or her preferences (or perhaps "informed" preferences) were fulfilled. Similarly, individual preferences (or perhaps informed preferences) were widely held to be the primary starting points for the justification of institutions and moral principles.

Both of these views seemed to me mistaken. I set out in "Preference and Urgency" (essay 4) to explain why, and to call attention to the problem of explaining the basis of morally significant claims about individual interests and well-being. I pursued these questions in a series of further articles, including "Value, Desire, and Quality of Life" (essay 9). As I indicate in that essay, it now seems to me that the task of giving an overall account of well-being and that of explaining the basis of morally significant interests are less closely related than I at first supposed.[3]

Consent is another idea that is often held to play a central role in the justification of institutions. Fundamental economic and political institutions cannot be justified simply on the ground that those to whom they apply have consented to their authority. Nonetheless, in order to be justifiable, institutions must give individuals the power to shape many of their particular obligations through the choices they make. The fact that an individual has chosen a certain outcome, or could have avoided it by choosing differently, is often an important reason why that outcome is legitimate. Essays 12 and 13 deal with different ways in which this is the case. In "Punishment and the Rule of Law" (essay 12) I take issue with an account according to which the legitimacy of punishment derives from the fact that the criminal, in breaking the law, has consented to the legal consequences of his doing so. I offer an alternative explanation of the way in which the justification of punishment depends on the fact that individuals can avoid punishment by choosing appropriately. In "Promises and Contracts" (essay 13) I offer a similar explanation of the role that the value of choice plays in the justification of the enforcement of legal contracts, and I raise some questions about appeals to the notion of voluntariness in this justification.

These essays were written over a thirty-year period, from the late 1960s to the late 1990s. They are printed here in the order in which they were written, and with only minor editorial changes. Rereading them, I find many points where much more needs to be said, and many where I would say something different if I were writing today. I expect that other readers will have similar reactions, and I hope this will inspire or provoke them to carry these inquiries further.

---

[3] My current view of these matters is set out in chapter 3 of *What We Owe to Each Other* (Cambridge, MA: Harvard University Press, 1998).

A theory of freedom of expression

Persecution for the expression of opinions seems to me perfectly logical. If you have no doubt of your premises or your power and want a certain result with all your heart you naturally express your wishes in law and sweep away all opposition. To allow opposition by speech seems to indicate that you think the speech impotent, as when a man says that he has squared the circle, or that you do not care wholeheartedly for the result, or that you doubt either your power or your premises. But...

Oliver Wendell Holmes[1]

I

The doctrine of freedom of expression is generally thought to single out a class of "protected acts" which it holds to be immune from restrictions to which other acts are subject. In particular, on any very strong version of the doctrine there will be cases where protected acts are held to be immune from restriction despite the fact that they have as consequences harms which would normally be sufficient to justify the imposition of legal sanctions. It is the existence of such cases which makes freedom of expression a significant doctrine and which makes it appear, from a certain point of view, an irrational one. This feeling of irrationality is vividly portrayed by Justice Holmes in the passage quoted.

To answer this charge of irrationality is the main task of a philosophical defense of freedom of expression. Such an answer requires, first, a clear account of what the class of protected acts is, and then an explanation of the nature and grounds of its privilege. The most common defense of the doctrine of freedom of expression is a consequentialist one. This

---

This paper is derived from one presented to the Society for Ethical and Legal Philosophy, and I am grateful to the members of that group, as well as to a number of other audiences willing and unwilling, for many helpful comments and criticisms.
[1] Dissenting in *Abrams* v. *United States*, 250 U.S. 616 (1919).

may take the form of arguing with respect to a certain class of acts, e.g. acts of speech, that the good consequences of allowing such acts to go unrestricted outweigh the bad. Alternatively, the boundaries of the class of protected acts may themselves be *defined* by balancing good consequences against bad, the question of whether a certain species of acts belongs to the privileged genus being decided in many if not all cases just by asking whether its inclusion would, on the whole, lead to more good consequences than bad. This seems to be the form of argument in a number of notable court cases, and at least some element of balancing seems to be involved in almost every landmark First Amendment decision.[2] Thus one thing which an adequate philosophical account of freedom of expression should do is to make clear in what way the definition of the class of protected acts and the justification for their privilege depend upon a balancing of competing goals or interests and to what extent they rest instead on rights or other absolute, i.e. nonconsequentialist, principles. In particular, one would like to know to what extent a defender of freedom of expression must rest his case on the claim that the long-term benefits of free discussion will outweigh certain obvious and possibly severe short-run costs, and to what extent this calculation of long-term advantage depends upon placing a high value on knowledge and intellectual pursuits as opposed to other values.

A further question that an adequate account of freedom of expression should answer is this: to what extent does the doctrine rest on natural moral principles and to what extent is it an artificial creation of particular political institutions? An account of freedom of expression might show the doctrine to be artificial in the sense I have in mind if, for example, it identified the class of protected acts simply as those acts recognized as legitimate forms of political activity under a certain constitution *and* gave as the defense of their privilege merely a defense of that constitution as reasonable, just, and binding on those to whom it applied. A slightly different "artificial" account of freedom of expression is given by Meiklejohn,[3] who finds the basis for the privileged status of acts of expression in the fact that the right to perform such acts is necessary if the citizens of a democratic state are to perform their duties as self-governing citizens. On his view it appears that citizens not expected to "govern themselves" would lack (at least one kind of) right to freedom of expression. In contrast to either of these views, Mill's famous

---

[2] The balancing involved in such decisions is not always strictly a matter of maximizing good consequences, since what is "balanced" often includes personal rights as well as individual and social goods. The problems involved in "balancing" rights in this way are forcefully presented by Ronald Dworkin in "Taking Rights Seriously," *New York Review of Books*, December 17, 1970, pp. 23–31.

[3] Alexander Meiklejohn, *Political Freedom*, 2nd edn. (New York: Harper & Row, 1965). See esp. p. 79.

argument offers a defense of "the liberty of thought and discussion" which relies only on general moral grounds and is independent of the features of any particular laws or institutions. It seems clear to me that our (or at least my) intuitions about freedom of expression involve both natural and artificial elements. An adequate account of the subject should make clear whether these two kinds of intuitions represent rival views of freedom of expression or whether they are compatible or complementary.

Although I will not consider each of these questions about freedom of expression in turn, I hope by the end of this discussion to have presented a theory which gives answers to all of them. I begin with an oblique attack on the first.

II

The only class of acts I have mentioned so far is the class "acts of expression," which I mean to include any act that is intended by its agent to communicate to one or more persons some proposition or attitude. This is an extremely broad class. In addition to many acts of speech and publication it includes displays of symbols, failures to display them, demonstrations, many musical performances, and some bombings, assassinations, and self-immolations. In order for any act to be classified as an act of expression it is sufficient that it be linked with some proposition or attitude which it is intended to convey.

Typically, the acts of expression with which a theory of "free speech" is concerned are addressed to a large (if not the widest possible) audience, and express propositions or attitudes thought to have a certain generality of interest. This accounts, I think, for our reluctance to regard as an act of expression in the relevant sense the communication between the average bank robber and the teller he confronts. This reluctance is diminished somewhat if the note the robber hands the teller contains, in addition to the usual threat, some political justification for his act and an exhortation to others to follow his example. What this addition does is to broaden the projected audience and increase the generality of the message's interest. The relevance of these features is certainly something which an adequate theory of freedom of expression should explain, but it will be simpler at present not to make them part of the definition of the class of acts of expression.

Almost everyone would agree, I think, that the acts which are protected by a doctrine of freedom of expression will all be acts of expression in the sense I have defined. However, since acts of expression can be both violent and arbitrarily destructive, it seems unlikely that anyone would maintain that as a class they were immune from legal restrictions. Thus the class of protected acts must be some proper subset of this class. It is sometimes held that the relevant subclass consists of those acts of expression which are instances of "speech" as opposed to "action." But those who put forward such a view have generally wanted to include within the class of protected acts some which are not speech in any normal sense of the word (for instance, mime and certain forms of printed communication) and to exclude from it some which clearly are speech in the normal sense (talking in libraries, falsely shouting "fire" in crowded theaters, etc.). Thus if acts of speech are the relevant subclass of acts of expression, then "speech" is here functioning as a term of art which needs to be defined. To construct a theory following these traditional lines we might proceed to work out a technical correlate to the distinction between speech and action which seemed to fit our clearest intuitions about which acts do and which do not qualify for protection.[4]

To proceed in this way seems to me, however, to be a serious mistake. It seems clear that the intuitions we appeal to in deciding whether a given restriction infringes freedom of expression are not intuitions about which things are properly called speech as opposed to action, even in some refined sense of "speech." The feeling that we must look for a definition of this kind has its roots, I think, in the view that since any adequate doctrine of freedom of expression must extend to some acts a privilege not enjoyed by all, such a doctrine must have its theoretical basis in some difference between the protected acts and others, i.e. in some definition of the protected class. But this is clearly wrong. It could be, and I think is, the case that the theoretical bases of the doctrine of freedom of expression are multiple and diverse, and while the net effect of these elements taken together is to extend to some acts a certain privileged status, there is no theoretically interesting (and certainly no simple and intuitive) definition of the class of acts which enjoys this privilege. Rather than trying at the outset to carve out the privileged subset of acts of expression, then, I propose to consider the class as a whole and to look for ways in which the charge of irrationality brought against the doctrine of freedom of expression might be answered without reference to a single class of privileged acts.

As I mentioned at the start, this charge arises from the fact that under any nontrivial form of the doctrine there will be cases in which acts of expression are held to be immune from legal restriction despite the fact

---

[4] This task is carried out by Thomas Emerson in *Toward a General Theory of the First Amendment* (New York: Random House, 1966). See esp. pp. 60–2.

that they give rise to undoubted harms which would in other cases be sufficient to justify such restriction. (The "legal restriction" involved here may take the form either of the imposition of criminal sanctions or of the general recognition by the courts of the right of persons affected by the acts to recover through civil suits for damages.) Now it is not in general sufficient justification for a legal restriction on a certain class of acts to show that certain harms will be prevented if this restriction is enforced. It might happen that the costs of enforcing the restriction outweigh the benefits to be gained, or that the enforcement of the restriction infringes some right either directly (e.g. a right to the unimpeded performance of exactly those acts to which the restriction applies) or indirectly (e.g. a right which under prevailing circumstances can be secured by many only through acts to which the restriction applies). Alternatively, it may be that while certain harms could be prevented by placing legal restrictions on a class of acts, those to whom the restriction would apply are not responsible for those harms and hence cannot be restricted in order to prevent them.

Most defenses of freedom of expression have rested upon arguments of the first two of these three forms. In arguments of both these forms factors which taken in isolation might have been sufficient to justify restrictions on a given class of acts are held in certain cases to be overridden by other considerations. As will become clear later, I think that appeals both to rights and to the balancing of competing goals are essential components of a complete theory of freedom of expression. But I want to begin by considering arguments which, like disclaimers of responsibility, have the effect of showing that what might at first seem to be reasons for restricting a class of acts cannot be taken as such reasons at all.

My main reason for beginning in this way is this: it is easier to say what the classic violations of freedom of expression have in common than it is to define the class of acts which is protected by that doctrine. What distinguishes these violations from innocent regulation of expression is not the character of the acts they interfere with but rather what they hope to achieve – for instance, the halting of the spread of heretical notions. This suggests that an important component of our intuitions about freedom of expression has to do not with the illegitimacy of certain restrictions but with the illegitimacy of certain justifications for restrictions. Very crudely, the intuition seems to be something like this: those justifications are illegitimate which appeal to the fact that it would be a bad thing if the view communicated by certain acts of expression were to become generally believed; justifications which are legitimate, though they may sometimes be overridden, are those that appeal to features of acts of expression (time, place, loudness) other than the views they communicate.

As a principle of freedom of expression this is obviously unsatisfactory as it stands. For one thing, it rests on a rather unclear notion of "the view communicated" by an act of expression; for another, it seems too restrictive, since, for example, it appears to rule out any justification for laws against defamation. In order to improve upon this crude formulation, I want to consider a number of different ways in which acts of expression can bring about harms, concentrating on cases where these harms clearly can be counted as reasons for restricting the acts that give rise to them. I will then try to formulate the principle in a way which accommodates these cases. I emphasize at the outset that I am not maintaining in any of these cases that the harms in question are always sufficient justification for restrictions on expression, but only that they can always be taken into account.

1. Like other acts, acts of expression can bring about injury or damage as a direct physical consequence. This is obviously true of the more bizarre forms of expression mentioned above, but no less true of more pedestrian forms: the sound of my voice can break glass, wake the sleeping, trigger an avalanche, or keep you from paying attention to something else you would rather hear. It seems clear that when harms brought about in this way are intended by the person performing an act of expression, or when he is reckless or negligent with respect to their occurrence, then no infringement of freedom of expression is involved in considering them as possible grounds for criminal penalty or civil action.

2. It is typical of the harms just considered that their production is in general quite independent of the view which the given act of expression is intended to communicate. This is not generally true of a second class of harms, an example of which is provided by the common law notion of assault. In at least one of the recognized senses of the term, an assault (as distinct from a battery) is committed when one person intentionally places another in apprehension of imminent bodily harm. Since assault in this sense involves an element of successful communication, instances of assault may necessarily involve expression. But assaults and related acts can also be part of larger acts of expression, as for example when a guerrilla theater production takes the form of a mock bank robbery which starts off looking like the real thing, or when a bomb scare is used to gain attention for a political cause. Assault is sometimes treated as inchoate battery, but it can also be viewed as a separate offense which consists in actually bringing about a specific kind of harm. Under this analysis, assault is only one of a large class of possible crimes which consist in the production in others

of harmful or unpleasant states of mind, such as fear, shock, and perhaps certain kinds of offense. One may have doubts as to whether most of these harms are serious enough to be recognized by the law or whether standards of proof could be established for dealing with them in court. In principle, however, there seems to be no alternative to including them among the possible justifications for restrictions on expression.

3. Another way in which an act of expression can harm a person is by causing others to form an adverse opinion of him or by making him an object of public ridicule. Obvious examples of this are defamation and interference with the right to a fair trial.

4. As Justice Holmes said, "The most stringent protection of free speech would not protect a man in falsely shouting fire in a theater and causing a panic."[5]

5. One person may through an act of expression contribute to the production of a harmful act by someone else, and at least in some cases the harmful consequences of the latter act may justify making the former a crime as well. This seems to many people to be the case when the act of expression is the issuance of an order or the making of a threat or when it is a signal or other communication between confederates.

6. Suppose some misanthropic inventor were to discover a simple method whereby anyone could make nerve gas in his kitchen out of gasoline, table salt, and urine. It seems just as clear to me that he could be prohibited by law from passing out his recipe on handbills or broadcasting it on television as that he could be prohibited from passing out free samples of his product in aerosol cans or putting it on sale at Abercrombie & Fitch. In either case his action would bring about a drastic decrease in the general level of personal safety by radically increasing the capacity of most citizens to inflict harm on each other. The fact that he does this in one case through an act of expression and in the other through some other form of action seems to me not to matter.

It might happen, however, that a comparable decrease in the general level of personal safety could be just as reliably predicted to result from the distribution of a particularly effective piece of political propaganda which would undermine the authority of the government, or from the publication of a theological tract which would lead to a schism and a bloody civil war. In these cases the matter seems to me to be entirely different, and the harmful consequence seems clearly not to be a justification for restricting the acts of expression.

[5] In *Schenck v. United States*, 249 U.S. 47 (1919).

What I conclude from this is that the distinction between expression and other forms of action is less important than the distinction between expression which moves others to act by pointing out what they take to be good reasons for action and expression which gives rise to action by others in other ways, e.g. by providing them with the means to do what they wanted to do anyway. This conclusion is supported, I think, by our normal views about legal responsibility.

If I were to say to you, an adult in full possession of your faculties, "What you ought to do is rob a bank," and you were subsequently to act on this advice, I could not be held legally responsible for your act, nor could my act legitimately be made a separate crime. This remains true if I supplement my advice with a battery of arguments about why banks should be robbed or even about why a certain bank in particular should be robbed and why you in particular are entitled to rob it. It might become false – what I did might legitimately be made a crime – if certain further conditions held: for example, if you were a child, or so weak-minded as to be legally incompetent, and I knew this or ought to have known it; or if you were my subordinate in some organization and what I said to you was not advice but an order, backed by the discipline of the group; or if I went on to make further contributions to your act, such as aiding you in preparations or providing you with tools or giving you crucial information about the bank.

The explanation for these differences seems to me to be this. A person who acts on reasons he has acquired from another's act of expression acts on what *he* has come to believe and has judged to be a sufficient basis for action. The contribution to the genesis of his action made by the act of expression is, so to speak, superseded by the agent's own judgment. This is not true of the contribution made by an accomplice, or by a person who knowingly provides the agent with tools (the key to the bank) or with technical information (the combination of the safe) which he uses to achieve his ends. Nor would it be true of my contribution to your act if, instead of providing you with reasons for thinking bank robbery a good thing, I issued orders or commands backed by threats, thus changing your circumstances so as to *make* it a (comparatively) good thing for you to do.

It is a difficult matter to say exactly when legal liability arises in these cases, and I am not here offering any positive thesis about what constitutes being an accessory, inciting, conspiring, etc. I am interested only in maintaining the negative thesis that whatever these crimes involve, it has to be something more than merely the communication of persuasive reasons for action (or perhaps some special circumstances, such as diminished capacity of the person persuaded).

I will now state the principle of freedom of expression which was promised at the beginning of this section. The principle, which seems to me to be a natural extension of the thesis Mill defends in chapter 2 of *On Liberty*, and which I will therefore call the Millian Principle, is the following:

There are certain harms which, although they would not occur but for certain acts of expression, nonetheless cannot be taken as part of a justification for legal restrictions on these acts. These harms are: (a) harms to certain individuals which consist in their coming to have false beliefs as a result of those acts of expression; (b) harmful consequences of acts performed as a result of those acts of expression, where the connection between the acts of expression and the subsequent harmful acts consists merely in the fact that the act of expression led the agents to believe (or increased their tendency to believe) these acts to be worth performing.

I hope it is obvious that this principle is compatible with the examples of acceptable reasons for restricting expression presented in 1 through 6 above. (One case in which this may not be obvious, that of the man who falsely shouts "fire," will be discussed more fully below.) The preceding discussion, which appealed in part to intuitions about legal responsibility, was intended to make plausible the distinction on which the second part of the Millian Principle rests and, in general, to suggest how the principle could be reconciled with cases of the sort included in 5 and 6. But the principle itself goes beyond questions of responsibility. In order for a class of harms to provide a justification for restricting a person's act it is not necessary that he fulfill conditions for being legally responsible for any of the individual acts which actually produce those harms. In the nerve-gas case, for example, to claim that distribution of the recipe may be prevented one need not claim that a person who distributed it could be held legally responsible (even as an accessory) for any of the particular murders the gas is used to commit. Consequently, to explain why this case differs from sedition it would not be sufficient to claim that providing means involves responsibility while providing reasons does not.

I would like to believe that the general observance of the Millian Principle by governments would, in the long run, have more good consequences than bad. But my defense of the principle does not rest on this optimistic outlook. I will argue in the next section that the Millian Principle, as a general principle about how governmental restrictions on the liberty of citizens may be justified, is a consequence of the view, coming down to us from Kant and others, that a legitimate government is one whose authority citizens can recognize while still regarding themselves as equal, autonomous, rational agents. Thus, while it is not a principle about legal responsibility, the Millian Principle has its origins in a certain view of human agency from which many of our ideas about responsibility also derive.

Taken by itself, the Millian Principle obviously does not constitute an adequate theory of freedom of expression. Much more needs to be said about when the kinds of harmful consequences which the principle allows us to consider can be taken to be sufficient justification for restrictions on expression. Nonetheless, it seems to me fair to call the Millian Principle the basic principle of freedom of expression. This is so, first, because a successful defense of the principle would provide us with an answer to the charge of irrationality by explaining why certain of the most obvious consequences of acts of expression cannot be appealed to as a justification for legal restrictions against them. Second, the Millian Principle is the only plausible principle of freedom of expression I can think of which applies to expression in general and makes no appeal to special rights (e.g. political rights) or to the value to be attached to expression in some particular domain (e.g. artistic expression or the discussion of scientific ideas). It thus specifies what is special about acts of expression as opposed to other acts and constitutes in this sense the usable residue of the distinction between speech and action.

I will have more to say in section IV about how the Millian Principle is to be supplemented to obtain a full account of freedom of expression. Before that, however, I want to consider in more detail how the principle can be justified.

III

As I have already mentioned, I will defend the Millian Principle by showing it to be a consequence of the view that the powers of a state are limited to those that citizens could recognize while still regarding themselves as equal, autonomous, rational agents. Since the sense of autonomy to which I will appeal is extremely weak, this seems to me to constitute a strong defense of the Millian Principle as an exceptionless restriction on governmental authority. I will consider briefly in section V, however, whether there are situations in which the principle should be suspended.

To regard himself as autonomous in the sense I have in mind a person must see himself as sovereign in deciding what to believe and in weighing competing reasons for action. He must apply to these tasks his own canons of rationality, and must recognize the need to defend his beliefs and decisions in accordance with these canons. This does not mean, of course, that he must be perfectly rational, even by his own standard of rationality, or that his standard of rationality must be exactly ours. Obviously the content of this notion of autonomy will vary according to the range of variation we are willing to allow in canons of rational decision. If just anything counts as such a canon then the requirements I have mentioned will become mere tautologies: an autonomous man believes what he believes and decides to do what he decides to do. I am sure I could not describe a set of limits on what can count as canons of rationality which would secure general agreement, and I will not try, since I am sure that the area of agreement on this question extends far beyond anything which will be relevant to the applications of the notion of autonomy that I intend to make. For present purposes what will be important is this. An autonomous person cannot accept without independent consideration the judgment of others as to what he should believe or what he should do. He may rely on the judgment of others, but when he does so he must be prepared to advance independent reasons for thinking their judgment likely to be correct, and to weigh the evidential value of their opinion against contrary evidence.

The requirements of autonomy as I have so far described them are extremely weak. They are much weaker than the requirements Kant draws from essentially the same notion,[6] in that being autonomous in my sense (like being free in Hobbes's) is quite consistent with being subject to coercion with respect to one's actions. A coercer merely changes the considerations which militate for or against a certain course of action; weighing these conflicting considerations is still up to you.

An autonomous man may, if he believes the appropriate arguments, believe that the state has a distinctive right to command him. That is, he may believe that (within certain limits, perhaps) the fact that the law requires a certain action provides him with a very strong reason for performing that action, a reason which is quite independent of the consequences, for him or others, of his performing it or refraining. How strong this reason is – what, if anything, could override it – will depend on his view of the arguments for obedience to law. What is essential to the person's remaining autonomous is that in any given case his mere recognition that a certain action is required by law does not settle the question of whether he will do it. That question is settled only by his own decision, which may take into account his current

---

[6] Kant's notion of autonomy goes beyond the one I employ in that for him there are special requirements regarding the reasons which an autonomous being can act on. (See the second and third sections of *Foundations of the Metaphysics of Morals*.) While his notion of autonomy is stronger than mine, Kant does not draw from it the same limitations on the authority of states (see *Metaphysical Elements of Justice*, sections 46–9).

assessment of the general case for obedience and the exceptions it admits, consideration of his other duties and obligations, and his estimate of the consequences of obedience and disobedience in this particular case.[7]

Thus, while it is not obviously inconsistent with being autonomous to recognize a special obligation to obey the commands of the state, there are limits on the *kind* of obligation which autonomous citizens could recognize. In particular, they could not regard themselves as being under an "obligation" to believe the decrees of the state to be correct, nor could they concede to the state the right to have its decrees obeyed without deliberation. The Millian Principle can be seen as a refinement of these limitations.

The apparent irrationality of the doctrine of freedom of expression derives from its apparent conflict with the principle that it is the prerogative of a state – indeed, part of its duty to its citizens – to decide when the threat of certain harms is great enough to warrant legal action, and when it is, to make laws adequate to meet this threat. (Thus Holmes's famous reference to "substantive evils that Congress has a right to prevent.")[8] Obviously this principle is not acceptable in the crude form in which I have just stated it; no one thinks that Congress can do *anything* it judges to be required to save us from "substantive evils." The Millian Principle specifies two ways in which this prerogative must be limited if the state is to be acceptable to autonomous subjects. The argument for the first part of the principle is as follows.

The harm of coming to have false beliefs is not one that an autonomous man could allow the state to protect him against through restrictions on expression. For a law to provide such protection it would have to be in effect and deterring potential misleaders while the potentially misled remained susceptible to persuasion by them. In order to be protected by such a law a person would thus have to concede to the state the right to decide that certain views were false and, once it had so decided, to prevent him from hearing them advocated even if he might wish to. The conflict between doing this and remaining autonomous would be direct if a person who authorized the state to protect him in this way necessarily also bound himself to accept the state's judgment about which views were false. The matter is not quite this simple, however, since it is conceivable that a person

---

[7] I am not certain whether I am here agreeing or disagreeing with Robert Paul Wolff (*In Defense of Anarchism* [New York: Harper & Row, 1970]). At any rate I would not call what I am maintaining anarchism. The limitation on state power I have in mind is that described by John Rawls in the closing paragraphs of "The Justification of Civil Disobedience," in Hugo Bedau, ed., *Civil Disobedience: Theory and Practice* (New York: Pegasus Books, 1969).

[8] In *Schenck* v. *United States*.

might authorize the state to act for him in this way while still reserving to himself the prerogative of deciding, on the basis of the arguments and evidence left available to him, where the truth was to be found. But such a person would be "deciding for himself" only in an empty sense, since in any case where the state exercised its prerogative he would be "deciding" on the basis of evidence preselected to include only that which supported one conclusion. While he would not be under an obligation to accept the state's judgment as correct, he would have conceded to the state the right to deprive him of grounds for making an independent judgment.

The argument for the second half of the Millian Principle is parallel to this one. What must be argued against is the view that the state, once it has declared certain conduct to be illegal, may when necessary move to prevent that conduct by outlawing its advocacy. The conflict between this thesis and the autonomy of citizens is, just as in the previous case, slightly oblique. Conceding to the state the right to use this means to secure compliance with its laws does not immediately involve conceding to it the right to require citizens to believe that what the law says ought not to be done ought not to be done. Nonetheless, it is a concession that autonomous citizens could not make, since it gives the state the right to deprive citizens of the grounds for arriving at an independent judgment as to whether the law should be obeyed.

These arguments both depend on the thesis that to defend a certain belief as reasonable a person must be prepared to defend the grounds of his belief as not obviously skewed or otherwise suspect. There is a clear parallel between this thesis and Mill's famous argument that if we are interested in having truth prevail we should allow all available arguments to be heard.[9] But the present argument does not depend, as Mill's may appear to, on an empirical claim that the truth is in fact more likely to win out if free discussion is allowed. Nor does it depend on the perhaps more plausible claim that, given the nature of people and governments, to concede to governments the power in question would be an outstandingly poor strategy for bringing about a situation in which true opinions prevail.

It is quite conceivable that a person who recognized in himself a fatal weakness for certain kinds of bad arguments might conclude that everyone would be better off if he were to rely entirely on the judgment of his friends in certain crucial matters. Acting on this conclusion, he might enter into an agreement, subject to periodic review by him, empowering them to shield him from any sources of information likely to divert him from their counsel

---

[9] In chapter 2 of *On Liberty*.

on the matters in question. Such an agreement is not obviously irrational, nor, if it is entered into voluntarily, for a limited time, and on the basis of the person's own knowledge of himself and those he proposes to trust, does it appear to be inconsistent with his autonomy. The same would be true if the proposed trustees were in fact the authorities of the state. But the question we have been considering is quite different: could an autonomous individual regard the state as having, not as part of a special voluntary agreement with him but as part of its normal powers qua state, the power to put such an arrangement into effect without his consent whenever *it* (i.e. the legislative authority) judged that to be advisable? The answer to this question seems to me to be quite clearly no.

Someone might object to this answer on the following grounds. I have allowed for the possibility that an autonomous man might accept a general argument to the effect that the fact that the state commands a certain thing is in and of itself a reason why that thing should be done. Why couldn't he also accept a similar argument to the effect that the state qua state is in the best position to decide when certain counsel is best ignored?

I have already argued that the parallel suggested here between the state's right to command action and a right to restrict expression does not hold. But there is a further problem with this objection. What saves temporary, voluntary arrangements of the kind considered above from being obvious violations of autonomy is the fact that they can be based on a firsthand estimation of the relative reliability of the trustee's judgment and that of the "patient." Thus the person whose information is restricted by such an arrangement has what he judges to be good grounds for thinking the evidence he does receive to be a sound basis for judgment. A principle which provided a corresponding basis for relying on the state qua state would have to be extremely general, applying to all states of a certain kind, regardless of who occupied positions of authority in them, and to all citizens of such states. Such a principle would have to be one which admitted variation in individual cases and rested its claim on what worked out best "in the long run." Even if some generalization of this kind were true, it seems to me altogether implausible to suppose that it could be rational to rely on such a general principle when detailed knowledge of the individuals involved in a particular case suggested a contrary conclusion.

A more limited case for allowing states the power in question might rest not on particular virtues of governments but on the recognized fact that under certain circumstances individuals are quite incapable of acting rationally. Something like this may seem to apply in the case of the man who falsely shouts "fire" in a crowded theater. Here a restriction on expression is justified by the fact that such acts would lead others (give them reason) to perform harmful actions. Part of what makes the restriction acceptable is the idea that the persons in the theater who react to the shout are under conditions that diminish their capacity for rational deliberation. This case strikes us as a trivial one. What makes it trivial is, first, the fact that only in a very farfetched sense is a person who is prevented from hearing the false shout under such circumstances prevented from making up his own mind about some question. Second, the diminished capacity attributed to those in the theater is extremely brief, and applies equally to anyone under the relevant conditions. Third, the harm to be prevented by the restriction is not subject to any doubt or controversy, even by those who are temporarily "deluded." In view of all of these facts, the restriction is undoubtedly one which would receive unanimous consent if that were asked.[10]

This is not true, however, of most of the other exceptions to the Millian Principle that might be justified by appeal to "diminished rationality." It is doubtful, for example, whether any of the three conditions I have mentioned would apply to a case in which political debate was to be suspended during a period of turmoil and impending revolution. I cannot see how nontrivial cases of this kind could be made compatible with autonomy.

The arguments I have given may sound like familiar arguments against paternalism, but the issue involved is not simply that. First, a restriction on expression justified on grounds contrary to the Millian Principle is not necessarily paternalistic, since those who are to be protected by such a restriction may be other than those (the speaker and his audience) whose liberty is restricted. When such a restriction is paternalistic, however, it represents a particularly strong form of paternalism, and the arguments I have given are arguments against paternalism only in this strong form. It is quite consistent with a person's autonomy, in the limited sense I have employed, for the law to restrict his freedom of action "for his own good," for instance by requiring him to wear a helmet while riding his motorcycle. The conflict arises only if compliance with this law is then promoted by forbidding, for example, expression of the view that wearing a helmet isn't worth it, or is only for sissies.

It is important to see that the argument for the Millian Principle rests on a limitation of the authority of states to command their subjects rather than on a right of individuals. For one thing, this explains why this particular principle of freedom of expression applies to governments rather than to

---

[10] This test is developed as a criterion for justifiable paternalism by Gerald Dworkin in his essay "Paternalism," in Richard Wasserstrom, ed., *Morality and the Law* (Belmont, CA: Wadsworth, 1971).

individuals, who do not have such authority to begin with. There are surely cases in which individuals have the right not to have their acts of expression interfered with by other individuals, but these rights presumably flow from a general right to be free from arbitrary interference, together with considerations which make certain kinds of expression particularly important forms of activity.

If the argument for the Millian Principle were thought to rest on a right, "the right of citizens to make up their own minds," then that argument might be thought to proceed as follows. Persons who see themselves as autonomous see themselves as having a right to make up their own minds, hence also a right to whatever is necessary for them to do this; what is wrong with violations of the Millian Principle is that they infringe this right.

A right of this kind would certainly support a healthy doctrine of freedom of expression, but it is not required for one. The argument given above was much more limited. Its aim was to establish that the authority of governments to restrict the liberty of citizens in order to prevent certain harms does not include authority to prevent these harms by controlling people's sources of information to insure that they will maintain certain beliefs. It is a long step from this conclusion to a right which is violated whenever someone is deprived of information necessary for him to make an informed decision on some matter that concerns him.

There are clearly cases in which individuals have a right to the information necessary to make informed choices and can claim this right against the government. This is true in the case of political decisions, for example, when the right flows from a certain conception of the relation between a democratic government and its citizens. Even where there is no such right, the provision of information and other conditions for the exercise of autonomy is an important task for states to pursue. But these matters take us beyond the Millian Principle.

IV

The Millian Principle is obviously incapable of accounting for all of the cases that strike us as infringements of freedom of expression. On the basis of this principle alone we could raise no objection against a government that banned all parades or demonstrations (they interfere with traffic), outlawed posters and handbills (too messy), banned public meetings of more than ten people (likely to be unruly), and restricted newspaper publication to one page per week (to save trees). Yet such policies surely strike us as intolerable. That they so strike us is a reflection of our belief that free expression is a good which ranks above the maintenance of absolute peace and quiet, clean streets, smoothly flowing traffic, and rock-bottom taxes.

Thus there is a part of our intuitive view of freedom of expression which rests upon a balancing of competing goods. By contrast with the Millian Principle, which provides a single defense for all kinds of expression, here it does not seem to be a matter of the value to be placed on expression (in general) as opposed to other goods. The case seems to be different for, say, artistic expression than for the discussion of scientific matters, and different still for expression of political views.

Within certain limits, it seems clear that the value to be placed on having various kinds of expression flourish is something which should be subject to popular will in the society in question. The limits I have in mind here are, first, those imposed by considerations of distributive justice. Access to means of expression for whatever purposes one may have in mind is a good which can be fairly or unfairly distributed among the members of a society, and many cases which strike us as violations of freedom of expression are in fact instances of distributive injustice. This would be true of a case where, in an economically inegalitarian society, access to the principal means of expression was controlled by the government and auctioned off by it to the highest bidders, as is essentially the case with broadcasting licenses in the United States today. The same might be said of a parade ordinance which allowed the town council to forbid parades by unpopular groups because they were too expensive to police.

But to call either of these cases instances of unjust distribution tells only part of the story. Access to means of expression is in many cases a necessary condition for participation in the political process of the country, and therefore something to which citizens have an independent right. At the very least the recognition of such rights will require governments to insure that means of expression are readily available through which individuals and small groups can make their views on political issues known, and to insure that the principal means of expression in the society do not fall under the control of any particular segment of the community. But exactly what rights of access to means of expression follow in this way from political rights will depend to some extent on the political institutions in question. Political participation may take different forms under different institutions, even under equally just institutions.

The theory of freedom of expression which I am offering, then, consists of at least four distinguishable elements. It is based upon the Millian Principle, which is absolute but serves only to rule out certain justifications for legal restrictions on acts of expression. Within the limits set by this principle the whole range of governmental policies affecting opportunities for expression, whether by restriction, positive intervention, or failure to intervene, are subject to justification and criticism on a number of diverse grounds. First, on grounds of whether they reflect an appropriate balancing of the value of certain kinds of expression relative to other social goods; second, whether they insure equitable distribution of access to means of expression throughout the society; and third, whether they are compatible with the recognition of certain special rights, particularly political rights.

This mixed theory is somewhat cumbersome, but the various parts seem to me both mutually irreducible and essential if we are to account for the full range of cases which seem intuitively to constitute violations of "free speech."

V

The failure of the Millian Principle to allow certain kinds of exceptions may seem to many the most implausible feature of the theory I have offered. In addition to the possibility mentioned earlier, that exceptions should be allowed in cases of diminished rationality, there may seem to be an obvious case for allowing deviations from the principle in time of war or other grave emergency.

It should be noticed that because the Millian Principle is much narrower than, say, a blanket protection of "speech," the theory I have offered can already accommodate some of the restrictions on expression which wartime conditions may be thought to justify. The Millian Principle allows one, even in normal times, to consider whether the publication of certain information might present serious hazards to public safety by giving people the capacity to inflict certain harms. It seems likely that risks of this kind which are worth taking in time of peace in order to allow full discussion of, say, certain scientific questions, might be intolerable in wartime.

But the kind of emergency powers that governments feel entitled to invoke often go beyond this and include, for example, the power to cut off political debate when such debate threatens to divide the country or otherwise to undermine its capacity to meet a present threat. The obvious justification for such powers is clearly disallowed by the Millian Principle, and the theory I have offered provides for no exceptions of this kind.

It is hard for me at the present moment to conceive of a case in which I would think the invocation of such powers by a government right. I am willing to admit that there might be such cases, but even if there are I do not think that they should be seen as "exceptions" to be incorporated within the Millian Principle.

That principle, it will be recalled, does not rest on a right of citizens but rather expresses a limitation on the authority governments can be supposed to have. The authority in question here is that provided by a particular kind of political theory, one which has its starting point in the question: how could citizens recognize a right of governments to command them while still regarding themselves as equal, autonomous, rational agents? The theory is normally thought to yield the answer that this is possible if, but only if, that right is limited in certain ways, and if certain other conditions, supposed to insure citizen control over government, are fulfilled. I have argued that one of the necessary limitations is expressed by the Millian Principle. If I am right, then the claim of a government to rule by virtue of this particular kind of authority is undermined, I think completely, if it undertakes to control its citizens in the ways that the Millian Principle is intended to exclude.

This does not mean, however, that it could not in an extreme case be right for certain people, who normally exercised the kind of authority held to be legitimate by democratic political theory, to take measures which this authority does not justify. These actions would have to be justified on some other ground (e.g. utilitarian), and the claim of their agents to be obeyed would not be that of a legitimate government in the usual (democratic) sense. Nonetheless most citizens might, under the circumstances, have good reason to obey.

There are a number of different justifications for the exercise of coercive authority. In a situation of extreme peril to a group, those in the group who are in a position to avert disaster by exercising a certain kind of control over the others may be justified in using force to do so, and there may be good reason for their commands to be obeyed. But this kind of authority differs both in justification and extent from that which, if democratic political theory is correct, a legitimate democratic government enjoys. What I am suggesting is that if there are situations in which a general suspension of civil liberties is justified – and, I repeat, it is not clear to me that there are such – these situations constitute a shift from one kind of authority to another. The people involved will probably continue to wear the same hats, but this does not mean that they still rule with the same title.

It should not be thought that I am here giving governments license to kick over the traces of constitutional rule whenever this is required by the "national interest." It would take a situation of near catastrophe to justify a move of the kind I have described, and if governments know what they are doing it would take such a situation to make a move of this sort inviting. For a great deal is given up in such a move, including any notion that the commands of government have a claim to be obeyed which goes beyond the relative advantages of obedience and disobedience.

When the situation is grave and the price of disorder enormous, such utilitarian considerations may give the government's commands very real binding force. But continuing rule on this basis would be acceptable only for a society in permanent crisis or for a group of people who, because they could see each other only as obedient servants or as threatening foes, could not be ruled on any other.

2

Rights, goals, and fairness

Critics of utilitarianism frequently call attention to the abhorrent policies that unrestricted aggregative reasoning might justify under certain possible, or even actual, circumstances. They invite the conclusion that to do justice to the firm intuition that such horrors are clearly unjustifiable one must adopt a deontological moral framework that places limits on what appeals to maximum aggregate well-being can justify. As one who has often argued in this way, however, I am compelled to recognize that this position has its own weaknesses. In attacking utilitarianism one is inclined to appeal to individual rights, which mere considerations of social utility cannot justify us in overriding. But rights themselves need to be justified somehow, and how other than by appeal to the human interests their recognition promotes and protects? This seems to be the uncontrovertible insight of the classical utilitarians. Further, unless rights are to be taken as defined by rather implausible rigid formulae, it seems that we must invoke what looks very much like the consideration of consequences in order to determine what they rule out and what they allow. Thus, for example, in order to determine whether a given policy violates the right of freedom of expression it is not enough to know merely that it restricts speech. We may need to consider also its effects: how it would affect access to the means of expression and what the consequences would be of granting to government the kind of regulatory powers it confers.

I am thus drawn toward a two-tier view: one that gives an important role to consequences in the justification and interpretation of rights but which takes rights seriously as placing limits on consequentialist reasoning

The original version of this paper was presented at the Reisensberg Conference on Decision Theory and Social Ethics and appeared in an issue of *Erkenntnis* devoted to papers from that conference. This revised version is used with the permission of the editors of that journal and D. Reidel & Co. I am indebted to a number of people for critical comments and helpful discussion, particularly to Ronald Dworkin, Derek Parfit, Gilbert Harman, Samuel Scheffler, and Milton Wachsberg. Work on this paper was supported in part by a fellowship from the National Endowment for the Humanities.

at the level of casuistry. Such a view looks like what has been called rule utilitarianism, a theory subject to a number of very serious objections. First, rule utilitarians are hard pressed to explain why, if at base they are convinced utilitarians, they are not thoroughgoing ones. How can they square their utilitarianism with the acceptance of individual actions that are not in accord with the utilitarian formula? Second, rule utilitarianism seems to be open to some of the same objections leveled against utilitarianism in its pure form; in particular it seems no more able than act utilitarianism is to give a satisfactory place to considerations of distributive justice. Third, in attempting to specify which rules it is that are to be applied in the appraisal of acts and policies, rule utilitarians of the usual sort are faced with an acute dilemma. If it is some set of ideal rules that are to be applied – those rules general conformity to which would have the best consequences – then the utilitarian case for a concern with rules, rather than merely with the consequences of isolated acts, appears lost. For this case must rest on benefits that flow from the general observance of rules but not from each individual act, and such benefits can be gained only if the rules are in fact generally observed. But if, on the other hand, the rules that are to be applied must be ones that are generally observed, the critical force of the theory seems to be greatly weakened.

The problem, then, is to explain how a theory can have, at least in part, a two-tier structure; how it can retain the basic appeal of utilitarianism, at least as it applies to the foundation of rights, and yet avoid the problems that have plagued traditional rule utilitarianism. As a start towards describing such a theory I will consider three questions. (1) What consequences are to be considered, and how is their value to be determined? (2) How do considerations of distributive justice enter the theory? (3) How does one justify taking rights (or various moral rules) as constraints on the production of valued consequences?

I. CONSEQUENCES AND THEIR VALUES

Here I have two remarks, one of foundation, the other of content. First, as I have argued elsewhere[1] but can here only assert, I depart from the classical utilitarians and many of their modern followers in rejecting subjective preferences as the basis for the valuation of outcomes. This role is to be played instead by an ethically significant, objective notion of the relative importance of various benefits and burdens.

---

[1] In "Preference and Urgency" (1975), in this volume, essay 4, pp. 70–83.

Second, as to content, the benefits and burdens with which the theory is concerned must include not only the things that may happen to people but also factors affecting the ability of individuals to determine what will happen. Some of these factors are the concern of what are generally called rights, commonly[2] distinguished into (claim-)rights to command particular things, where others have a correlative duty to comply; liberties to do or refrain from certain things, where others have no such correlative duties; powers to change people's rights or status; and immunities from powers exercised by others. I take it to be the case that the familiar civil rights, as well as such things as rights of privacy and "the right to life," are complexes of such elements. The de facto ability effectively to choose among certain options and the de facto absence of interference by others with one's choices are not the same thing as rights, although if it is generally believed that a person has a particular right, say a claim-right, this may contribute to his having such de facto ability or lack of interference. But, however they are created, such abilities and protections are important goods with which any moral theory must be concerned, and the allocation of rights is one way in which this importance receives theoretical recognition.

Any theory of right, since it deals with what agents should and may do, is in a broad sense concerned with the assignment of rights and liberties. It is relevant to ask, concerning such a theory, how much latitude it gives a person in satisfying moral requirements and how much protection it gives a person through the constraints it places on the actions of others. Traditional utilitarianism has been seen as extreme on both these counts. It is maximally specific in the requirements it imposes on an agent, and, since there are no limits to what it may require to be done, it provides a minimum of reliable protection from interference by others. Objections to utilitarianism have often focused on its demanding and intrusive character,[3] and other theories of right may grant individuals both greater discretion and better protection. But these are goods with costs. When one individual is given a claim-right or liberty with respect to a certain option, the control that others are able to exercise over their own options is to some degree diminished. Further, if we take the assignment of rights to various individuals as, in at least

---

[2] Following Hohfeld and others. See W. N. Hohfeld, *Fundamental Legal Conceptions* (New Haven, 1923), and also Stig Kanger, "New Foundations for Ethical Theory," in Risto Hilpinen, ed., *Deontic Logic: Introductory and Systematic Readings* (Dordrecht, 1971), pp. 36–58. On the distinction between concern with outcomes and concern with the allocation of competences to determine outcomes see Charles Fried, "Two Concepts of Interests: Some Reflections on the Supreme Court's Balancing Test," *Harvard Law Review* 76 (1963), 755–78.

[3] See Bernard Williams, "A Critique of Utilitarianism," in J. J. C. Smart and B. Williams, *Utilitarianism: For and Against* (Cambridge, 1973).

some cases, an end-point of justification, then we must be prepared to accept the situation resulting from their exercise of these rights even if, considered in itself, it may be unattractive or at least not optimal. Both these points have been urged by Robert Nozick,[4] the latter especially in his attack on "end-state" and "patterned" theories. What follows from these observations, however, is not Nozick's particular theory of entitlements but rather a general moral about the kind of comparison and balancing that a justification of rights requires: the abilities and protections that rights confer must be assigned values that are comparable not only with competing values of the same kind but also with the values attached to the production of particular end-results.

The same moral is to be drawn from some of Bernard Williams's objections to utilitarianism.[5] Williams objects that utilitarianism, in demanding total devotion to the inclusive goal of maximum happiness, fails to give adequate recognition to the importance, for each individual, of the particular projects which give his life content. The problem with such an objection is that taken alone it may be made to sound like pure self-indulgence. Simply to demand freedom from moral requirements in the name of freedom to pursue one's individual projects is unconvincing. It neglects the fact that these requirements may protect interests of others that are at least as important as one's own. To rise clearly above the level of special pleading these objections must be made general. They must base themselves on a general claim about how important the interests they seek to protect are for any person as compared with the interests served by conflicting claims.

The two preceding remarks – of foundation and of content – are related in the following way. Since the ability to influence outcomes and protection from interference or control by others are things people care about, they will be taken into account in any subjective utilitarian theory. I will later raise doubts as to whether such a theory can take account of them in the right way, but my present concern is with the question what value is to be assigned to these concerns. On a subjective theory these values will be determined by the existing individual preferences in the society in question. I would maintain, however, that prevailing preferences are not an adequate basis for the justification of rights. It is not relevant, for example, to the determination of rights of religious freedom that the majority group in a society is feverishly committed to the goal of making its practices universal while the minority is quite tepid about all matters of religion.

---

[4] In *Anarchy, State and Utopia* (New York, 1974), esp. pp. 32–5 and ch. 7.
[5] In sec. 5 of "A Critique of Utilitarianism."

This is of course just an instance of the general objection to subjective theories stated above. The equally general response is that one has no basis on which to "impose" values that run contrary to individual preferences. This objection draws its force from the idea that individual autonomy ought to be respected and that it is offensive to frustrate an individual's considered preferences in the name of serving his "true interests." This idea does not itself rest on preferences. Rather, it functions as the objective moral basis for giving preferences a fundamental role as the ground of ethically relevant valuations. But one may question whether this theoretical move is an adequate response to the intuitive idea from which it springs. To be concerned with individual autonomy is to be concerned with the rights, liberties, and other conditions necessary for individuals to develop their own aims and interests and to make their preferences effective in shaping their own lives and contributing to the formation of social policy. Among these will be rights protecting people against various forms of paternalistic intervention. A theory that respects autonomy will be one that assigns all of these factors their proper weight. There is no reason to think that this will be accomplished merely by allowing these weights, and all others, to be determined by the existing configuration of preferences.

II. FAIRNESS AND EQUALITY

Rather than speaking generally of "distributive justice," which can encompass a great variety of considerations, I will speak instead of fairness, as a property of processes (e.g. of competitions), and equality, as a property of resultant distributions. The question is how these considerations enter a theory of the kind I am describing. One way in which a notion of equality can be built into a consequentialist theory is through the requirement that, in evaluating states of affairs to be promoted, we give equal consideration to the interests of every person. This principle of equal consideration of interests has minimal egalitarian content. As stated, it is compatible with classical utilitarianism which, after all, "counts each for one and none for more than one." Yet many have felt, with justification, that utilitarianism gives insufficient weight to distributive considerations. How might this weight be increased? Let me distinguish two ways. The first would be to strengthen the principle of equal consideration of interests in such a way as to make it incompatible with pure utilitarianism. "Equal consideration" could, for example, be held to mean that in any justification by appeal to consequences we must give priority to those individual interests that are "most urgent." To neglect such interests in order to serve instead less urgent interests even of a greater number of people would, on this interpretation, violate "equality of consideration." Adoption of this interpretation would ward off some objections to utilitarianism based on its insensitivity to distributive considerations but would at the same time preserve other characteristic features of the doctrine, e.g. some of its radically redistributive implications. Such a "lexical interpretation" has, of course, its own problems. Its strength (and plausibility) is obviously dependent on the ranking we choose for determining the urgency of various interests.

The nature of such a ranking is an important problem, but one I cannot pursue here. Whatever the degree of distributive content that is built into the way individual interests are reckoned in moral argument, however, there is a second way in which distributive considerations enter a theory of the kind I wish to propose: equality of distributions and fairness of processes are among the properties that make states of affairs worth promoting. Equality in the distribution of particular classes of goods is at least sometimes of value as a means to the attainment of other valued ends, and in other cases fairness and equality are valuable in their own right.

Classical utilitarianism, of course, already counts equality as a means, namely as a means to maximum aggregate utility. Taken alone, this seems inadequate – too instrumental to account for the moral importance equality has for us. Yet I do think that in many of the cases in which we are most concerned with the promotion of equality we desire greater equality as a means to the attainment of some further end. In many cases, for example, the desire to eliminate great inequalities is motivated primarily by humanitarian concern for the plight of those who have least. Redistribution is desirable in large part because it is a means of alleviating their suffering (without giving rise to comparable suffering elsewhere). A second source of moral concern with redistribution in the contemporary world lies in the fact that great inequalities in wealth give to those who have more an unacceptable degree of control over the lives of others. Here again the case for greater equality is instrumental. Were these two grounds for redistribution to be eliminated (by, say, greatly increasing the standard of living of all concerned and preventing the gap between rich and poor, which remains unchanged, from allowing the rich to dominate) the moral case for equality would not be eliminated, but I believe that it would seem less pressing.

Beyond these and other instrumental arguments, fairness and equality often figure in moral argument as independently valuable states of affairs. So considered, they differ from the ends promoted in standard utilitarian theories in that their value does not rest on their being good things *for* particular individuals: fairness and equality do not represent ways in which individuals may be *better off*.[6] They are, rather, special morally desirable features of states of affairs or of social institutions. In admitting such moral features into the evaluation of consequences, the theory I am describing departs from standard consequentialist theories, which generally resist the introduction of explicitly moral considerations into the maximand. It diverges also from recent deontological theories, which bring in fairness and equality as specific moral requirements rather than as moral goals. I am inclined to pursue this "third way" for several reasons.

First, it is not easy to come up with a moral argument for substantive equality (as distinct from mere formal equality or equal consideration of interests) which makes it look like an absolute moral requirement. Second, considerations of fairness and equality are multiple. There are many different processes that may be more or less fair, and we are concerned with equality in the distribution of many different and separable benefits and burdens. These are not all of equal importance; the strength of claims of equality and fairness depends on the goods whose distribution is at issue. Third, these claims do not seem to be absolute. Attempts to achieve equality or fairness in one area may conflict with the pursuit of these goals in other areas. In order to achieve greater equality we may, for example, change our processes in ways that involve unfairness in the handling of some individual cases. Perhaps the various forms of fairness and equality can be brought together under one all-encompassing notion of distributive justice which is always to be increased, but it is not obvious that this is so. In any event, it would remain the case that attempts to increase fairness and equality can have costs in other terms; they may interfere with processes whose efficiency is important to us, or involve unwelcome intrusions into individuals' lives. In such cases of conflict it does not seem that considerations of fairness and equality, as such, are always dominant. An increase in equality may in some cases not be worth its cost; whether it is will depend in part on what it is equality *of*.

Economists often speak of "trade-offs" between equality and other concerns (usually efficiency). I have in the past been inclined, perhaps intolerantly, to regard this as crassness, but I am no longer certain that it is in principle mistaken. The suggestion that equality can be "traded-off" against other goods arouses suspicion because it seems to pave the way for defenses of the status quo. Measures designed to decrease inequality in

---

[6] Here I am indebted to Kurt Baier. Defending the claim that fairness and equality are intrinsically valuable is of course a further difficult task. Perhaps all convincing appeals to these notions can be reduced to instrumental arguments, but I do not at present see how. Such a reduction would move my theory even closer to traditional utilitarianism.

present societies are often opposed on the ground that they involve too great a sacrifice in efficiency or in individual liberty, and one way to head off such objections is to hold that equality is to be pursued whatever the cost. But one can hold that appeals to liberty and efficiency do not justify maintaining the status quo – and in fact that considerations of individual liberty provide some of the strongest arguments in favor of increased equality of income and wealth – without holding that considerations of equality are, as such, absolute and take priority over all other values.

III. RIGHTS

Why give rights a special place in a basically consequentialist theory? How can a two-tier theory be justified? One common view of the place of rights, and moral rules generally, within utilitarianism holds that they are useful as means to the coordination of action. The need for such aids does not depend on imperfect motivation; it might exist even in a society of perfect altruists. A standard example is a rule regulating water consumption during a drought. A restriction to one bucket a day per household might be a useful norm for a society of utilitarians even though their reasons for taking more water than this would be entirely altruistic. Its usefulness does not depend on self-interest. But the value of such a rule does depend on the fact that the agents are assumed to act independently of one another in partial ignorance of what the others have done or will do. If Dudley knows what others will do, and knows that this will leave some water in the well, then there is no utilitarian reason why he should not violate the rule and take more than his share for some suitable purpose – as the story goes, to water the flowers in the public garden.

I am of two minds about such examples. On the one hand, I can feel the force of the utilitarian's insistence that if the water is not going to be used how can we object to Dudley's taking it? On the other hand, I do not find this line of reply wholly satisfying. Why should *he* be entitled to do what others were not? Well, because he knows and they didn't; he alone has the opportunity. But just because he has it, does that mean he can exercise it unilaterally? Perhaps, to be unbearably priggish, he should call the surplus to the attention of the others so that they can all decide how to use it. If this alternative is available is it all right for him to pass it up and act on his own? A utilitarian might respond here that he is not saying that Dudley is entitled to do whatever he wishes with the surplus water; he is entitled to do with it what the principle of utility requires and nothing else.

Here a difference of view is shown. Permission to act outside the rule is seen by the nonutilitarian as a kind of freedom for the agent, an exemption, but it is seen by a utilitarian as a specific moral requirement. Dudley is required to do something that is different from what the others do because his situation is different, but he has no greater latitude for the exercise of discretion or personal preference than anyone else does. This suggests that one can look at an assignment of rights in either of two ways: as a way of constraining individual decisions in order to promote some desired further effect (as in the case of a system of rules defining a division of labor between co-workers) or as a way of parceling out valued forms of discretion over which individuals are in conflict. To be avoided, I think, is a narrow utilitarianism that construes all rights on the first model, e.g. as mechanisms of coordination or as hedges against individual errors in judgment. So construed, rights have no weight against deviant actions that can be shown to be the most effective way of advancing the shared goal.

If, however, the possibility of construing some rights on the second model is kept open, then rights can be given a more substantial role within a theory that is still broadly utilitarian. When, as seems plausible on one view of the water-shortage example, the purpose of an assignment of rights is to ensure an equitable distribution of a form of control over outcomes, then these rights are supported by considerations which persist even when contrary actions would promote optimum results. This could remain true for a society of conscientious (though perhaps not single-minded) consequentialists, provided that they are concerned with "consequences" of the sort I have described above. But to say that a rule or a right is not in general subject to exceptions justified on act-utilitarian grounds is not to say that it is absolute. One can ask how important it is to preserve an equitable distribution of control of the kind in question, and there will undoubtedly be some things that outweigh this value. There is no point in observing the one-bucket restriction when the pump-house is on fire. Further, the intent of an assignment of rights on the second model is apt to be to forestall certain particularly tempting or likely patterns of behavior. If this is so, there may be some acts which are literally contrary to the formula in which the right is usually stated but which do not strike us as actual violations of the right. We are inclined to allow them even though the purposes they serve may be less important than the values the right is intended to secure. Restrictions on speech which nonetheless are not violations of freedom of expression are a good example of such "apparent exceptions."

Reflections of this kind suggest to me that the view that there is a moral right of a certain sort is generally backed by something like the following:

(i) An empirical claim about how individuals would behave or how institutions would work in the absence of this particular assignment of rights (claim-rights, liberties, etc.).

(ii) A claim that this result would be unacceptable. This claim will be based on valuation of consequences of the sort described in section I above, taking into account also considerations of fairness and equality.

(iii) A further empirical claim about how the envisaged assignment of rights will produce a different outcome.

The empirical parts of this schema play a larger or at least more conspicuous role in some rights than in others. In the case of the right to freedom of expression this role is a large one and fairly well recognized. Neglecting this empirical element leads rights to degenerate into implausible rigid formulae. The impossibility of taking such a formula literally, as defining an absolute moral bar, lends plausibility to a "balancing" view, according to which such a right merely represents one important value among others, and decisions must be reached by striking the proper balance between them. Keeping in mind the empirical basis of a right counters this tendency and provides a ground (1) for seeing that "apparent exceptions" of the kind mentioned above are not justified simply by balancing one right against another; (2) for seeing where genuine balancing of interests is called for and what its proper terms are; and (3) for seeing how the content of a right must change as conditions change. These remarks hold, I think, not only for freedom of expression but also for other rights, for example, rights of due process and rights of privacy. In each of these cases a fairly complex set of institutional arrangements and assumptions about how these arrangements operate stands, so to speak, between the formula through which the right is identified and the goals to which it is addressed. This dependence on empirical considerations is less evident in the case of rights, like the right to life, that lie more in the domain of individual morality. I will argue below, however, that this right too can profitably be seen as a system of authorizations and limitations of discretion justified on the basis of an argument of the form just described.

This view of rights is in a broad sense consequentialist in that it holds rights to be justified by appeal to the states of affairs they promote. It seems to differ from the usual forms of rule utilitarianism, however, in that it does not appear to be a maximizing doctrine. The case for most familiar rights – freedom of expression, due process, religious toleration – seems to be more concerned with the avoidance of particular bad consequences than with promoting maximum benefit. But this difference is in part only apparent. The dangers that these rights are supposed to ward off are major ones, not likely to be overshadowed by everyday considerations. Where they are overshadowed, the theory I have described allows for the rights in question to be set aside. Further, the justification for the particular form that such a right takes allows for the consideration of costs. If a revised form of some right would do the intended job as well as the standard form at clearly reduced costs to peripheral interests, then this form would obviously be preferred. It should be noted, however, that if something is being maximized here it cannot, in view of the role that the goals of fairness and equality play in the theory, be simply the sum of individual benefits. Moreover, this recognition of an element of maximization does not mean that just any possible improvement in the way people generally behave will become the subject of a right. Rights concern the alleviation of certain major problems, and incremental gains in other goods become relevant to rights in the way just mentioned only when they flow from improvements in our ways of dealing with such problems.

I have suggested that the case for rights derives in large part from the goal of promoting an acceptable distribution of control over important factors in our lives. This general goal is one that would be of importance to people in a wide range of societies. But the particular rights it calls for may vary from society to society. Thus, in particular, the rights we have on the view I have proposed are probably not identical with the rights that would be recognized under the system of rules, general conformity to which in our society would have the best consequences. The problems to which our rights are addressed are ones that arise given the distribution of power and the prevailing patterns of motivation in the societies in which we live. These problems may not be ones that would arise were an ideal code of behavior to prevail.[7] (And they might not be the same either as

---

[7] How much this separates my view of rights from an ideal rule-utilitarian theory will depend on how that theory construes the notion of an ideal system of rules being "in force" in a society. In Brandt's sophisticated version, for example, what is required is that it be true, and known in the society, that a high proportion of adults subscribe to these rules, that is, chiefly, that they are to some extent motivated to avoid violating the rules and feel guilty when they believe they have done so. ("Some Merits of One Form of Rule Utilitarianism," in Gorovitz, ed., *Mill: Utilitarianism, with Critical Essays* [Indianapolis, IN, 1971].) This may not ensure that the level of conformity with these rules is much greater than the level of moral behavior in societies we are familiar with. If it does not, then Brandt's theory may not be much more "ideal" than the theory of rights offered here. The two theories appear to differ, however, on the issues discussed in sections I and II above. These issues also divide my view from R. M. Hare's version of rule utilitarianism, with which I am otherwise in much agreement. See his "Ethical Theory and Utilitarianism," in H. D. Lewis, ed., *Contemporary British Philosophy, Fourth Series* (London, 1976). Like these more general theories, the account of rights offered here has a great deal in common with the view put forward by Mill in the final chapter of *Utilitarianism* (particularly if Mill's remarks about "justice" are set aside).

those we would face in a "state of nature.") Concern with rights does not involve accepting these background conditions as desirable or as morally unimpeachable; it only involves seeing them as relatively fixed features of the environment with which we must deal.

Which features of one's society are to be held fixed in this way for purposes of moral argument about rights? This can be a controversial moral question and presents a difficult theoretical issue for anyone holding a view like rule utilitarianism. As more and more is held fixed, including more about what other agents are in fact doing, the view converges toward act utilitarianism. If, on the other hand, very little is held fixed then the problems of ideal forms of rule utilitarianism seem to loom larger: we seem to risk demanding individual observance of rights when this is pointless given the lack of general conformity.

This dilemma is most acute to the degree that the case for rights (or moral rules) is seen to rest on their role in promoting maximum utility through the coordination of individual action. Where this is actually the case – as it is with many rules and perhaps some rights – it is of undoubted importance what others are in fact doing – to what degree these rights and rules are generally observed and how individual action will affect general observance. I suggest, however, that this is not the case with most rights. On the view I propose, a central concern of most rights is the promotion and maintenance of an acceptable distribution of control over important factors in our lives. Where a certain curtailment of individual discretion or official authority is clearly required for this purpose, the fact that this right is not generally observed does not undermine the case for its observance in a given instance. The case against allowing some to dictate the private religious observances of others, for example, does not depend on the existence of a general practice of religious toleration. Some of the benefits at which rights of religious freedom are aimed – the benefits of a general climate of religious toleration – are secured only when there is general compliance with these rights. But the case for enforcing these rights does not depend in every instance on these benefits.

For these reasons, the view of rights I have proposed is not prey to objections often raised against ideal rule-utilitarian theories. A further question is whether it is genuinely distinct from an act-consequentialist doctrine. It may seem that, for reasons given above, it cannot be: if an act in violation of a given right yields some consequence that is of greater value than those with which the right is concerned, then on my view the right is to be set aside. If the act does not have such consequences then, in virtue of its conflict with the right and the values that right protects, it seems that the act would not be justifiable on act-consequentialist grounds anyway. But this rests on a mistake. The values supporting a particular right need not all stand to be lost in every case in which the right is violated. In defending the claim that there is a right of a certain sort, e.g. a particular right of privacy, we must be prepared to compare the advantages of having this right – the advantages, e.g. of being free to decline to be searched – against competing considerations – e.g. the security benefits derived from a more lenient policy of search and seizure. But what stands to be gained or lost in any given instance in which a policeman would like to search me need not coincide with either of these values. It may be that in that particular case I don't care.[8]

There is, then, no incoherence in distinguishing between the value of having a right and the cost of having it violated on a particular occasion. And it is just the values of the former sort that we must appeal to in justifying a two-tier view. What more can be said about these values? From an act-consequentialist point of view the value attached to the kind of control and protection that rights confer seems to rest on mistrust of others. If everyone could be relied upon to do the correct thing from an act-consequentialist standpoint would we still be so concerned with rights? This way of putting the matter obscures several important elements. First, it supposes that we can all agree on the best thing to be done in each case. But concern with rights is based largely on the warranted supposition that we have significantly differing ideas of the good and that we are interested in the freedom to put our own conceptions into practice. Second, the objection assumes that we are concerned only with the correct choice being made and have no independent concern with who makes it. This also seems clearly false. The independent value we attach to being able to make our own choices should, however, be distinguished from the further value we may attach to having it recognized that we are *entitled* to make them. This we may also value in itself as a sign of respect and personhood, but there is a question to what degree this value is an artifact of our moral beliefs and customs rather than a basis for them. Where a moral framework of rights is established and recognized, it will be important for a person to have his status as a right holder generally acknowledged. But is there something analogous to this importance that is lost for everyone in a society of conscientious act consequentialists where no one holds rights? It is not clear to me that there is, but, however this may be, my account emphasizes

---

[8] On the importance of establishing the proper terms of balancing see Fried, "Two Concepts of Interests," p. 758.

the value attached to rights for the sake of what they may bring rather than their value as signs of respect.

If the factors just enumerated were the whole basis for concern with rights then one would expect the case for them to weaken and the force of act-consequentialist considerations to grow relatively stronger as (1) the importance attached to outcomes becomes absolutely greater and hence, presumably, also relatively greater as compared with the independent value of making choices oneself, and as (2) the assignment of values to the relevant outcomes becomes less controversial. To some extent both these things happen in cases where life and death are at stake, and here mistrust emerges as the more plausible basis for concern with rights.

IV. CASES OF LIFE AND DEATH

From the point of view suggested in this paper, the right to life is to be seen as a complex of elements including particular liberties to act in one's own defense and to preserve one's life, claim-rights to aid and perhaps to the necessities of life, and restrictions on the liberty of others to kill or endanger. Let me focus here on elements in these last two categories, namely limits on the liberty to act in ways that lead to a person's death. An act-consequentialist standard could allow a person to take action leading to the death of another whenever this is necessary to avoid greater loss of life elsewhere. Many find this policy too permissive, and one explanation of this reaction is that it represents a kind of blind conservatism. We know that our lives are always in jeopardy in many ways. Tomorrow I may die of a heart attack or a blood clot. I may be hit by a falling tree or discover that I have a failing liver or find myself stood up against a wall by a group of terrorists. But we are reluctant to open the door to a further form of deadly risk by licensing others to take our life should this be necessary to minimize loss of life overall. We are reluctant to do this even when the effect would be to increase our net chances of living a long life by decreasing the likelihood that we will actually die when one of the natural hazards of life befalls us. We adopt, as it were, the attitude of hoping against hope not to run afoul of any of these hazards, and we place less stock on the prospect of escaping alive should we be so unlucky. It would not be irrational for a person to *decide* to increase his chances of survival by joining a transplant-insurance scheme, i.e. an arrangement guaranteeing one a heart or kidney should he need one provided he agrees to sacrifice himself to become a donor if he is chosen to do so. But such a decision is sufficiently controversial and the stakes so high that it is not a decision that can be taken to have been made for us as part of a unanimously acceptable basis for the assignment of rights. What I have here called conservatism is, however, uncomfortably close to a bias of the lucky against the unlucky insofar as it rests on a conscious turning of attention away from the prospect of our being one of the unlucky ones.

A substitute for conservatism is mistrust. We are reluctant to place our life in *anyone's* hands. We are even more reluctant to place our lives in *everyone's* hands as the act-consequentialist standard would have us do. Such mistrust is the main factor supporting the observed difference between the rationality of joining a voluntary transplant-insurance scheme and the permissibility of having a compulsory one (let alone the universally administered one that unrestricted act consequentialism could amount to). A person who joins a voluntary scheme has the chance to see who will be making the decisions and to examine the safeguards on the process. In assessing the force of these considerations one should also bear in mind that what they are to be weighed against is not "the value of life itself" but only a small increase in the probability of living a somewhat longer life.

These appeals to "conservatism" and mistrust, if accepted, would support something like the distinction between killing and letting die: we are willing to grant to others the liberty not to save us from threat of death when this is necessary to save others, but we are unwilling to license them to put us under threat of death when we have otherwise escaped it. As is well known, however, the killing/letting die distinction appears to permit some actions leading to a person's death that are not intuitively permissible. These are actions in which an agent refrains from aiding someone already under threat of death and does so because that person's death has results he considers advantageous. (I will assume that they are thought advantageous to someone other than the person who is about to die.) The intuition that such actions are not permitted would be served by a restriction on the liberty to fail to save, specifying that this course of action cannot be undertaken on the basis of conceived advantages of having the person out of the way. Opponents of the law of double effect have sometimes objected that it is strange to make the permissibility of an action depend on quite subtle features of its rationale. In the context of the present theory, however, the distinction just proposed is not formally anomalous. Conferrals of authority and limitations on it often take the form not simply of licensing certain actions or barring them but rather of restricting the grounds on which actions can be undertaken. Freedom of expression embodies restrictions of this kind, for example, and this is one factor responsible for the distinction between real and apparent violations mentioned above.[9]

Reasons for such a restriction in the present case are easy to come by. People have such powerful and tempting reasons for wanting others removed from the scene that it is obviously a serious step to open the door to calculations taking these reasons into account. Obviously, what would be proposed would be a qualified restriction, allowing consideration of the utilitarian, but not the purely self-interested, advantages to be gained from a person's death. But a potential agent's perception of this distinction does not seem to be a factor worth depending on.

The restriction proposed here may appear odd when compared to our apparent policy regarding mutual aid. If, as seems to be the case, we are prepared to allow a person to fail to save another when doing so would involve a moderately heavy sacrifice, why not allow him to do the same for the sake of a much greater benefit, to be gained from that person's death? The answer seems to be that, while a principle of mutual aid giving less consideration to the donor's sacrifice strikes us as too demanding, it is not nearly as threatening as a policy allowing one to consider the benefits to be gained from a person's death.

These appeals to "conservatism" and mistrust do not seem to me to provide adequate justification for the distinctions in question. They may explain, however, why these distinctions have some appeal for us and yet remain matters of considerable controversy.

---

[9] For a view of freedom of expression embodying this feature, see Scanlon, "A Theory of Freedom of Expression" (1972), in this volume, essay 1, pp. 6–25.

3

Due process

In this essay I will offer a general account of how the absence of due process can give rise to legitimate claims against institutional actions. I will be concerned particularly to show in what ways claims to due process are grounded in moral principles of political right and how far they depend rather on strategic judgments about the prudent design of social institutions. My account will provide a demarcation of the area within which due process claims are appropriate – an area much broader than "state action" – and provide at least a rough framework for determining when given procedures are adequate responses to these claims. I will also offer an account of substantive due process and undertake to explain why it is that when a legal right to due process is recognized, courts, in enforcing this right, will find themselves making substantive as well as merely procedural decisions.

The account I will offer sticks close to the truism that due process is concerned with protection against arbitrary decisions, and one can find a place in my account for many of the phrases that have been used in interpreting the Fifth and Fourteenth Amendments to the United States Constitution. But while I will have a certain amount to say in the abstract about the role of courts in providing and enforcing due process, my account is a philosophical and not a legal one. It is grounded in a conception of the moral requirements of legitimacy for social institutions and not on what the law of the United States or any other country actually is. I hope that what I have to say may be of some use in legal arguments about constitutional rights to due process of law, but I have not undertaken to defend my theory as an interpretation of the Constitution.

In revising this paper I have benefited from the responses of the commentators and discussants at the meeting at which the first version of the paper was delivered and from comments by members of the Society for Ethical and Legal Philosophy and members of Ronald Dworkin's seminar on the philosophy of law, all of whom heard later versions. I am grateful to the members of these audiences for their patience and help, and especially to Bruce Ackerman and Ronald Dworkin for many helpful discussions on the subject of this essay.

I

The requirement of due process is one of the conditions of moral acceptability for institutions that give some people power to control or intervene in the lives of others. Institutions create such power in several ways. They do so directly by giving some the authority to command others and providing the force to compel obedience to these commands. Less directly, but no less effectively, institutions give some people a measure of control over others by securing their control over resources or opportunities that are important ingredients in the kind of life that people in the society want to live. I have referred to these forms of control in terms that emphasize their negative and threatening aspects, but they are an aspect of social life one could not reasonably seek to avoid altogether. To begin with, some dependence of this kind is in a trivial sense unavoidable. To the extent that any one person has the right and ability to determine how some choice is to be made, others are to that degree "subject to his will." In addition, nontrivial forms of authority are important and valuable means to many social goals.

But even if rights and powers giving some people a measure of control over others must be a feature of any plausible system of social institutions, the way in which these rights and powers are distributed is one of the features of social institutions that is most subject to moral criticism and most in need of justification. Questions of due process become interesting only on the supposition that such justifications can be given. The importance of due process arises from the fact that these justifications are in general limited and conditional. Even a person's rights to move his body and to dispose of his possessions as he sees fit are limited by requirements that he not bring specified kinds of harm to others. More interestingly, the authority of public officials is, typically, not only limited (e.g. by their jurisdiction) but also conditional. Thus they are empowered not simply to disburse a certain benefit or impose a certain burden but rather to do so *provided* certain specified conditions are met. For example, the authority of a judge to order penalties or fines, and the authority to issue or revoke licenses are both of this form. Authority not tied to special justifying conditions is in fact quite rare. (Perhaps the presidential power to pardon is an example.)

This conditional character is typical not only of the authority of public officials but also of that of persons occupying positions of special power in nongovernmental institutions such as schools, colleges, and businesses. School administrators have the authority to suspend or expel students on academic or disciplinary grounds and to impose other disciplinary penalties.

Employers have the right (absent specific contractual bars) to fire workers when this is required by considerations of economic efficiency, and perhaps also when it is necessary as a means of discipline within the firm. In each case, these limits and conditions on a given form of authority flow from the nature of the justification for that authority. The authority of school administrators and employers is presumably to be defended on the ground that it is crucial to the effective functioning of these enterprises.[1] But there would be no prospect of constructing on this basis a defense for unconditional authority to fire or suspend someone for any reason whatever, for example, because you didn't like his looks, his politics, or his religion, or because he was unwilling to bribe you.

But once de facto power to suspend or fire is conferred, one may ask what reason there is to believe that it will not be exercised in these unjustifiable ways. Thus, beyond the requirement of institutions that the power they confer be morally justifiable, there is the further moral requirement that there be some effective guarantee that these powers will be exercised only within the limits and subject to the conditions implied by their justification. In some cases, nothing need be done to provide such a guarantee. It may happen that, given the motives and the scruples which those in a particular position of power can be expected to have, and given the structural features of their position (e.g. the competitive pressures active on them), there is little reason to expect that they will act outside their authority. Where this is not the case – when obvious temptations or even just clear opportunities for laxness or capriciousness exist – an effective counter may be provided by a system of retrospective justice, levying penalties for the improper use of power and requiring compensation for those injured.

Beyond (or in addition to) this, further guarantees may be provided by introducing special requirements on the way in which those who exercise power make their decisions. Due process is one version of this latter strategy. It aims to provide some assurance of nonarbitrariness by requiring those who exercise authority to justify their intended actions in a public proceeding by adducing reasons of the appropriate sort and defending these against critical attack. The idea of such proceedings presupposes, of course, publicly known and reasonably specific rules with respect to which official actions are to be justified.

The authority to decide whether the reasons advanced are adequate may be assigned to different persons or bodies by different procedures. If the grounds and limits of a given decision maker's authority are well known

---

[1] Of course one also has to justify *having* such institutions given their costs.

and taken seriously in a community, then even a hearing procedure that allows him to preside and pronounce the verdict may be a nonnegligible check on the arbitrary use of his power since he will presumably place some value on not being publicly seen to flout the accepted standards for the performance of his job. But in general the assurances provided by a system of due process will be credible only if there is the possibility of appeal to some independent authority which can invoke the coercive power of the state to support its decisions.

Appeal to the courts offers greater assurance against arbitrariness, in part, because of the expectation that the judge will be less a party to the original dispute than the decision maker himself, but also because a judge is presumed to have a greater commitment to an ideal of procedural justice and a greater long-term stake in his reputation as a maker of decisions that are well founded in the relevant rules and principles. At each stage in the appeals process other than the last, these factors of personal motivation will be supplemented by the more explicit threat of being overruled. When we reach the ultimate legal authority, of course, we will in practice be relying on personal commitment, pride, and aspiration alone and on the existence of a public conception of the ground and limits of this authority, which serves as a basis for public approbation or disapprobation of the way it is exercised.

II

Due process is only one of the strategies for avoiding arbitrary power by altering the conditions under which decisions are made. It may be contrasted with strategies that seek to make power less arbitrary by making the motives with which it is exercised more benign; for example, by allowing decisions to be made by elected representatives of those principally affected. Rule by such elected representatives is an acceptably nonarbitrary form of authority in a given situation to the extent that it is reasonable to believe that the complex of motives under which representatives act – the desire to be reelected, the need for financial support, loyalty to and shared feelings with one's region or group, the desire to be a "good representative" in the generally accepted sense of this phrase, the desire to be esteemed in the society of representatives and politicians, etc. – will add up to produce decisions reasonably in accord with the rights and wishes of those governed.

As I have mentioned, a system of due process also depends upon motives, e.g. on the professionalism of judges. But such a system need not in general attempt to make the authority whose decisions it is supposed to control responsive to the interests of the affected parties. Indeed, the notion of due process is most often invoked in cases (such as the employment case discussed above, or cases of school or prison discipline) where it is assumed that the decision-making authority whose actions are to be checked will be moved (quite properly) by considerations largely separate from the interests of the persons most directly affected. The idea of a right to due process is thus much broader in application than that of a right to participation or representation; it involves the recognition of those subject to authority as entitled to demand justification for its uses and entitled to protection against its unjustified use but not necessarily as entitled to share in the making of decisions affecting them.[2]

The fact that requirements of due process thus involve minimal alteration in the established relations of power makes them a particularly easy remedy for courts to invoke. Their acceptability is also increased in a society like our own by the extraordinarily high public regard for legal institutions and the procedures that are typical of them. Given these facts, one might expect that insofar as it falls to the judiciary to deal with important social conflicts the remedy of due process is likely to be overused.

I have not attempted to say what the *right* to due process is. The moral basis of my account of due process lies in something like a right, namely the idea that citizens have a legitimate claim against institutions which make them subject in important ways to the arbitrary power of others. But it is not easy to say in general when those who have such a claim are entitled specifically to what I have called a mechanism of due process. I described above a range of controls on the exercise of power extending from cases in which authority can be regarded as self-policing to systems of retrospective justice to systems of due process with increasing levels of judicial review.

Moral principles of political philosophy do not determine which of these mechanisms is required in any given case. This is a question of strategy that can be answered only on the basis of an analysis of the factors active in a particular setting. The situation is analogous to the case of representation. One might set forth as a principle of political philosophy that just institutions should provide means for people to participate effectively in decisions affecting them provided that power is distributed equally and that its exercise will not enable some to override the rights of others. But political

---

[2] Contrast Philip Selznick, *Law, Society and Industrial Justice* (New York: Sage Foundation, 1969), p. 275: "there is latent in the law of governance [as exemplified by due process] a norm of participation . . . a legal order should be seen as transitional to a polity."

philosophy can tell us little about what kinds of participatory and/or representative institutions will satisfy the requirement of effective and equal participation in a given case. The choice of suitable forms may depend on local tradition, the distribution of economic and social power in the society, the nature of other primary divisive conflicts, and other variables.

In deciding whether mechanisms of due process are required, and in assessing the adequacy of particular mechanisms, the main questions seem to be these:

(1) How likely is it that a given form of power – if unchecked – will be used outside the limits of its justification?

(2) How serious are the harms inflicted by its misuse?

(3) Would due process be an effective check on the exercise of this power?

(4) Would the costs of a requirement of due process in cases of this kind be excessive? Is the additional effectiveness of due process over other forms of control worth the additional cost?

The costs at issue here will include, in addition to the delay of decisions and the costs of mounting the procedures themselves, the personal and social costs of depersonalizing decisions and reducing them to rules and procedures.

Due process, as I have characterized it, will be most effective where there exist reasonably clear, generally understood standards for exercise of the authority in question, standards which can serve as the background for public justification and defense of decisions. As the relevant standards – and even the starting points for arguments for and against the propriety of a given decision – become less and less clear, the constraints on the decision maker in a due process proceeding become progressively weaker, and the power of these decision makers itself comes to seem more and more arbitrary. The same thing may be true when the relevant standards – although they may be quite precise – become less and less generally understood until finally they are the preserve of a small group including only the hearing examiners, their staff, and the main combatants.

The variation in the forms of due process mechanism that are appropriate to different situations is not due solely to the different ways in which effective protection against arbitrary decisions can best be given. The procedures with which we are familiar in civil and criminal trials, disciplinary proceedings, and administrative hearings serve a variety of different functions in addition to the general one of providing protection against arbitrary power; and some of the features of these proceedings may be explained by these additional purposes. Thus, for example, many hearings are not merely fact-finding or rule-applying mechanisms; they also serve an important symbolic function as public expressions of the affected parties' right to demand that official acts be explained and justified. If the hearing is to serve this function, the procedures followed should be ones that take the complainants' objections seriously and place them on a par with the claims of authority. This provides an argument for adversary proceedings, for the right to counsel, and for the rights to call witnesses and cross-examine opposing witnesses – reasons which go beyond whatever advantages these procedures may have as mechanisms for ensuring a "correct outcome."[3] An argument of this kind is at its strongest in the case of a criminal trial or other proceedings in which a person is accused of wrongdoing. An accused person has an interest in having the opportunity to respond to the charges against him and to present what he takes to be the best defense of his action. This interest would not be met merely by ensuring that all the facts and the relevant legal arguments in the defendant's favor will somehow be brought before the court. There is a crucial difference between having these facts presented and having them presented as a defense by the accused or by someone speaking for him with his consent and participation. To the extent that this interest is a component in the rationale for the procedures of a criminal trial, it would be a mistake automatically to take these procedures as a model for what due process requires generally.

A different mix of purposes is represented in disciplinary proceedings in a school or university. Officials of an educational institution have, in addition to general duties to treat students coming before them fairly and not to use their power in an arbitrary manner, special obligations to be concerned with students' intellectual and personal needs.[4] It is therefore not sufficient merely that disciplinary proceedings follow clear and fair rules and that accused students be informed of their rights and given the opportunity to rebut charges against them. The institution may also be itself obligated (in a way that the state in a criminal trial is not) to investigate cases with the aim of uncovering evidence favorable to the defendant. It should also undertake to inform an accused student of the various alternatives open to him and counsel him in deciding what course to follow.[5] One would

---

[3] The inadequacies of a purely instrumental justification for trial procedures is pointed out by Laurence Tribe in "Trial by Mathematics," *Harvard Law Review* 84 (1971), 1329–93.

[4] See W. A. Seavey, "Dismissal of Students: 'Due Process,'" *Harvard Law Review* 70 (1957), 1406–10; also, the unsigned note "Judicial Control of Actions of Private Associations," *Harvard Law Review* 76 (1963), 983–1100, esp. pp. 1002 ff.; and Z. Chafee, "The Internal Affairs of Associations Not for Profit," *Harvard Law Review* 43 (1930), 993–1029. I am grateful to Owen Fiss, who called my attention to the last two articles after the original version of this paper had been written.

[5] This implies that what would normally be regarded as fair adversary proceedings may not be enough. It is sometimes suggested that, for reasons like those considered here, adversary procedures are

expect to see these special obligations reflected in differences between the procedures followed in cases of student discipline and in cases where faculty members or other employees face dismissal. But the requirements of *due process* in these cases are the same.[6]

III

I have described due process as one of the conditions for the moral legitimacy of power-conferring institutions. Suppose that a right to due process as I have described it were to be recognized as a legal right within a given legal system. What might a court be deciding in determining in a certain case that this right had been violated? There seem to be three possibilities:

(1) The court may decide that, given the nature of the authority in question, the nature of the harms likely to result from its improper use, and the likelihood of its being used improperly, procedural safeguards are required that were not followed in the given case. Here the court is appraising the decision-making process from the outside in its capacity as the guarantor of the legal right to (procedural) due process.

(2) On the other hand, the court may decide that while the procedures followed in the given case were formally adequate the reasoning accepted in these tribunals was faulty or in any case insufficient to justify the decision in question on the required grounds. Here the court is playing a role as one of the appeals stages in an established system of due process. Whether judicial authority to make decisions of this kind is required as a deterrent against tendentious verdicts at earlier stages is itself a question of procedural due process of type (1).

(3) Finally, the court may decide that, while the procedures followed in the given case were formally adequate and the reasoning offered in support of decisions unexceptionable, the rules that were applied in these proceedings must themselves be rejected because they exceed the assigned authority of the decision maker in question. Such rules (e.g. the disciplinary code of a school, prison, or labor union) might be struck down on the ground that their enforcement would infringe some specific

---

not appropriate at all for university discipline and that something more like traditional avuncular "dean's justice" better allows for the appropriate combination of concerned investigation, personal counseling, and rendering of justice. But the potential for arbitrariness here is apparent and familiar. One obvious alternative is a division of labor between (probably adversary) tribunals to apply the rules and separate officials to counsel and assist in uncovering the facts.

[6] An alternative explanation of these differences would be that due process itself requires something different where the accused persons are young. But the special obligations of school officials seem to go beyond what general paternalistic arguments are usually taken to require.

constitutional guarantee (e.g. some First Amendment right), but this is just one way in which it might be shown that a given rule exceeded the authority of the agency in question. This same conclusion could also be reached by arguing that, given the nature of the institution in question, the given rule could not possibly be taken as part of its authority.

This third case is substantive due process as I understand it. Substantive due process decisions in their most characteristic and controversial form are those based not on any explicit constitutional limitation but rather on appeal to the nature of the authority whose power is in question. The notion of the nature of an institution is one likely to raise legal and philosophical eyebrows. It appears to be an attempt to resolve legal or moral issues by appeal to definitions, and it is apt to provoke questions as to where such definitions are supposed to come from. Surely, it will be urged, social institutions do not have "essences" which can be discovered and used as the basis for authoritative resolution of philosophical or legal controversies. But an important social institution enabling some to wield significant power over others is unlikely to exist without some public rationale – at the very least an account put forth for public consumption of why this institution is legitimate and rational. This will include some conception of the social goals the institution is taken to serve and of the way in which the authority exercised by participants in the institution is rationally related to those goals. If the institution is not merely rationalized by those wishing to maintain its power, but in fact generally accepted as legitimate then some conception of this sort will be fairly generally accepted in the society and rendered coherent with other aspects of the prevailing views. Such a conception may be more or less clearly articulated. It is almost certain to be vague and incomplete in some areas and may be gradually shifting and changing. But something of this kind will almost surely exist and can serve as a basis for argument.

In an argument of the kind I have in mind, an appeal to the current conception of an institution – even in its clearest and most explicit features – need not be final. One must also be prepared to argue that the social goals appealed to are in fact valuable and to defend the forms of authority defined by the institution as rational means to those goals and as acceptable given the costs they involve. When a defense of this kind is given within the context of a due process proceeding, the social goals and judgments of relative value to which it appeals must themselves be defended by appeal to contemporary standards (or by an argument about what standards in the relevant area ought to be, given other beliefs and values people in the society hold.[7]) But while the limits of debate are in this sense set by prevailing views, the fact that the dominant conception of an institution is not taken at face value but must be shown to be coherent and consistent with other social values provides a measure of independence and allows for criticism through which the prevailing conception of an institution can be extended, clarified, and altered.

Such appeals to the nature of a social institution lie behind many quite convincing commonsense political arguments, and even though our conception of an institution is often partly in doubt and in places controversial such appeals can yield quite definite conclusions. It seems to me clear, for example, that a labor union could not use its power of expulsion to collect dues to be used to support a particular religious group but that it could, at least in some cases, compel dues members to pay to support a political candidate or party. And this conclusion follows, I think, from our conception of the nature and purposes of a union rather than from any specific constitutional or statutory limitation.

Such arguments by appeal to the nature of an institution occupy a kind of gray area between considerations of rights and considerations of good policy. Take, for example, the question of academic freedom. It seems to me that the doctrine of academic freedom has its basis in the idea that the purposes of academic institutions are the pursuit and teaching of the truth about certain recognized academic subjects as defined by the prevailing canons of those subjects.[8] Relative to this conception of the purposes of academic institutions, it is rational that they be organized in such a way that the primary motivation of scholars and teachers will be to report and to teach whatever appears to them to be the truth about their subjects. In particular, if teachers and scholars are subject to power which is likely to be used to influence them to teach and report doctrines favored by certain people whether or not these doctrines appear to them to be the truth about their subjects, then it is rational to shield them from this power.

The doctrine of academic freedom is generally defended as one such shield. The restraints it imposes on the authority of administrators and trustees over teachers are directly tied to a particular conception of the purposes of an academic institution. They would make no sense (or only a different and more limited kind of sense) as applied to a religious school whose main purpose was the dissemination of a particular faith or to a

---

[7] A class of arguments of this form is discussed in section v below.

[8] Canons which may themselves be revised and altered of course. The following discussion draws on my essay, "Academic Freedom and the Control of Research," in E. Pincoffs, ed., *The Concept of Academic Freedom* (Austin: University of Texas Press, 1975), pp. 237–54.

school founded for the purpose of offering an education which included a nonstandard version of some recognized subject, e.g. biology without evolution or some unorthodox version of history.

As I have described it, academic freedom appears more as a counsel for the rational design and wise administration of certain kinds of academic institutions than as a matter of right. But such a counsel of rationality may be transformed into a right through the application of a general moral or legal principle of due process, limiting the authority of academic officials to those powers and prerogatives that are consistent with and rationally related to the rationale for and purposes of their institutions. To defend the right of academic freedom so conceived, one must be prepared to defend the relevant kind of academic institutions as worth having and their activities as worth the costs of safeguarding them through this means.

Decisions of substantive due process and decisions of procedural due process both involve appeal to a conception of the institutions in question, their rationale and purposes. In making a procedural due process decision of the first type described above, a court must estimate the risk that the power exercised by an institution will be used in ways that go beyond its authority. The court must therefore employ, as a standard, some conception of what that authority is. In making a decision of substantive due process, however, a court goes further and appeals to such a conception in order itself to declare a particular exercise of power illegitimate.

The distinction between substantive due process decisions and procedural due process decisions may seem to coincide with that between judicial scrutiny of rule-making authority and judicial scrutiny of rule-applying authority, but the two distinctions are not the same. Rule-making authority may come under judicial scrutiny on grounds falling clearly within what I have called procedural due process. There may be serious doubts whether, in a particular situation, given rule-making power will be used only in a nonarbitrary fashion, and special procedures for the making of rules may be required to ensure this. What is special about substantive due process scrutiny is not that it is directed to the limits of rule-making authority but rather that in exercising it courts directly apply a conception of what the rules of a particular institution may or may not be.

The potentially controversial grounds on which substantive due process decisions may be based – a conception of the nature and purposes of a particular institution – are thus already presupposed by decisions of procedural due process. Nonetheless, decisions of substantive due process deserve to be considered a more controversial form of judicial activity, for in making them courts exercise a further and more intrusive form of authority over the institutions concerned. Whether it is proper for courts to exercise this kind of authority is itself a question of procedural due process (type [1]) in the broad sense I have described. In its favor, one might maintain that judicial oversight of rule-making and rule-applying procedures, however careful, is empty as a protection against arbitrary authority if the authorities in question are free to make and apply whatever rules they wish. This would be an overstatement. Strong traditions, the opinion of a public informed by a clear conception of the limits of the authority in question, and the likely resistance of those affected by arbitrary rules all may provide some check on rule-making authority, a check whose effectiveness may be enhanced by an enforced requirement of appropriate rule-making procedures. But these same factors also provide a check on the manner in which rules are applied, and this check is not always sufficient, even when the relevant procedural safeguards are observed. This is shown by the fact that in at least some cases we think that courts should have the power not only to require due process at the level of original decisions but also to reverse the results of such procedures when they are clearly misapplications of the relevant rules. Thus the argument that substantive due process is sometimes called for is parallel to the argument that procedural due process of type (2) described above is sometimes called for.

It is very implausible to suggest that, while the threat of arbitrariness for which the second form of procedural due process is a possible remedy often occurs, the corresponding threat of misuse of rule-making authority never exists. But even where this threat exists, it is a further question whether substantive judicial review is called for, or even effective, as a protection against it.

One reason for doubting its effectiveness rests on skepticism about arguments by appeal to the nature of an institution. If such arguments are thought to be insubstantial rhetoric – not arguments at all but a mode of discourse in which there are virtually no useful standards and in which almost anything can be defended with equal plausibility – then a process of review based on such arguments would itself constitute a highly arbitrary form of authority, perhaps as arbitrary as that which is sought to be checked. I have expressed above, and tried to defend by example, the view that for most significant social institutions "the nature of the institution" is something one can argue about in a rational way. But even if this is conceded, there may be objections to empowering judges to strike down rules or other enactments of, for example, private associations on the basis of the court's judgment that these fall outside of and cannot be defended by appeal to the current conception of the nature of the organizations in question. It may be thought preferable to allow organizations (through means meeting procedural due process standards) to define and alter their own purposes and rationale. Crudely described, what is at issue here seems to be a question of balancing – of finding the proper trade-off between the goal of protecting people from arbitrary regulations and requirements and that of allowing them to associate for common purposes and define the terms of their own association. I will have more to say about this problem and about the claims of institutional autonomy in the next section.

IV

I have argued that the basis of due process requirements lies in a condition on the legitimacy of power-conferring institutions. Since the state is only one such institution among many, it follows that the range of possible application of due process requirements is much broader than the extent of "state action." This conclusion seems to me to be in accord with our intuitions about particular cases. In considering rights to due process in cases of suspension or expulsion of students, for example, it seems arbitrary to distinguish between institutions on the basis of whether or not they receive state or federal funds. This seems arbitrary, first, because the very serious dislocation of a student's career – which in our society can result from expulsion from college – is not significantly different in the two cases. Nor is the likelihood of arbitrary action by administrators acting in the absence of procedural safeguards less in one case than the other. Given the importance attached to gaining admission to college, and the lack of real bargaining power on the part of applicants, students' freedom of choice in deciding what college to attend can scarcely be expected to serve as an effective check on administrators' authority, and the decision to attend a particular school can scarcely be taken as authorization of whatever powers the administrators of that school may wish to claim. At any rate, there seems to be little difference with respect to these matters between private and public institutions.

But while judicial enforcement of due process requirements does not seem to me to be limited to cases of state action, there does seem to me to be an area of activity, which might be called the sphere of purely voluntary organizations, within which due process requirements apply only with reduced force. In this section I will attempt to characterize this area more clearly and examine the ways in which the claims of due process seem to be reduced.[9] I will also indicate how the notion of state action retains some content and force even though it does not mark the outer limits of due process enforcement.

Even given the similarities noted above, the difference between state-supported institutions and private institutions might still be crucial for due process if the costs of imposing due process requirements on the two kinds of institutions were significantly different. But, at least as long as we confine our attention to procedural due process, and as long as we are concerned with colleges and universities in the traditional sense, this is not the case. One can imagine a religious school in which the tenets of the faith required relations of authority which would be entirely inconsistent with due process requirements of the usual kind. In such a case, the cost of imposing due process rights would be quite high, amounting to the serious alteration, if not the destruction, of valued aspects of institutional life. A school of this kind would be extremely special in offering not merely education of the kind required for the careers at which most members of the society aim but rather a special form of life chosen for its own sake by those who happen to value it. Those who attend such an institution thus accept its requirements voluntarily in a stronger sense than those who accept the requirements of, say, Princeton or the University of Michigan or Harvard Law School, institutions which are principal means of access to some of the most highly desired positions in the society.

But as far as the weakening of procedural due process requirements is concerned, it is the former feature – the direct clash between the forms of due process and the goals of the institution – rather than its high degree of voluntariness that is crucial. For even where institutions are thoroughly voluntary, if the costs to individuals of the misuse of official authority are high and the chance of such misuse significant then there will be a prima facie case for procedural due process safeguards. In the present example, this prima facie case is overridden by the unusually disruptive consequences of due process forms.

---

[9] For a discussion of the law relating to voluntary associations, in which many of the intuitive distinctions used here are clearly and perceptively drawn, see the sources referred to in footnote 4 above.

By distinguishing, in the following discussion, between "purely voluntary" institutions and institutions that are "not fully voluntary" I do not mean to suggest that those who participate in institutions of the latter sort, e.g. as students in universities, do so *involuntarily*. All I am saying about such institutions is that, given the costs of refusal to participate in them, the authority they exercise over their members cannot be defended simply by appeal to the members' consent as expressed in their willingness to "join."

In voluntary institutions of this kind, it is at least partly accurate to see the authority of institutional officers to order, discipline, and expel members as arising from a contract, and to see the limits and conditions of this authority as fixed by the terms on which members (voluntarily) enter. Since even full voluntariness at time of entry into membership does not preclude great inequality in the power unilaterally to interpret and act on the terms of the membership "contract," the need to impose procedural due process is not eliminated by the voluntary nature of the institution.

But substantive due process is very different. It amounts to the power of a court to arrive at an independent judgment of the limits and conditions of the authority of the group and its officers, a judgment based on a conception of the nature of the institution that need not be determined by the understanding of its members. Where an institution is truly voluntary, this represents a serious inroad into the freedom of individuals to enter into such arrangements as they wish and to define the terms of their own association.

But few of the most significant institutions of society are voluntary in this strong sense. When institutions are not fully voluntary, there are limits on the degree to which it is permissible to allow present members or present officers freely to determine the conditions under which others may have access to the benefits their institution provides. These limits are in part determined by the nature of the institution in the sense described above.

Let me return to the case of traditional colleges and universities. Some limits on changes in university requirements and policies may arise from the requirement of fair warning and the obligation to comply with the legitimate expectations of students already enrolled. In determining what expectations are (or were) legitimate, we may appeal to "the idea of a university" as it was understood at the time these students enrolled. Here appeal to the nature of an institution helps us to fill in a vague or incompletely articulated agreement. But the idea of a university may be invoked in a stronger sense in setting the limits on requirements for admission or requirements that are to apply only to students who enroll in the future.

It seems at the outset that almost any requirements of this kind would be immune from substantive due process review provided they were plausibly related to normal educational purposes or could be brought under the heading of educational experimentation. For requirements that are evidently idle or perverse, the matter is not so clear. I am thinking here of such things as a policy of restricting admission to persons over six feet tall or a university policy requiring freshmen to speak only when spoken to and to serve as lackeys to older students and faculty.

If we think that courts should not intervene to review and possibly strike down such policies, this is presumably because we feel that freedom to try out new and different educational forms is a good thing, that competitive pressures between institutions will curb excesses, and that the existence of many comparable alternative institutions prevents idiosyncratic policies adopted by one school from imposing a very high cost on would-be applicants. Such considerations are crucial to the case for nonintervention given the place universities occupy as means of access to the most desired positions in our society. If these conditions should fail to hold – if certain restrictions on admission unrelated to plausible academic purposes should cease to be merely the idiosyncrasy of a few particular institutions among many and should come to be quite general, thereby effectively excluding a group of people from university education and all those careers to which it is the main avenue of approach – then the case for judicial intervention on substantive due process grounds would be strong.

This is what has happened in cases of discrimination. What once was or might have been an idle preference which some institutions could be allowed to cater to – like a preference for people over six feet tall – comes to have unacceptable consequences once it becomes a general pattern. This preference then ceases to be an acceptable ground for admissions decisions. Antidiscrimination judgments of this kind can be seen as substantive due process decisions based on arguments about the nature of an institution in the sense discussed above. The judgment that university admissions officers cannot follow a white-only policy is based on the judgment that a university cannot take being an all-white institution as one of its defining purposes. It cannot do so because the cost of allowing educational (and other) institutions so to define themselves is, in the circumstances, unacceptable. What is the cost? It is, first, that a whole group of people will be effectively blocked from important areas of social life. Of course, any set of criteria – if uniformly employed by all the institutions in a given category (e.g. all universities) – will act as a bar to some "group," namely those who fail to meet these particular criteria. Perhaps any such exclusion, when it is sufficiently uniform, always represents a cost which must be considered. But it is crucial to the costs typical of cases striking us as discrimination that the criteria of exclusion express attitudes that are demeaning to those towards whom they are directed. Once circumstances arise in which such attitudes are widespread and have been generally acted upon – once, that is, discrimination of a certain kind has become a problem – the cost of allowing institutions to define themselves as excluding the group discriminated against become very high. This may provide grounds for refusing to allow institutions so to define themselves even in areas of national life in which such a definition would pose no threat of systematic exclusion. For example, it would not be acceptable to form a lily-white professional sports team in 1975 even though this would pose no threat to black athletes.

The conclusion of a substantive due process argument of this kind barring institutional discrimination against blacks is not that institutional policies must be "color blind." A university admitting blacks only would not be objectionable on the grounds I have mentioned: there is at present no risk of whites being excluded from higher education generally or from any important range of institutions within it. A policy of excluding whites need not be based on antiwhite attitudes, and, even if it were, the threat posed to their self-respect and standing in the society would be insignificant. Finally, an institution with such a policy could conceivably be thought to serve significant cultural value. (A similar asymmetry exists in the United States of 1975 between institutions excluding women and institutions for women only.)

I have suggested that the conclusion of a substantive due process argument against discrimination is to be stated negatively as the judgment that there are certain purposes which institutions may not be allowed to adopt as part of their defining rationale or to appeal to in justifying their policies.[10] It might be suggested that such judgments could as well be stated positively as, for example, the judgment that universities must employ only admission criteria rationally related to their central academic purpose. I want to make two comments about this alternative formulation.

First, if this requirement is understood narrowly, as the claim that since the central purpose of universities is education, they must employ academic excellence, demonstrated or projected, as their sole criterion for admission, then the proposal is one that has never been imposed and should not be. But colleges and universities should be able to choose their own special character and be free in choosing students to supplement strictly academic criteria with other desiderata related to the kind of institution they wish to be. Substantive due process decisions which ruled out this kind of variation, even to the extent of requiring that nonacademic criteria be restricted to a tie-breaking role in admissions, would be mistaken. This shows, I think, that the correct arguments must be understood negatively – as ruling out certain purposes and standards rather than demanding others.

[10] My analysis of discrimination is in this way similar to that offered by Ronald Dworkin in his "The Right to Go to Law School – the DeFunis Case," *New York Review of Books* 23 (Feb. 5, 1976), pp. 29–33. But I do not proceed, as he does, from a general theoretical distinction according to which all preferences to associate with or not to associate with others are suspect.

Second, it is a mistake to think that criteria of academic excellence are themselves sacrosanct. I have stressed the fact that universities are gateways to the most generally desired position in our society. Criteria of academic success bear some relation to plausible efficiency-based criteria for selection to these positions. But this connection certainly can be, and for many positions no doubt commonly is, overrated. In any event, the general use of standard academic criteria for admission to colleges, universities, and professional schools has costs, both in tending to preserve some forms of discrimination and in creating its own form of stratification, and these have to be weighed against its value as a means to increased efficiency. I am not here arguing that this balancing comes out against academic criteria. I am only pointing out that the standard of merit which they represent, while it may have great appeal both for its own sake and as a hard-won refuge from arbitrary and discriminating practices, still has to be defended as worth the costs it involves.[11]

Let me summarize the discussion of this section. There is an important distinction between those institutions of a society that are truly voluntary and those that, because they are the means of access to benefits people in that society have reason to want are so important to life in the society that their power cannot plausibly be justified merely by saying that anyone who does not wish to deal with them on their own terms may simply refrain from dealing with them. Obviously, an institution that is truly voluntary at one time can cease to be so at another as conditions and mores change. Perhaps colleges and universities were once truly voluntary in our society; now they are not. Procedural due process requirements apply to voluntary as well as to nonvoluntary institutions, but for substantive due process the distinction is crucial. The authority that truly voluntary institutions have over their members can plausibly be seen as derived from consent, and their more general justification lies simply in the value of allowing individuals to associate for whatever purposes they may choose.[12]

But as an institution ceases to be truly voluntary and comes to be the mechanism for providing some important good, some further justification for its power is required. This justification typically rests on the institution's role in providing the good in question, and the authority of individuals

[11] See Thomas Nagel, "Equal Treatment and Compensatory Discrimination," *Philosophy and Public Affairs* 2 (1973), 348–63.

[12] In deciding how large a price nonmembers may be asked to bear in order that we can associate for our own private purposes one may, of course, have to take into account what those purposes are. The point is only that with respect to the substance of its power over *members*, the particular purposes of a voluntary association do not have the same justificatory role as they do in the case of nonvoluntary institutions.

within the institution must then be defended as part of a rational and acceptable mechanism for providing that good. Thus, in the case of non-voluntary institutions, there arises a basis for criticism on substantive due process grounds. But this does not mean that a court would be justified in imposing on any such institution its conception of what is required by the central function of that institution. Institutional autonomy and variety among institutions providing the same good remain important values. Even where institutions of a certain kind are not fully voluntary, the ability of individuals to choose among various institutions of this kind may constitute an adequate safeguard against capricious restrictions or unwarranted requirements. But when the exercise of institutional autonomy leads to systematic exclusion or to the imposition of other unacceptable social costs then judicial intervention may be called for to delimit the purposes with respect to which institutional policies are to be justified.

A remark on "state action." The state is a nonvoluntary institution of the strongest kind. Everyone in the society is subject to its requirements, and most are required to support its activities whether they wish to or not. The activities of the state, however, are varied. Some of these, when considered with respect to their particular purposes, are in themselves what I have called nonvoluntary institutions (state-supported universities are an example); others are more akin to voluntary institutions (national parks and the support of scholarly research seem to me to fall into this category).[13]

But all of these activities, since they are supported by tax money, are the undertakings of a particular nonvoluntary institution. Accordingly, they are subject to conditions and limitations flowing from the nature of this institution, conditions and limitations that may not apply to other (voluntary or nonvoluntary) organizations pursuing the same purposes (e.g. nonpublic universities, private recreational areas, or foundations for the support of scholarly research). Thus, for example, tax-supported institutions may be

---

[13] Some clarification of the notion of a voluntary institution is needed. Our concern is with forms of power some people are able to wield over others, and within a single institution several different forms of power may be involved. Thus, for example, a social club exercises one form of power over members, another over those who seek membership, and another over its employees. With respect to the first two, it is a purely voluntary institution; with respect to the last not so. Thus, the governmental agencies referred to are like voluntary organizations in the power they have over beneficiaries but like businesses or other employers in their authority over those they hire.

What about research-supporting agencies like NSF and NEH? Are the recipients of their grants like beneficiaries or like employees? The answer to this question depends on the role such support has in the economy of the relevant branch of academia. If grants provide temporary support for breaks within other long-term employment, they seem to belong to the voluntary sphere; but not so if they constitute continuing support without which a career of research in the field would be economically impossible.

barred from adopting religious or political activities as part of their function even though comparable private institutions may do so, and tax-supported institutions may be subject to especially stringent requirements of fairness in the distribution of their benefits. These conditions and limitations could be enforced under the heading of substantive due process as applied to the particular nonvoluntary institution of the state. But, since the state is only one nonvoluntary institution among many, this is a special case of substantive due process. To show that substantive due process applies to a given institution one need not show that it is an activity of the state but only that it, like the state, should be recognized as not truly voluntary.

v

Probably the most controversial substantive due process decisions are those in which a court overturns the action of a legislature. According to the general framework presented in section III, such a decision could take either of two forms: the piece of legislation might conflict with a specific constitutional prohibition or it might be found to exceed the authority of the legislature in a more general sense as determined by an argument about the nature of legislative authority. Decisions of the first kind are, in themselves, relatively uncontroversial; although the way in which I have presented them may seem odd insofar as it suggests that any instance of judicial review is an example of substantive due process. I will return to this point. Decisions of the second kind are subject to the two objections to substantive due process discussed above – skepticism about arguments appealing to the "nature" of an institution and the belief that institutional autonomy is preferable to the imposition of judicial authority – which apply here in slightly modified form and with apparent added strength.

The first objection appears to be strengthened because the question at issue has become not merely whether there is some ground on which claims about the nature of an institution (in this case the nature of the legislature and its power) can rationally be established but rather whether such claims can be established by appeals to and interpretation of the Constitution. After all, it is the Constitution which is supposed to define the limits of governmental authority, and which therefore ought to be the only ground on which a court can delimit that authority. The second objection is also strengthened, since what is to be overridden by a substantive due process decision is now not merely the desire of some small group of people to be allowed to associate for their own purposes but a decision of the legislature which, after all, is supposed to be the political voice of all the people.

If we were to stipulate for the moment that the due process clauses of the Constitution can be taken to require due process in the sense I have outlined, then we might take a short way with the first objection. For on this assumption substantive due process arguments of the kind I have described would be, in a formal sense, arguments about what the Constitution requires just as much as, say, arguments about freedom of speech are: in each case there is a brief constitutional formula. In both cases, the subject at issue concerns the distribution of authority (in the case of the First Amendment, authority to regulate expression, in the other case, authority more generally). In neither case does the Constitution literally specify what constitutes an acceptable system of authority of the relevant kind. Thus, in applying either formula, a court must be working with some conception of authority not explicitly supplied by the Constitution, and it must defend these conceptions as tenable under prevailing conditions, arguing by appeal to the Constitution and to generally accepted principles of political morality.[14]

There are, of course, a number of differences between the two cases I have just compared. One particularly relevant here is the difference in scope of the two principles. Freedom of expression is a fairly specific question, and only one of many with which the Constitution deals. But substantive due process, as I have described it, deals with the basis and bounds of authority in all branches of government (and even outside of it), i.e. with the subject matter of the Constitution as a whole. So it seems that either substantive due process arguments are just arguments about what the rest of the Constitution as a whole requires, in which case the due process clauses add nothing to the rest of the Constitution beyond procedural guarantees, or else the authority to make substantive due process decisions opens the door to general theoretical argument about what the powers of government ought to be, i.e. to judicial revision and extension of the Constitution.

Obviously the Constitution, which embodies fundamental political principles of our society, plays a central role in substantive due process arguments as I have described them. But in order to decide which of the alternatives just presented follows from my view, one would have to know how far the forms of argument I have described are included within an adequate account of

---

[14] Here I am close to the distinction between concepts and conceptions drawn by Ronald Dworkin. See his article, "Nixon's Jurisprudence," *New York Review of Books* (May 4, 1972), pp. 27–35.

the methods of constitutional interpretation. For this one would require a general theory of constitutional adjudication, which I cannot provide.[15]

But arguments against substantive due process decisions and in favor of judicial modesty vis-à-vis legislative judgments have often been put forward not just as arguments about what our Constitution and legal traditions require but as arguments in political theory about what constitutes a proper distribution of authority in a democratic system.[16] So considered, these arguments fall within the framework I have been presenting: as I have already remarked, the question they are concerned with is a question of procedural due process of type (1) (as indeed are all questions about the propriety of various forms of judicial review). These arguments may be approached within my framework by considering the four questions presented above, these being (1) the likelihood of misuse[17] of the power in question; (2) the magnitude of the harms involved; (3) the degree to which substantive due process review would offer an improvement, and (4) the costs involved in invoking it.

Questions of types (1) and (2), about the likelihood of legislative excess and the degree to which legislative self-restraint can be relied upon, play some role in arguments against substantive due process, as do questions of type (4), concerned mainly with a feared loss of popular sovereignty to a dictatorial judiciary. But the most prominent role has been played by questions of type (3): is substantive due process review itself an acceptably nonarbitrary form of authority? This question divides into two: are there acceptably clear standards for substantive due process arguments? And is there sufficient reason to think that courts will be held to these standards in making their decisions? Here the relation between "interpretation of the Constitution" and what I have called "argument about the nature of an institution" comes to be of putative importance as a matter of political theory

[15] Appeal to such a theory would also be required to decide whether the alternatives presented are fairly described. For a theory of adjudication that seems to encompass much of the kind of argument I have been describing, see Ronald Dworkin, "Hard Cases," *Harvard Law Review* 88 (1975) 1057–109.

[16] Insofar as these are distinct. Of course, arguments of the latter sort are apt to play an important role in arguments about what our constitution and political system requires. Here I am proposing only to pursue the questions of political theory without inquiring into how they figure in this larger argument.

[17] There is here a slight problem of circularity in the interpretation of (1). Since what is at issue is the extent of legislative authority and the degree to which the word of legislatures is final, we cannot presuppose agreement on what constitutes misuse of legislative power. In order for the argument to proceed, therefore, we have to suppose that there is at least some agreement on the kinds of legislative action which are highly undesirable and which, if frequent, would at least raise questions about the acceptability of legislative authority. (Some such agreement seems generally to be asserted by proponents of judicial modesty who, while arguing against judicial intervention, usually profess to deplore the legislation under attack.)

as well as of law. For the idea behind some arguments against substantive due process in this more extended form seems to be that judicial review is an acceptably nonarbitrary form of authority only insofar as it consists in the application of reasonably specific constitutional formulas.

This idea may sometimes be motivated by the view that in reaching substantive due process decisions a court must either be (a) applying some relatively clear constitutional formula; or (b) registering what it takes to be prevailing public opinion; or (c) enacting into law its own personal philosophical views. It is then maintained that, since (c) is unacceptably arbitrary and (b) something better done by an elective representative body than by a court, (a) represents the only acceptable alternative. The strength of this conclusion depends, of course, on how the notion of "application" as used in (a) is understood. I cannot here go into the question of whether there is a plausible interpretation of (a) that would encompass what is generally accepted as legitimate constitutional adjudication in non-due process areas yet exclude the kind of reasoning I have described in discussing substantive due process. I have maintained above that if (a) is interpreted narrowly, then (a), (b), and (c) do not exhaust the relevant alternatives. It is possible to argue rationally about the acceptable distribution of authority in society, and the requirement that a court resolve issues by engaging in public debate of this kind may in some instances be a less arbitrary method of decision than the alternative of unrestrained legislative authority.

Of course, if courts have the authority to reach decisions on this ground, it is likely that they will sometimes do it wrongly. But one cannot infer from the fact that certain decisions are egregiously wrong that they would best be avoided by the adoption of a formal principle (e.g. a principle of judicial modesty) barring courts from undertaking such decisions at all. Such a principle is analogous to a formal principle of legislative behavior, say, one requiring representatives to vote the expressed wishes of their constituents or, alternatively, permitting them to vote their own consciences. Individual decisions can be outstandingly wrong on substantive grounds without violating any such formal principle.[18] Such a principle has to be argued for on general grounds of the kind just discussed by showing that, given the conditions under which decisions are made, the pressures on decision makers and the methods open to them, the adoption of the principle is a needed curb on arbitrariness or a valuable contribution to the efficiency or reliability of the process.

---

[18] This is true, I would argue, of the famous substantive due process cases of the *Lochner* era. The view of liberty and of freedom of contract on which they are based could not be given a coherent defense of the kind required for a substantive due process decision on my account.

Rather than pursue this general controversy any further, let me close by considering one special case of the argument for judicial modesty. On my view, substantive due process decisions involve an element of balancing. In reaching such a decision a court may often have to decide, for example, whether the instrumental value of allowing an institution to operate in a certain way or to pursue a particular purpose justifies allowing it to exercise a certain form of authority despite the costs of its doing so. It is often maintained that such questions are ones which a representative body is particularly designed to resolve, and that a court, in undertaking to reweigh a balancing decision previously arrived at by the legislature, is either inefficiently undertaking to act as a better barometer of public feeling than the legislature is or else placing its own preferences above those of the people as a whole in a way that is repugnant to democratic principles. I want to maintain, against this argument, that questions properly resolved by balancing come in different forms, and that for some balancing questions there is both an acceptable method of judicial determination and a reason why this method should be preferred to purely legislative resolution.

In the sense in which the term "balancing" is used in most legal (and some philosophical) theory, almost anything can be "balanced" against almost anything else. With no claim to exhaustiveness (or even to mutual exclusiveness), let me roughly distinguish three different forms of decision making in which competing considerations are balanced against one another. The first, which I will call "aggregative balancing," is the form typical of traditional utilitarian arguments. In this form, the sum of the advantages of those who may be expected to gain from a particular act or policy is compared to the sum of the disadvantages of those who will lose by it. It is an essential mark of aggregative balancing that the outcome can always be influenced by altering the *number* of people on each side, for example, by sufficiently increasing the gainers or decreasing the losers.

One method of individual decision making that is parallel to aggregative balancing as a method of social choice might be called "individual probabilistic balancing." Here a single person, when faced with a choice between alternative actions leading to uncertain outcomes, considers, for each alternative, the sum of the values for him of the outcomes associated with that alternative, discounted in each case by the probabilities he assigns to these outcomes actually occurring. He then chooses the alternative with the greatest sum of values. Thus, for example, a person considering the desirability from his point of view of various policies concerning police searches may take into account, for each policy, the contribution that policy will make to his safety balanced against the negative value he attaches to being searched, this discounted by the likelihood under that policy of his being subjected to such a search. If, as may be the case in this example, a large number of people think it extremely unlikely that the disadvantageous consequences of a given policy will actually accrue to them, while this probability is much higher for a certain much smaller group, then, if each person reaches his decision on the basis of individual probabilistic balancing and the group decision is made by majority vote, the result is likely to be the same as if aggregative balancing were used.

I suggest that there are questions which, intuitively, strike us as questions of balancing but for which such aggregative arguments do not strike us as appropriate. They are not appropriate, for example, as a way of deciding where the line between reasonable and unreasonable searches and seizures is to be drawn. Surely this line *is* arrived at by a kind of balancing, and this is a balancing which involves the relative strengths of people's interests. This is shown by the fact that, as customs and patterns of life change, it may become proper to draw this line differently; the difference reflecting changes in the value people place on keeping various areas of their lives free from intervention.

But neither aggregative considerations nor estimates of probability are relevant to the kind of balancing that is involved here. To strike the relevant kind of balance, a person must ask himself not what his chances are of being searched, but what *he* would accept as adequate justification for having a certain intervention into his life *actually* take place.

Let me call this "personal balancing." Here we are typically balancing, on the one hand, the importance of the benefits to be gained by allowing officials to exercise a certain power, for example, the power to carry out searches under specific conditions. Determination of this value may involve some aggregation, since we are concerned not with what will be gained by allowing a search to be carried out on a single particular occasion but the value of having such search power in general.[19] On the other hand, we have the value to *an* individual of being free from this kind of invasion. Here we are dealing not with the value to any particular individual but with a

---

[19] The question is one of allocation of competences; hence, in the terms of Charles Fried's distinction ("Two Concepts of Interests: Some Reflections on the Supreme Court's Balancing Test," *Harvard Law Review* 76 [1963], 755–78), we are concerned with a balancing of interests rather than of wants. My distinction is not the same as Fried's, since I am concerned with what is balanced against the benefits of allocating a competence in a given way. But another central distinction in Fried's article (p. 771), that between a court's assigning itself a certain role and its playing that role, appears to be the same as the distinction drawn above between due process decisions of type (1) and those of other types.

"normal" value – the value most people in the society would assign to being free from such searches.

If we were all perfect utilitarians, then perhaps the question posed in personal balancing is one we would settle by aggregative balancing. But utilitarianism is not an adequate account of our normal outlook. There is certainly an area of public policy choices within which aggregative considerations are generally thought, perhaps correctly, to have a dominant role. It seems appropriate, for example, that the goal of bringing the greatest benefit to the greatest number should guide decisions as to how funds available for medical research are to be allocated among the campaigns against various diseases. But a particularly high ratio of benefits to burdens would not, I think, generally be taken as in and of itself sufficient to justify a policy of compulsory organ donation (with monetary compensation) or a policy giving medical authorities the right to compel participation in (not at all dangerous but somewhat unpleasant) medical experiments.

Now there is no reason why legislatures could not reach judgments of the nonaggregative kind I have been calling personal balancing. But there is good evidence for thinking that they characteristically operate in a fashion more likely to yield aggregative judgments. Certainly this seems to be true of the behavior of many legislatures in civil liberties matters. But, even given well-founded suspicion of legislative judgments in areas where personal balancing is called for, a case for giving final judgment in these areas to the courts requires some account of how judges are equipped to do better.

What a court must ask in these cases is whether the benefits that are taken as grounds for a particular exercise of authority are really sufficient to justify it, given the value people generally set on being free from interventions of the kind in question. In determining what this value is, judges need not refer primarily to their own tastes and values. Ample evidence is available in the lengths to which people generally go in their private lives to protect themselves against such interventions, the ways in which they react when they suffer them, and the kinds of legal remedies (claims for damages, etc.) that they consider appropriate. When this evidence makes it clear that the value placed on being free from interventions of the given kind is indeed very high, then a court has an objective basis on which to claim that the authority to carry out such interventions cannot be justified by marginal considerations of social advantage (e.g. the expectation of a slight increase in convictions for certain crimes). An argument of this form would seem to me to support, for example, due process decisions of the kind sometimes based on the test of "conduct that shocks the conscience" while avoiding the subjective aura of that slogan. What is relevant is not that a given exercise of authority (e.g. certain searches) outrages a judge, but rather that it should outrage anyone because the grounds on which it purports to be justified manifestly fail to match the value we ourselves demonstrably place on being free from such interventions.

Arriving at a judgment by the method I have suggested is not the same thing as making an estimate of public opinion. Public opinion may clearly be that the law in question should be passed. In the kind of argument I am suggesting a court would offer evidence for a claim about the value most people demonstrably do set on the sanctity of the relevant aspects of their lives and argue that, given what this value is, the proffered justification for the law in question does not hold up. The conclusion to be drawn is that public opinion and the judgment of the legislature reflected an unacceptable willingness to set a lower value on the concerns of the assignable minority who would suffer from this law than they do on their own, i.e. to engage in aggregative balancing in a case in which this is not an appropriate method.

What is the area within which it is proper for a court to look behind expressed preferences and make judgments of this sort? One answer is that it consists of those cases in which the burden of a piece of legislation is being borne by a clearly identifiable minority that is unlikely to be able to defend itself effectively in legislative decision making (the classical "discrete and insular minority"[20]); but before this criterion becomes applicable one must, on the view I have sketched, already have determined that the question at issue is one of balancing and that it is one for which personal balancing is the required form. But which questions are these?

Here I have no clear-cut answer. One natural suggestion is that personal balancing is required where rights are at issue, but I am unsatisfied with this answer for several reasons. First, some issues of rights are not questions of balancing at all but rather arguments of principle which mark the limits of permissible balancing. Second, within these limits it is not clear that every question of balancing that concerns the subject matter of a recognized right is one for which purely aggregative methods are inappropriate. It may be, for example, that "the greatest happiness of the greatest number" is a proper ground for settling some policy questions about the regulation of expression but not the proper ground for others. Obviously this question of limits – as well as the definition of personal balancing itself – requires further clarification before this distinction can be considered an adequate theoretical device. I offer it here in a tentative way as an example of how

[20] Cf. footnote 4 of Justice Stone's opinion in *U.S. v. Carolene Products Co.*, 304 *U.S.* 144 (1938) at 152.

the judicial balancing that would form a part of substantive due process decisions as I have described them might be distinguished from the kinds of balancing properly reserved to legislatures.

I have tried here to give a general account of due process and to show how much of what seems to fall under this heading can be traced to a single intuitive idea – the unacceptability of arbitrary power – which constitutes its moral foundation. In giving an exposition and anatomy of the idea of due process as I understand it, I have probably given more emphasis to the appeal of this notion than to its problems and dangers. (This is particularly true of my discussion of substantive due process.) This emphasis is perhaps the natural tendency in a theoretical discussion, where intellectual coherence is an overriding goal and where relatively little can be said about questions of strategy and political judgment. The fact that the notion of due process is so situated as naturally to serve as a point of conflict between the pure demands of justificatory coherence and the real world of political institutions is no doubt one reason why this notion continues to be a subject of interest and an object of intense controversy.

4

Preference and urgency

Arguments in moral philosophy frequently turn on appeals to some standard on the basis of which the benefits and sacrifices of different people can be compared. In applying principles of distributive justice, for example, we must appeal to some standard of this kind as a ground for measuring the equality or inequality of shares, and similar appeals must be made in defending systems of rights, and institutionally defined prerogatives and protections. Such appeals to the comparison of benefits and burdens will of course be most direct in those theories which are, broadly speaking, utilitarian, but they also play a crucial role in theories that diverge from utilitarianism. Comparisons of this kind are, for example, crucial to the argument from Rawls's Original Position, and, in general, criteria of relative well-being and relative sacrifice will have a central place in any moral theory that does not start with a system of rights taken as standing in need of no defense.

In this paper I want to describe and discuss some problems concerning the way in which criteria of well-being are to be formulated and defended and the ways in which they enter into moral arguments. Let me begin by stating some properties which it seems that criteria of well-being should have if they are to play the role commonly assigned to them in moral argument. First, if they are to serve as one of the starting points for the criticism and justification of institutions, it appears that criteria of well-being must represent a kind of consensus, at least among those to whom this criticism or justification is addressed. Second, adequate criteria must allow for the fact of individual variation in taste and interest. (I leave aside for the moment consideration of the various ways in which this might be "allowed for.") Finally, on a slightly different level, it seems that an adequate criterion of well-being will have to be result-oriented; that is,

Presented in an APA symposium on Equality, December 28, 1975. The author is indebted to Thomas Nagel for a number of very helpful discussions of this topic.

it will not merely take the form of a ranking of particular "bundles" of goods, but will provide an evaluation of the ways in which individuals may be affected by having these goods. This is so, for one reason, because an adequate criterion will have to be sensitive to variations in needs, e.g. variations arising from physical disabilities. But even if everyone could be assumed to have the same physical condition and the same tastes it could still be the case that a particular good, e.g. a certain legal right, would affect people quite differently depending on where they were situated in society. Different people are able in differing degrees to take advantage of particular legal prerogatives and stand in need to different degrees of the protection that particular legal rights provide. At least this is the case in the societies with which we are familiar. So, if a criterion of relative well-being is to be an adequate basis for the criticism of the institutions of such societies, it must enable us to describe and compare these different gains and losses.

Moral and political theories are often not very explicit about the criteria of well-being that they invoke. Those criteria which have been most explicitly invoked and most clearly formulated are what I will call "subjective criteria." By a *subjective criterion* I mean a criterion according to which the level of well-being enjoyed by a person in given material circumstances or the importance for that person of a given benefit or sacrifice is to be estimated by evaluating those material circumstances or that benefit or sacrifice solely from the point of view of that person's tastes and interests. Hedonistic utilitarianism rests upon a criterion which is subjective in this sense (at least if the relevant notions of pleasure and pain are not understood too narrowly). So also does the "New Utilitarianism" of welfare economists and others. John Harsanyi,[1] for example, advocates a principle of maximum average utility, where "utility" is taken to be an interpersonally comparable notion obtained by first constructing, for each individual, a set of von Neumann–Morgenstern utility functions based on his preferences and then forming these into a single interpersonal system via the following method of interpersonal comparison: the utility level of person A in given material circumstances is the same as that of person B in his material circumstances if an impartial third party would be indifferent between the prospect of assuming A's material circumstances together with A's tastes, interests, etc., and the prospect of assuming B's total material condition together with *his* subjective outlook.

---

[1] "Cardinal Welfare, Individualist Ethics, and Interpersonal Comparisons of Utility," *Journal of Political Economy* 63 (1955), 309–21, and "Can the Maximin Principle Serve as a Basis for Morality? A Critique of John Rawls's Theory," *American Political Science Review* 69 (1975), 594–606.

Given the desiderata listed above, it is easy to see why subjective criteria should be attractive. First, they appear to give maximum recognition to the sovereignty of individual tastes. Subjective criteria may vary in the way in which they identify individual preferences: a criterion might take at face value a person's preferences as he would sincerely report them, or it might be based on his preferences as they would be if corrected for factual mistakes and rendered consistent through a process of careful deliberation. Presumably any plausible criterion will allow for some correction of this kind. Thus, even on a subjective criterion, a person can be mistaken about his level of well-being and how various prospects would affect it. But it remains true on such a criterion that a person's preferences "as they really are" constitute the ultimate standard for judgments about his well-being.

Second, subjective criteria are obviously result-oriented and can clearly accommodate variations in need. That subjective criteria can be held to represent a consensus on which moral criticism of social institutions and social policies can be based is less apparent. I suspect that what proponents of subjective criteria would maintain here is that relative strength of individual preference is the only basis for appraisal of institutions and policies which could be the object of a consensus consistent with the sovereignty of individual tastes. Therefore it would be agreed upon by people to the extent that they seek a principle recognizing them as equal, independent agents whose judgment must be accorded equal weight.

In addition to these considerations, subjective criteria may seem to have a kind of theoretical primacy. How, after all, would any other criteria of relative well-being be defended if not, ultimately, by appeal to individual preferences? For all these reasons, then, there is a natural tendency to take subjective criteria as basic and to hold that, insofar as other criteria are ever an appropriate basis for the moral appraisal of institutions and policies, this is so only for practical reasons – because individual preferences are too many and various to be taken into account and these other criteria represent the best usable approximation to them.

Despite these considerations, it seems clear that the criteria of well-being that we actually employ in making moral judgments are objective. By an *objective criterion* I mean a criterion that provides a basis for appraisal of a person's level of well-being which is independent of that person's tastes and interests, thus allowing for the possibility that such an appraisal could be correct even though it conflicted with the preferences of the individual in question, not only as he believes they are but even as they would be if rendered consistent, corrected for factual errors, etc. In speaking of "objective" criteria I do not mean to deny that these criteria may be socially relative. Nor do I mean to exclude the possibility that, according to such a criterion, the same allotment of goods and opportunities may be judged to represent different levels of well-being for two different people because of differences in their condition. As long as these differences in condition are not merely differences in preferences, a criterion can admit this kind of variation while still remaining objective in my sense. Thus objective criteria can be result-oriented.

The proponent of an objective criterion of well-being need not deny the relevance of subjective preference altogether. A high objective value may be attached to providing those conditions which are necessary to allow individuals to develop their own preferences and interests and to make these felt in the determination of social policy. It may also be important on objective grounds that people should be free to make agreements through which they exchange their allotted shares for others more in line with their preferences. What I take to be central to the objectivist position, however, is the idea that, insofar as we are concerned with moral claims that some interests should be favored at the expense of others in the design of distributive institutions or in the allocation of other rights and prerogatives, it is an objective evaluation of the importance of these interests, and not merely the strength of the subjective preferences they represent, that is relevant. Thus, on an objective criterion we can "allow for" variations in individual preference and give individual autonomy an important place without making the relative strength of subjective preference the foundation of our theory.

That the objectivist position is correct as a description of our actual moral intuitions is evident from the following considerations. Consider first cases of distributive justice. One, admittedly extreme, principle of distributive justice formulated on a subjective basis is the principle of maximum equal satisfaction. This principle requires institutions to be so arranged as to effect distributions that give citizens the same level of utility, where utility is understood in the way described above, and to make this level as high as possible. This principle would have the effect, roughly speaking, of requiring social resources to flow in the direction of the least efficient users: if it takes a greater commitment of material resources to raise A to a given level of well-being than it takes to raise B to a comparable level, then the principle will require a greater expenditure of resources on A than on B. This consequence is directly advocated by A. K. Sen,[2] and it is not implausible in every instance. It seems right, for example, that a person

---

[2] *On Economic Inequality* (New York: Norton, 1973), pp. 18–19, 77–8.

who suffers from physical disabilities making it difficult and expensive for him to enjoy any of the normal pleasures of life should receive special assistance, and an adequate notion of equal treatment might well require such assistance. There may be controversies about the level of aid justified by such disabilities, and the principle of equal satisfaction may set this level too high, but the general tendency to recognize such claims does not seem wrong.

But the principle of equal satisfaction as I have stated it would give this same kind of special consideration to a person who, because of special interests or unusually refined or expensive tastes, could not be raised to a "normal level of satisfaction" without very high expenditures. Examples of this kind are, of course, just the correlates of familiar objections to classical utilitarianism on the ground that it would require us to favor in the distribution of social resources those people, if there are any, who are unusually *efficient* consumers of goods – those whose level of utility rises most rapidly in response to a given expenditure of resources. What the examples show, however, is not that there is anything wrong with maximizing doctrines or with egalitarian doctrines per se but rather that a subjective criterion of well-being seems insensitive to differences between preferences that are of great relevance when these preferences are taken as the basis for moral claims.

The same thing can be seen as well in the case of duties of mutual aid. The strength of a stranger's claim on us for aid in the fulfillment of some interest depends upon what that interest is and need not be proportional to the importance he attaches to it. The fact that someone would be willing to forgo a decent diet in order to build a monument to his god does not mean that his claim on others for aid in his project has the same strength as a claim for aid in obtaining enough to eat (even assuming that the sacrifices required of others would be the same). Perhaps a person does have some claim on others for assistance in a project to which he attaches such great importance. Whether such a claim has significant weight can be debated. All I need maintain is that it does not have the weight of a claim to aid in the satisfaction of a truly urgent interest even if the person in question assigns these interests equal weight.

Even if it is the case that in assessing moral claims we discriminate among "equally strong" preferences, it requires to be explained on what basis we do this and how the use of this basis is to be supported. Let me first try to describe what I take to be the content of the morally relevant notion of "urgency" or "importance" of preferences as we commonly employ it. To begin with, what is the structure of this notion; i.e. what things stand in the relation of greater or lesser urgency? It seems true in a general sense that, say, health is more important than amusement, but little follows from this. It does not follow, for example, either as a matter of individual rational choice or as a matter of defensible social policy, that any activity promoting health is to take precedence over any matter of entertainment. A more adequate outline would be this. We have various general concerns, of which health and amusement might be two. Associated with each of these there is a scale of the various levels or degrees to which the concern might be fulfilled at a given time. Various combinations of such levels represent different levels of well-being. The relation of urgency, then, will be a relation between various increments or decrements along one or more of these scales. This relation allows us to compare the importance for a person in certain circumstances of not undergoing a certain sacrifice with the importance of some competing benefit for a person under different circumstances.

My claim, then, is that, when we set out to compare two such conflicting interests with the aim of supporting a moral judgment as to which should be allowed to prevail, what we do is not compare how strongly the people in question feel about these interests (as determined, perhaps, by what they would be willing to sacrifice to get their way) but rather inquire into the reasons for which these benefits are considered desirable. Even if the goods in question are quite foreign to us and of no value in our society, we can understand why they are of value to someone else if we can bring the reasons for their desirability under familiar general categories. These reasons might, for example, concern material comfort, status, or security; or they might concern health or protection against injury. An alleged benefit which we could not understand as falling under any familiar category of this sort and which was not regarded by the person as having the arbitrariness typical of something he "just happened to take an interest in" would be totally opaque to us. But once we can understand the desirability of a benefit in this way we can begin to place it in a rough hierarchy of relative urgency. The urgency of a benefit will obviously not depend only on the category of the reason for which it is desirable. It will also be relevant how well off the person would be in respect to this category without the benefit, in particular what alternatives are available to him and what sacrifices would be involved in shifting to one of these alternatives. Thus, for example, a person might be interested in having X for reasons of a type that are in general important. Perhaps it is a way of protecting his health. But if X is a very inefficient way of pursuing this goal, or just has little to recommend it as compared with other alternatives available to him, then his preference for X over these other means may have little urgency unless some new reasons for this preference can be adduced. (It should be clear here that a judgment that two courses of action are "alternatives" or that one is a "more efficient" alternative will depend upon what may be a fairly detailed account of the reasons for which these pursuits are valued and of the relative importance of these reasons.)

An account of the various concerns that may move people, of the ways in which a person's interest in these concerns may originate and change, and of the various forms of activity people may undertake in pursuit of these interests would constitute a kind of schematic picture of a range of variation of normal lives.[3] Within such a picture some concerns and some pursuits will appear as relatively peripheral – as things a person might or might not be moved by depending on his choices or on chance factors in his life and upbringing. Other interests will appear as more central – as things virtually anyone must be concerned with. (But, to repeat, from the fact that something advances a central interest it does not follow that it is itself a matter of urgency.)

A picture of this kind can be more or less general; it can represent the range of variation of normal lives in a particular society or the range of lives that might be accessible to people in societies of a given general type (e.g. at a given level of development at a given period in history). How general a picture it is appropriate to employ as the background for judgments of relative urgency will depend on the questions we are addressing. When we are appraising the urgency of a certain benefit for a particular individual, a narrower, socially specific view will normally have priority, since the significance of this benefit will depend on the range of alternatives actually available to the person in his society. But we can also criticize social institutions for, among other things, making available only an unduly limited or particularly inefficient class of ways of pursuing natural human goods. In making such judgments we fall back on a more general conception of the range of possibilities.

A more troubling form of social relativity arises when the relative importance attached to certain concerns in a particular society diverges sharply from the standard we would apply. It might seem that, insofar as we are appraising only a society's internal arrangements, it is that society's standard of relative urgency which is relevant. But this is so only so long as we

---

[3] I admit this is an extravagantly general and abstract notion, but it seems to me to be required for arguments we make. Something like it would be required, I think, either to defend or to attack Rawls's claim that his primary social goods are "socially strategic," i.e. that, if they are fairly distributed, then the claims of the various needs and interests people have will have been fairly met. See his "Fairness to Goodness," *Philosophical Review* 84, no. 4 (October 1975), sec. V.

take these standards to be the object of genuine, society-wide agreement. When there is disagreement on standards within the society we have to make up our own minds who is right; thus we base our appraisal of its institutions on our own conception of relative importance. Similarly, in the reverse direction, whenever there is a sharp divergence between the standards of relative importance that appear to us to be correct and those which are apparently accepted in a given society, we are apt to require strong positive evidence for the claim that the alleged consensus is genuine and unmanufactured.

These general remarks can be illustrated by the following example.[4] Even if the distribution of income in a society were strictly equal, it might be felt that true equality required special allowance for those with expensive medical needs. But how much is required? There must come a point beyond which the concern with ensuring health and prolonging life ceases to take objective priority over other concerns. At this point the requirements of equality are fulfilled, and it is up to each individual whether he wishes to sacrifice other goods in order to give himself additional forms of protection. But how is this point determined? One answer would be that each society can set this threshold wherever it likes. It all depends on how the members of that society value health and the prolongation of life, and to what extent they are willing to take chances. But this presupposes that there is some consensus in the society on the relevant values – that there is some value that "everyone sets" on various increments of health protection. If there is no such consensus then the question of what equality requires can be settled only by an independent determination of the relevant value. This raises a general problem concerning the objective notion of urgency and its relation to consensus, which I shall return to at the end of the paper.

I have so far argued that the criteria of well-being that we commonly employ in moral judgment are objective, and I have tried to describe in a general way the content of these criteria. I have also claimed that these objective criteria are acceptably result-oriented and that they allow in an appropriate way for variations in individual taste and preference. The question remains, however, whether there are reasons why we should employ such objective criteria rather than subjective ones as the interpersonal measure of benefit and sacrifice. One argument to this effect proceeds as follows. In the examples presented above it seemed as though a principle of mutual aid

---

[4] This case is discussed by Charles Fried in his "Difficulties in the Economic Analysis of Rights with Application to the Case of Health," in Gerald Dworkin, Gordon Bermant, and Peter G. Brown, eds., *Markets and Morals* (New York: John Wiley, 1977), pp. 175–95. Fried draws a distinction between objective and subjective criteria of well-being very similar to the distinction I employ.

or of distributive justice based on a subjective criterion would leave us open to being "held up" by people who had unusually expensive tastes or who attached inordinate importance to some relatively minor concern. This objection might be put by saying that preferences are too nearly voluntary to be an appropriate basis for the adjudication of competing claims.[5] Rawls may be referring to something like this objection when he says, in arguing in favor of an objective criterion, "We are assuming that people are able to control and to revise their wants and desires in the light of circumstances and that they are to have responsibility for doing so... Persons do not take their wants and desires as determined by happenings beyond their control. We are not, so to speak, assailed by them, as we are perhaps by disease and illness so that wants and desires fail to support claims to the means of satisfaction in the way that disease and illness support claims to medicine and treatment."[6]

The appeal of this objection cannot lie in the possibility of contemporaneous choice, since a person's preferences are not directly subject to his will. "Preference," insofar as it is a highly individualistic notion (a person's preferences are "his own" and to be respected as such), seems also to have a voluntarist ring. But this is partly a verbal illusion. That we do not see our wants and desires as things that "assail us" may come to this: something does not count as one of our desires or at least not as one of our preferences unless we identify with it. Still, this is only a necessary condition for preferences. We cannot determine what our preference is or adjust the relative strength of two preferences by a single act of "identification" or choice in the way we can determine which of two alternative courses of action we will opt for. Indeed, it seems likely that in order to be a preference in the sense that could plausibly be taken as a basis for moral argument something must either be firmly felt (something we are "assailed by") or else linkable to other preferences and beliefs by appropriate reasoning.

So the appeal of the voluntariness objection must lie elsewhere. One possible place is in the malleability of preferences over time. The development of our tastes and interests is to a certain extent subject to our conscious direction, and perhaps we think that it should be to a greater extent than it actually is. Perhaps the force of the voluntariness objection lies in that

---

[5] Richard Brandt voices an objection of this sort to a criterion of well-being based on a notion of preference so inclusive as to allow moral opinions to be the ground of preferences. But a notion of preference restricted to wants and desires appears to satisfy him. See his "Personal Values and the Justification of Institutions," in S. Hook, ed., *Human Values and Economic Policy* (New York: New York University Press, 1967), pp. 22–40. A similar view is expressed in Kurt Baier's contribution to the same volume.

[6] "A Kantian Conception of Equality," *Cambridge Review* 96, 2225 (February, 1975), 97.

it is possible for unusually strong or unusually expensive preferences to be "manufactured" by the person who has them. Just the fact that this is a possibility might make a standard of interpersonal comparison that took preferences at face value unacceptably subject to manipulation. But if this were the whole basis for the voluntariness objection one would expect that, at least in principle, the actual genesis of a person's preferences would be relevant to the strength of their claim to be satisfied. The very same intense interest might have arisen out of a conscious decision to "take up" a certain activity, or it might have grown almost unnoticed as the result of a series of chance encounters. Which of these is the case does not, however, seem to matter for the purposes of determining the strength of the person's claim on others for aid in the satisfaction of this interest. (Although it may be relevant to the assessment of his claim for aid in getting rid of the interest should he come to regard it as an obsession which cripples him in the pursuit of his normal activities.) That no difference shows up here may be a reflection of the fact that, as Rawls says, we take the view (literally false) that *all* a person's wants and desires are things he controls and is responsible for. My interest at the moment, however, is in seeing what lies behind this view.

The fact that an interest, given its content, could have arisen in either of the two ways suggested above already tells us something about it, namely that it is a concern that the person need not have developed. Things could have been otherwise; he could have taken up some other pursuit; and in either case he would have lacked this particular concern or at least would not assign it the importance he now does. How are these "could"s to be understood? I suggest that they refer to the existence of alternative possibilities within the framework of what we consider to be a normal life. It may be possible for a person to succeed to some degree in controlling and greatly reducing or even eliminating some desire which is generally regarded as basic to a normal life. But in general the preferences that are plausibly thought of as subject to the control of the person who has them are those which concern interests that are peripheral rather than central in the sense described above. To say that a preference falls into this class is thus to say something about the reasons supporting it. Suppose a person's preference has this character – the reasons supporting it are "peripheral" – but the person equates this preference with others of much greater objective urgency. This additional strength may be said, speaking loosely, to be something the agent is "responsible for" not because he has in fact chosen to feel this way (perhaps he has not) but because it is merely a reflection of something about him, unsupported by objective reasons.

There are problems with this analysis of the voluntariness objection. From the fact that an interest is not central it may not follow that particular preferences flowing from it lack urgency. Could there be an interest which was not of a central category – an interest people might or might not happen to have – but which, if a person had it, would be the basis for urgent claims? It is not clear to me that there could be no such interest, but I cannot come up with an example. The claims of variable need are not an instance, since the interests that support them are interests everyone has. Religion might seem to be an example. In our society some people are concerned with religion, others are not. Yet the claims of one's religious preferences not to be interfered with are thought to have a special urgency. But would this be so if it were not thought that religion *or something like it* has a central place in anyone's life?

If the analysis I have offered of the appeal of the voluntariness objection is accurate then this objection presupposes something like the objective notion of urgency of preference which I described above. It therefore cannot be taken as an argument for this notion; rather, they are two parts of the same view. Given this view, it is natural that the adoption of a thoroughgoingly subjective criterion as the basis for moral assessment of institutions and individual claims will seem unacceptable. It would be unacceptable, given this view, to allow the structure of a person's preferences to justify elevating an objectively minor concern of his to the same level of moral importance as the urgent concerns of someone else. But subjective preferences could enter in a less radical way. Why shouldn't the appropriate moral principle be one which, in adjudicating between claims of the same urgency, gives greater weight to those to which greater subjective importance is attached?

The reasons for rejecting a principle giving even this more modest role to subjective criteria involve further appeal to the appropriateness, in social decision making, of the idea that each person's preferences are his own concern. There is no reason why a person may not assign an unusually high value to what would normally be considered a trivial concern, or why he should not become devoted to some inordinately expensive way of satisfying a common need. But others may properly say that the shares of scarce social goods available to them for needs of the same urgency should not be reduced as a result. That something like this is the view we actually take explains part of our reaction to Mill's doctrine of higher and lower pleasures. Leaving aside the elitist overtones of this doctrine and the empirical question of whether the unanimity of opinion claimed by Mill actually exists, Mill's position fails to be at all convincing for a further reason. Even if everyone who had tried both pursuits did agree that poetry was much to be preferred to pushpin and worth a much greater sacrifice, this fact would be irrelevant to a determination of the respective rights of poets and pushpin players. As long as we see these as two alternative pursuits of the same level of urgency, the desire to pursue one has the same moral claim not to be interfered with as the desire to pursue the other, and the people who would pursue them have the same claim to share in the social resources that are left over after more urgent interests have been taken care of.

This is not to say, of course, that if we were getting a present for a friend and had to choose between a pushpin game and a book of poetry we might not be advised on Millian grounds to prefer the poetry. In many of the examples commonly appealed to in support of utilitarian principles the balancing in question concerns what I have called "relative urgency." Harsanyi, for example, in arguing against Rawls, consistently stresses that the "more important" needs of one person should never be sacrificed to the less important or "minor" concerns of another whatever their overall levels of welfare may be.[7] It is significant, however, that, in those examples in which what is to be balanced really seems to be strength of preference, there are special features of the situation that make a concern with the tastes and preferences of the individuals involved particularly relevant, as they are, for example, when a person is choosing a gift for a friend or selecting a menu to please his guests. In defending the use of objective criteria one must claim that what is appropriate in these situations is not the right basis for adjudication between competing interests in a more impersonal situation.[8]

Urgency is a two-faced notion. In moral arguments appeals to relative urgency seem to be appeals to a consensus about how much people care about certain benefits, protections, etc. The structure of such arguments is first to claim that everyone admits in his own case that, say, being protected against a certain consequence is more important than enjoying some other benefit. One then imposes some moral framework, e.g. Rawls's Original Position, requiring that institutions be justified on grounds that give equal weight to everyone's concerns. The conclusion is then drawn that a morally acceptable allocation of rights would have to provide the protection in question at the expense of not providing the competing benefit. But when

---

[7] "Can the Maximin Principle Serve as a Basis for Morality?," p. 597. Consider also Mill's argument for rights on the basis of the importance of security, in ch. 5 of *Utilitarianism*.

[8] One response to such criticisms would be a consequentialist theory based on relative urgency rather than strength of preference. A theory of this kind might lack the reductive character claimed for some versions of utilitarianism, since the notion of urgency may itself have significant moral content. It seems likely that such a theory would preserve some of the radically redistributive consequences of utilitarianism, but the degree to which it would resemble utilitarianism in other respects would depend on the solution to the problem of how aggregative considerations and considerations of relative urgency can be combined in a systematic way, i.e. whether and when less urgent interests of many people can outweigh more urgent interests of a few. This is an important problem which must be faced in any event but which I have not attempted to deal with here.

this argument is considered from the perspective of individual preferences, the consensus appealed to is more doubtful. Relative urgency does not coincide either with the relative strength of expressed preferences or with that of preferences as they would be if rendered fully consistent, etc. From the point of view of individual preference, then, "urgency" as I have described it appears already to be a moral notion.

The notion of relative urgency is appealed to in both utilitarian and contract arguments, and in both its moral aspect enters in a veiled form. In Rawls, urgency enters through appeals to a consensus about the ordering of bundles of primary social goods. In forms of utilitarianism in which "utility" is left unspecified, urgency plays a large role in its interpretation. When "utility" is explicitly defined in terms of strength of preference, these preferences are generally assumed to have a structure that coincides with urgency as I have described it. But if urgency is an independent, morally significant notion that is neither a matter of literally unanimous agreement nor identical with the relative strength of subjective preferences, then this notion needs to be examined and the grounds of its moral relevance spelled out.

I see two approaches to this problem: roughly speaking, a naturalist and a conventionalist approach. The first would be to abandon the idea that the moral significance of relative urgency rests on consensus – on the fact that it is a ranking of concerns that everyone really agrees on. One would then seek to defend it as a morally significant notion in its own right, as the objective truth about which interests are more important and which are less so. The second approach would be to preserve the idea of consensus and to defend the notion of urgency as a construct put together for the purposes of moral argument. Such a construct coincides only approximately with actual individual preferences; its usefulness, however, stems not from the fact that these preferences are too many and diverse to be reckoned directly, but rather from the fact that it represents, under the circumstances, the best available standard of justification that is mutually acceptable to people whose preferences diverge.[9]

---

[9] The idea that a standard incorporating factors other than utility is required by the need for a mediating principle of this sort is similar to a suggestion made by Lester Thurow. What I have called "differences in urgency" enter in Thurow's theory through the "individual societal preferences" people have about how benefits are distributed. Thurow argues that such preferences, which make potential benefactors more interested in providing some benefits (e.g. medical care) than they are in providing others equally desired by the recipients, would have to be taken into account in an adequate social welfare function, along with the preferences of the beneficiaries. See his "Toward a Definition of Economic Justice," *The Public Interest* 31 (Spring 1973), 56–80, and also his contribution to the Dworkin et al. volume cited in footnote 4 above.

Some evidence as to which of these approaches is more promising might be derived from consideration of the voluntariness objection. If it is possible to offer a plausible instrumental argument for the standard of urgency, this would lend plausibility to the conventionalist view. If, on the other hand, such arguments wind up presupposing urgency, this would support its claim to being an objective notion that one cannot easily get behind.

5

Freedom of expression and categories of expression

I. INTRODUCTION

Freedom of expression, as a philosophical problem, is an instance of a more general problem about the nature and status of rights. Rights purport to place limits on what individuals or the state may do, and the sacrifices they entail are in some cases significant. Thus, for example, freedom of expression becomes controversial when expression appears to threaten important individual interests in a case like the Skokie affair, or to threaten some important national interest such as the ability to raise an army. The general problem is, if rights place limits on what can be done even for good reasons, what is the justification for these limits?

A second philosophical problem is how we decide what these limits are. Rights appear to be something we can reason about, and this reasoning process does not appear to be merely a calculation of consequences. In many cases, we seem to decide whether a given policy infringes freedom of expression simply by consulting our conception of what this right entails. And while there are areas of controversy, there is a wide range of cases in which we all seem to arrive at the same answer. But I doubt that any of us could write out a brief, noncircular definition of freedom of expression whose mechanical application to these clear cases would yield the answers on which we all agree. In what, then, does our agreement consist?

My aim in this essay is to present an account of freedom of expression that provides at least a few answers to these general questions. I will also address a more specific question about freedom of expression itself. What importance should a theory of freedom of expression assign to categories of expression such as political speech, commercial speech, libel, and pornography? These

Versions of this paper were presented at the University of Minnesota and the University of California at Berkeley as well as at the Pittsburgh symposium. I am grateful to members of all these audiences for helpful comments. I have also benefited greatly from discussions of this topic with Marshall Cohen, Clark Glymour, and Derek Parfit.

categories appear to play an important role in informal thought about the subject. It seems central to the controversy about the *Skokie* case, for example, that the proposed ordinance threatened the ability of unpopular *political* groups to hold demonstrations.[1] I doubt whether the residents of Skokie would have been asked to pay such a high price to let some other kind of expression proceed. To take a different example, laws against false or deceptive advertising and the ban on cigarette advertising on television suggest that we are willing to accept legal regulation of the form and content of commercial advertising that we would not countenance if it were applied to other forms of expression. Why should this be so?

While I do not accept all of these judgments, I find it hard to resist the idea that different categories of expression should to some degree be treated differently in a theory of freedom of expression. On the other hand some ideas of freedom of expression seem to apply across the board, regardless of category: intervention by government to stop the publication of what it regards as a false or misleading view seems contrary to freedom of expression whether the view concerns politics, religion, sex, health or the relative desirability of two kinds of automobile. So the question is, to what extent are there general principles of freedom of expression, and to what extent is freedom of expression category-dependent? To the degree that the latter is true, how are the relevant categories defined?

I will begin by considering the individual interests that are the basis of our special concern with expression. In section III I will consider how several theories of freedom of expression have been based on certain of these interests, and I will sketch an answer to the first two questions raised above. Finally, in sections IV and V, I will discuss the place of categories of expression within the framework I have proposed and apply this to the particular categories of political speech, commercial speech, and pornography.

II. INTERESTS

What are the interests with which freedom of expression is concerned? It will be useful to separate these roughly into those interests we have in being able to speak, those interests we have in being exposed to what others have to say, and those interests we have as bystanders who are affected by expression in other ways. Since, however, I want to make it clear that "expression" as I am using it is not limited to speech, I will refer to these three groups of

---

[1] *Village of Skokie* v. *National Socialist Party of America*, 69 Ill. 2d 605, 373 N.E. 2d 21 (1978).

interests as the interests of participants, the interests of audiences, and the interests of bystanders.

A. Participant interests

The actions to which freedom of expression applies are actions that aim to bring something to the attention of a wide audience. This intended audience need not be the widest possible audience ("the public at large"), but it must be more than one or two people. Private conversations are not, in general, a matter of freedom of expression, not because they are unimportant to us but because their protection is not the aim of this particular doctrine. (It is a matter, instead, of privacy or of personal liberty of some other sort.) But private conversations might be viewed differently if circumstances were different. For example, if telephone trees (or whispering networks) were an important way of spreading the word because we lacked newspapers and there was no way for us to gather to hear speeches, then legal restrictions on personal conversations could infringe freedom of expression as well as being destructive of personal liberty in a more general sense. What this shows, I think, is that freedom of expression is to be understood primarily in terms of the interests it aims to protect and only secondarily in terms of the class of actions whose protection is, under a given set of circumstances, an adequate way to safeguard these interests.

The most general participant interest is, then, an interest in being able to call something to the attention of a wide audience. This ability can serve a wide variety of more specific purposes. A speaker may be interested in increasing his reputation or in decreasing someone else's, in increasing the sales of his product, in promoting a way of life, in urging a change in government, or simply in amusing people or shocking them. From a social point of view, these interests are not all equally important, and the price that a society is required to pay in order to allow acts of expression of a particular kind to flourish will sometimes be a function of the value of expression of that kind.

This is one reason why it would be a mistake to look for a distinction between pure speech (or expression), which is protected by freedom of expression, and expression that is part of some larger course of action, which is not so protected. It is true that some acts of expression seem not to qualify for First Amendment protection because of the larger courses of action of which they are a part (assault, incitement). But what distinguishes these from other acts of expression is not just that they are part of larger courses of action (which is true of almost all acts of expression), but rather the character of the particular courses of action of which they form a part. Their exclusion from First Amendment protection should be seen as a special case of the more general phenomenon just mentioned: the protection to which an act of expression is entitled is in part a function of the value of the larger purposes it serves.

This cannot mean, of course, that the protection due a given act of expression depends on the actual value of the particular purposes at which it aims. It would be clearly antithetical to freedom of expression, for example, to accord greater protection to exponents of true religious doctrines than to exponents of false and misleading ones. Despite the fact that the objectives at which these two groups aim are of very different value, their acts of expression are (other things being equal) accorded equal status. This is so because the "further interest" that is at stake in the two cases is in fact the same, namely the interest we all have in being able to follow and promote our religious beliefs whatever they may be.

Here, then, is one way in which categories of expression arise. We are unwilling to bear the social costs of granting to just any expressive purpose the opportunities for expression that we would demand for those purposes to which we, personally, attach greatest importance. At the most concrete level, however, there is no agreement about the values to be attached to allowing particular acts of expression to go forward. It is just this lack of consensus, and the consequent unacceptability of allowing governments to regulate acts of expression on the basis of their perceived merits, that makes freedom of expression an important issue. In order to formulate a workable doctrine of freedom of expression, therefore, we look for something aproaching a consensus on the relative importance of interests more abstractly conceived – the interest in religious expression, the interest in political expression, etc. Even this more abstract consensus is only approximate,[2] however, and never completely stable. As people's values change, or as a society becomes more diverse, consensus erodes. When this happens, either the ranking of interests must change or the categories of interests must be redefined, generally in a more abstract manner.[3] Recent shifts in attitudes toward religion have

---

[2] How the existence of an approximate consensus, even though it is only approximate, can contribute to the legitimacy of the agreed-upon values as a basis for justification is a difficult problem which I cannot here discuss.

[3] I have assumed here that categories of interests are disrupted by a decrease in consensus and an increase in diversity of views since this is the course of change we are most familiar with. I suppose that the reverse process – in which increasing consensus makes an abstract category seem pointlessly abstract and leads to its being redefined to include what was before only a special case – is at least possible. On the former, more familiar kind of transition, see E. Durkheim, "Individualism and the Intellectuals," in R. Bellah, ed., *Emile Durkheim on Morality and Society* (Chicago: University of Chicago

provoked changes of both these kinds. As religion (or, as it is more natural to say here, *one's* religion) has come to be seen more as a matter of private concern on a par with other private interests, it has become harder to justify assigning religious concerns the preeminent value they have traditionally received. In order to make contemporary sense of this traditional assignment of values, on the other hand, there has been a tendency to redefine "religion" more abstractly as "a person's ultimate values and deepest convictions about the nature of life," thereby preserving some plausibility for the claim that we can all agree on the importance of religion in one's life even though we may have different beliefs.

The categories of participant interests I have been discussing are naturally identified with familiar categories of expression: political speech, commercial speech, etc. But we should not be too quick to make this identification. The type of protection that a given kind of expression requires is not determined by participant values alone. It also depends on such factors as the costs and benefits to nonparticipants and the reliability of available forms of regulation. Not surprisingly, these other factors also play a role in how categories of expression are defined. As will later become apparent, the lack of clarity concerning these categories results in part from the difficulty of seeing how these different elements are combined in their definition.[4]

B. Audience interests

The interests of audiences are no less varied than those of participants: interests in being amused, informed on political topics, made aware of the pros and cons of alternatives available in the market, and so on. These audience interests conflict with those of participants in an important way. While participants sometimes aim only at communicating with people who are already interested in what they have to present, in a wide range of important cases their aims are broader: they want to gain the attention of

---

Press, 1973), p. 43. See also E. Durkheim, *Division of Labor in Society*, trans. G. Simpson (1933). Perhaps Marx's view of the transition to a socialist society includes an instance of the latter kind.

[4] Here libel provides a good example. One reason for assigning it low status as a category of expressive acts is the low value attached to the participant interest in insulting people and damaging their reputations. This is something we sometimes want to do, but it gets low weight in our social calculus. Another reason is the high value we attach to not having our reputations damaged. These are not unrelated, but they do not motivate concern with the same class of actions. Other relevant considerations include the interest we may have in performing or having others perform acts which incidentally damage reputations. A defensible definition of libel as a category of expressive acts will be some resultant of all these factors, not simply of the first or the second alone.

people who would not otherwise consider their message. What audiences generally want, on the other hand, is to have expression available to them should they want to attend to it. Expression that grabs one's attention whether one likes it or not is generally thought of as a cost. But it should not be thought of only as a cost, even from the audience's point of view. As Mill rightly emphasized,[5] there is significant benefit in being exposed to ideas and attitudes different from one's own, though this exposure may be unwelcome. If we had complete control over the expression we are exposed to, the chances are high that we would use this power to our detriment. The important and difficult question, however, is, when unwanted exposure to expression is a good thing from the audience's point of view.

This question is relatively easy to answer if we think of it as a problem of balancing temporary costs of annoyance, shock or distraction against the more lasting benefits of a broadened outlook or deepened understanding. But it becomes more complicated if we take into account the possibility of more lasting costs such as being misled, having one's sensibilities dulled and cheapened, or acquiring foolish desires. This balancing task is simplified in the way we often think about expression by a further assumption about the audience's control. We are inclined to think that what would be ideal from the audience's point of view would be always to have the choice whether or not to be exposed to expression. Similarly, we have a tendency to assume that, having been exposed, an audience is always free to decide how to react: what belief to form or what attitude to adopt. This freedom to decide enables the audience to protect itself against unwanted long-range effects of expression. If we saw ourselves as helplessly absorbing as a belief every proposition we heard expressed, then our views of freedom of expression would be quite different from what they are. Certainly we are not like that. Nonetheless, the control we exercise over what to believe and what attitudes to adopt is in several respects an incomplete protection against unwarranted effects of expression.

To begin with, our decisions about what to believe are often mistaken, even in the best of circumstances. More generally, the likelihood of our not being mistaken, and hence the reliability of our critical rationality as a defense mechanism, varies widely from case to case depending on our emotional state, the degree of background information we possess, and the amount of time and energy we have to assess what we hear. As these things vary, so too does the value of being exposed to expression and the value of being able to avoid it. Commonly recognized cases of diminished

---

[5] J. Mill, *On Liberty*, ed. C. Shields (New York: Bobbs-Merrill, 1956), ch. 2.

rationality such as childhood, panic, and mental illness are just extreme instances of this common variation.

Quite apart from the danger of mistakenly believing what we hear, there is the further problem that a decision to disbelieve a message does not erase all the effects it may have on us. Even if I dismiss what is said or shown to me as foolish and exaggerated, I am slightly different for having seen or heard it. This difference can be trivial but it can also be significant and have a significant effect on my later decisions. For example, being shown powerful photographs of the horrors of war, no matter what my initial reaction to them may be, can have the effect of heightening (or ultimately of dulling) my sense of the human suffering involved, and this may later affect my opinions about foreign policy in ways I am hardly aware of.

Expression influencing us in this way is a good thing, from the point of view of our interests as audiences, if it affects our future decisions and attitudes by making us aware of good reasons for them, so long as it does not interfere with our ability to weigh these reasons against others. Expression is a bad thing if it influences us in ways that are unrelated to relevant reasons, or in ways that bypass our ability to consider these reasons. "Subliminal advertising" is a good example of this. What is bad about it is not just that it is "subliminal," i.e. that we are influenced by it without being aware of that influence. This, I think, happens all the time and is, in many cases, unobjectionable. What is objectionable about subliminal advertising, if it works, is that it causes us to act – to buy popcorn, say, or to read Dostoevsky – by making us think we have a good reason for so acting, even though we probably have no such reason. Suddenly finding myself with the thought that popcorn would taste good or that *Crime and Punishment* would be just the thing is often good grounds for acting in the relevant way. But such a thought is no reason for action if it is produced in me by messages flickered on the screen rather than by facts about my present state that indeed make this a good moment to go out for popcorn or to lie down with a heavy book.

I have assumed here that subliminal advertising works by leading us to form a false belief: we acquire a positive feeling toward popcorn which we then take, mistakenly, to be a sign that we would particularly enjoy some popcorn. One can easily imagine, however, that the effect is deeper.[6] Suppose that what the advertising does is to change us so that we both have a genuine desire for popcorn and will in fact enjoy it. One can still raise

---

[6] Here I am indebted to the discussion following the presentation of this paper at Berkeley and to comments by members of my graduate seminar for the Spring Term, 1979.

the question whether being affected in this way is a good thing for us, but an answer to it cannot rely on the claim that we are made to think that we have a reason to buy popcorn when in fact we do not. For in this case we will have as good a reason to buy popcorn as we ever do: we want some and will enjoy it if we get it. Advertising of this kind will be a bad thing from the audience's point of view if one is worse off for having acquired such a desire, perhaps because it leads one to eat unhealthily, or because it distracts one from other pursuits, or for some other reason.

It is particularly galling to think of such effects being produced in us by another agent whose aim is to have us benefit him through actions we would not otherwise choose. But the existence of a conscious manipulator is not essential to the objections I have presented. It is a bad thing to acquire certain desires or to be influenced by false reasons, and these things are bad whether or not they are brought about by other agents. But while the existence of a conscious manipulator is not essential to this basic objection, it can be relevant in two further ways. What we should want in general is to have our beliefs and desires produced by processes that are reliable – processes whose effectiveness depends on the grounds for the beliefs and on the goodness of the desires it produces. We prefer to be aware of how we are being affected partly because this critical awareness increases the reliability of the process; although, as I have said, this safeguard is commonly overrated. Particularly where effects on us escape our notice, the existence of an agent controlling these effects can decrease the reliability of the process: the effects produced will be those serving this agent's purposes, and there may be no reason to think that what serves his purposes will be good from our point of view. (Indeed, the reverse is suggested by the fact that he chooses surreptitious means.) So the existence of a controlling agent can be relevant because of its implications for the reliability of the process. Beyond the question of reliability, however, we may simply prefer to have the choice whether or not to acquire a given desire; we may prefer this even where there is no certainty as to which desire it is better to have. This provides a further reason for objecting to effects produced in us by others (although this reason seems to hold as well against effects produced by inanimate causes).

The central audience interest in expression, then, is the interest in having a good environment for the formation of one's beliefs and desires. From the point of view of this interest, freedom of expression is only one factor among many. It is important to be able to hear what others wish to tell us, but this is not obviously more important than having affirmative rights of access to important information or to basic education. Perhaps freedom of expression is thought to differ in being purely negative: it consists merely in not being denied something and is therefore more easily justified as a right than are freedom of information or the right to education, which require others to provide something for us. But this distinction does not withstand a careful scrutiny. To begin with, freedom of expression adequately understood requires affirmative protection for expression, not just the absence of interference. Moreover, even nonintervention involves costs, such as the annoyance and disruption that expression may cause. On the other side, restrictions on freedom of information include not only failures to provide information but also attempts to conceal what would otherwise become public. When a government makes such an attempt for the purpose of stopping the spread of undesirable political opinions, this contravenes the same audience interests as an attempt to restrict publication, and the two seem to be objectionable on the same grounds. The fact that there is in the one case no "participant" whose right to speak is violated, but only a fact that remains undiscovered, seems not to matter.

C. Bystander interests

I have mentioned that both participants and audiences can sometimes benefit from restrictions on expression as well as from the lack thereof. But the most familiar arguments for restricting expression appeal to the interests of bystanders. I will mention these only briefly. First are interests in avoiding the undesirable side effects of acts of expression themselves: traffic jams, the noise of crowds, the litter from leafletting. Second, and more important, are interests in the effect expression has on its audience. A bystander's interests may be affected simply by the fact that the audience has acquired new beliefs if, for example, they are beliefs about the moral character of the bystander. More commonly, bystanders are affected when expression promotes changes in the audience's subsequent behavior.

Regulation of expression to protect any of these bystander interests can conflict with the interests of audiences and participants. But regulation aimed at protecting bystanders against harms of the first type frequently strikes us as less threatening than that aimed at protecting bystanders against harmful changes in audience belief and behavior. This is true in part because the types of regulation supported by the two objectives are different. Protecting bystanders against harmful side effects of acts of expression calls for regulation only of the time, place, and manner of expression, and in many cases such regulation merely inconveniences audiences and participants. It *need* not threaten central interests in expression. Regulation to protect interests of the second kind, however, must, if it is successful, prevent effective communication of an idea. It is thus in direct conflict with the interests of participants and, at least potentially, of audiences as well. But this contrast is significant only to the degree that there are some forms of effective expression through which participant and audience interests can be satisfied without occasioning bystander harms of the first type: where there is no surplus of effective means of expression, regulation of time, place, and manner can be just as dangerous as restrictions on content.

III. THEORIES

Although "freedom of expression" seems to refer to a right of participants not to be prevented from expressing themselves, theoretical defenses of freedom of expression have been concerned chiefly with the interests of audiences and, to a lesser extent, those of bystanders. This is true, for example, of Mill's famous defense in *On Liberty*,[7] which argues that a policy of noninterference with expression is preferable to a policy of censorship on two grounds: first, it is more likely to promote the spread of true beliefs and, second, it contributes to the well-being of society by fostering the development of better (more independent and inquiring) individuals. A similar emphasis on audience values is evident in Alexander Meiklejohn's theory.[8] He argues that First Amendment freedom of speech derives from the right of citizens of a democracy to be informed in order that they can discharge their political responsibilities as citizens.

This emphasis can be explained, I think, by the fact that theories of freedom of expression are constructed to respond to what are seen as the most threatening arguments for restricting expression. These arguments have generally proceeded by calling attention to the harms that unrestricted expression may bring to audiences and bystanders: the harm, for example, of being misled, or that of being made less secure because one's neighbors have been misled or provoked into disaffection and unrest. The conclusion drawn is that government, which has the right and even the duty to protect its citizens against such harms, may and should do so by preventing the expression in question. Responding to this argument, theories of freedom of expression have tended to argue either that the interests in question are not best protected by restricting expression (Mill) or that "protecting" citizens in this way is illegitimate on other grounds (Meiklejohn).

The dialectical objective of Mill's argument helps to explain why, although he professes to be arguing as a utilitarian, he concentrates on just

---

[7] Mill, *On Liberty*, ch. 2. [8] A. Meiklejohn, *Political Freedom* (New York: Harper & Row, 1960).

two goods, true belief and individual growth, and never explicitly considers how these are to be balanced off against other goods that would have to be taken into account in a full utilitarian argument.

The surprising narrowness of Meiklejohn's theory can be similarly explained. Meiklejohn was reacting against the idea that a "clear and present danger" could justify a government in acting to protect its citizens by curbing the expression of threatening political ideas. This seemed to him to violate the rights of those it claimed to protect. Accordingly, he sought to explain the "absolute" character of the First Amendment by basing it in a right to be informed and to make up one's own mind. But is there such a right? Meiklejohn saw the basis for one in the deliberative role of citizens in a democratic political order. But a right so founded does not apply to all forms of expression. Debates over artistic merit, the best style of personal life, or the promotion of goods in the marketplace may have their importance, but Meiklejohn saw these forms of expression as pursuits on a par with many others, unable to claim any distinct right to immunity from regulation. He was thus led to concede that these activities, in the main, fall outside the area of fundamental First Amendment protection or, rather, that they qualify for it only insofar as their general importance makes them relevant to political decisions.

This narrowness is an unsatisfactory feature of what is in many ways an interesting and appealing theory. Moreover, given this emphasis on political rights as the basis of First Amendment protection of speech, it is particularly surprising that Meiklejohn's theory should take audience values – the right of citizens to be informed – as the only fundamental ones. For prominent among the political rights of democratic citizens is the right to participate in the political process – in particular, the right to argue for one's own interests and point of view and to attempt to persuade one's fellow citizens. Such rights of participation do not entirely derive from the need of one's fellow citizens to be informed; the right to press one's case and to try to persuade others of its validity would not evaporate if it could be assumed that others were already perfectly informed on the questions at issue. Perhaps Meiklejohn would respond by saying that what is at stake is not a matter of being informed in the narrow sense of possessing all the relevant information. Democratic citizens also need to have the arguments for alternative policies forcefully presented in a way that makes their strengths and weaknesses more apparent, stimulates critical deliberation and is conducive to the best decision. Surely, it might be asked, when political participation reaches the point where it becomes irrelevant to or even detracts from the possibility of good political decisions, what is the argument in its favor? I will return to this question of the relation between participant and nonparticipant interests in section v.[9]

Several years ago I put forward a theory of freedom of expression[10] that was very much influenced by Meiklejohn's views. Like him, I wanted to state a principle of freedom of expression which had a kind of absoluteness or at least a partial immunity from balancing against other concerns. But I wanted my theory to be broader than Meiklejohn's. I wanted it to cover more than just political speech, and I thought it should give independent significance to participant and audience interests. The basis of my theory was a single, audience-related principle applying to all categories of expression.

The Millian Principle
There are certain harms which, although they would not occur but for certain acts of expression, nonetheless cannot be taken as part of a justification for legal restrictions on these acts. These harms are: (a) harms to certain individuals which consist in their coming to have false beliefs as a result of those acts of expression; (b) harmful consequences of acts performed as a result of those acts of expression, where the connection between the acts of expression and the subsequent harmful acts consists merely in the fact that the act of expression led the agents to believe (or increased their tendency to believe) these acts to be worth performing.[11]

I undertook to defend this principle by showing it to be a consequence of a particular idea about the limits of legitimate political authority: namely that the legitimate powers of government are limited to those that can be defended on grounds compatible with the autonomy of its citizens – compatible, that is, with the idea that each citizen is sovereign in deciding what to believe and in weighing reasons for action.[12] This can be seen as a generalized version of Meiklejohn's idea of the political responsibility of democratic citizens.

The Millian Principle was intended to rule out the arguments for censorship to which Mill and Meiklejohn were responding. It did this by ruling that the harmful consequences to which these arguments appeal cannot count as potential justifications for legal restriction of expression. But there are other ways to arrive at policies that would strike us as incompatible with freedom of expression. One such way would be to restrict expression excessively, simply on the ground that it is a nuisance or has other undesirable consequences of a kind that the Millian Principle does allow to

---

[9] See pp. 105–112 below.
[10] Scanlon, "A Theory of Freedom of Expression" (1972), in this volume, essay 1.
[11] Ibid., p. 14.   [12] Ibid., pp. 15–21.

be weighed. So the second component in a theory of the type I described counters "excessive" restriction of this type by specifying that participant and audience interests in expression are to receive high values when they are balanced against competing goods. (As I have indicated, these values vary from one type of expression to another.) But freedom of expression does not only require that there should be "enough" expression. The two further components of the theory require that the goods of expression (for both participants and audiences) should be distributed in ways that are in accord both with the general requirements of distributive justice and with whatever particular rights there may be, such as rights to political participation, that support claims for access to means of expression.

This theory identifies the Millian Principle as the only principle concerned specifically with *expression* (as opposed to a general principle of justice) that applies with the same force to all categories of expression. If correct, then, it would answer one of the questions with which I began.[13] But is it correct? I now think that it is not.[14]

To begin with, the Millian Principle has what seem to be implausible consequences in some cases. For example, it is hard to see how laws against deceptive advertising or restrictions such as the ban on cigarette advertising on television could be squared with this principle. There are, of course, ways in which these objections might be answered. Perhaps the policies in question are simply violations of freedom of expression. If, on the other hand, they are acceptable this is because they are examples of justified paternalism, and my original theory did allow for the Millian Principle to be set aside in such cases.[15] But the theory provided for this exception only in cases of severely diminished rationality, because it took the view that any policy justified on grounds violating the Millian Principle would constitute paternalism of a particularly strong form.[16] The advertising cases seem to be clear counterexamples to this latter claim. More generally, clause (a) of the Millian Principle, taken as a limitation that can be set aside only in cases where our rational capacities are severely diminished, constitutes a rejection of paternalism that is too strong and too sweeping to be plausible. An acceptable doctrine of justified paternalism must take into account such factors as the value attached to being able to make one's own decisions, as well as the costs of so doing and the risks of empowering the government to make them on one's behalf. As the advertising examples show, these factors

---

[13] See p. 85 above.

[14] In what follows I am indebted to a number of criticisms, particularly to objections raised by Robert Amdur and by Gerald Dworkin.

[15] Scanlon, "A Theory of Freedom of Expression," pp. 19–20.   [16] Ibid., p. 20.

vary from case to case even where no general loss of rational capacities has occurred.

But the problems of the Millian Principle are not limited to cases of justified paternalism. The principle is appealing because it protects important audience interests – interests in deciding for oneself what to believe and what reasons to act on. As I have remarked earlier, these interests depend not only on freedom of expression, but also on other forms of access to information, education, and so on. Consideration of these other measures shows that there are in general limits to the sacrifices we are willing to make to enhance our decision-making capacity. Additional information is sometimes not worth the cost of getting it. The Millian Principle allows some of the costs of free expression to be weighed against its benefits, but holds that two important classes of costs must be ignored. Why should we be willing to bear unlimited costs to allow expression to flourish provided that the costs are of these particular kinds? Here it should be borne in mind that the Millian Principle is a restriction on the authority of legitimate governments. Now it may well be that, as I would argue, there is *some* restriction of this kind on the costs that governments may take as grounds for restricting expression, and that this is so because such a restriction is a safeguard that is more than worth the costs involved. But an argument for this conclusion, if it is to avoid the charge of arbitrariness and provide a convincing account of the exact form that the restriction takes, must itself be based on a full consideration of all the relevant costs.

What these objections mainly point to, then, is a basic flaw in the argument I offered to justify the Millian Principle. There are many ways in which the appealing, but notoriously vague and slippery notion of individual autonomy can be invoked in political argument. One way is to take autonomy, understood as the actual ability to exercise independent rational judgment, as a good to be promoted. Referring to "autonomy" in this sense is a vague, somewhat grandiloquent and perhaps misleading way of referring to some of the most important audience interests described in section II. The intuitive arguments I have offered in the present section appeal to the value of autonomy in this sense. These audience interests were also taken into account in the second component of my earlier theory. My argument for the Millian Principle, on the other hand, employed the idea of autonomy in a different way, namely as a constraint on justifications of authority. Such justifications, it was held, must be compatible with the thesis that citizens are equal, autonomous rational agents.[17]

---

[17] Ibid., p. 15.

The idea of such a constraint now seems to me mistaken. Its appeal derives entirely from the value of autonomy in the first sense, that is, from the importance of protecting central audience interests. To build these interests in at the outset as constraints on the process of justification gives theoretical form to the intuition that freedom of expression is based on considerations that cannot simply be outweighed by competing interests in the manner that "clear and present danger" or "pure balancing" theories of the First Amendment would allow. But to build these audience interests into the theory in this way has the effect of assigning them greater and more constant weight than we in fact give them. Moreover, it prevents us from even asking whether these interests might in some cases be better advanced if we could shield ourselves from some influences. In order to meet the objections raised to the Millian Principle, it is necessary to answer such questions, and, in general, to take account of the variations in audience interests under varying circumstances. But this is not possible within the framework of the argument I advanced.

Most of the consequences of the Millian Principle are ones that I would still endorse. In particular, I still think that it is legitimate for the government to promote our personal safety by restricting information about how to make your own nerve gas,[18] but not legitimate for it to promote our safety by stopping political agitation which could, if unchecked, lead to widespread social conflict. I do not think that my judgment in the latter case rests simply on the difficulty of predicting such consequences or on the idea that the bad consequences of allowing political controversy will in each such case be outweighed by the good. But I do not think that the difference between the two cases can be found in the distinction between restricting means and restricting reasons, as my original article suggested. The difference is rather that where political issues are involved governments are notoriously partisan and unreliable. Therefore, giving government the authority to make policy by balancing interests in such cases presents a serious threat to particularly important participant and audience interests. To the degree that the considerations of safety involved in the first case are clear and serious, and the participant and audience interests that might suffer from restriction are not significant, regulation could be acceptable.

In this way of looking at things, political speech stands out as a distinctively important category of expression. Meiklejohn's mistake, I think, was to suppose that the differences in degree between this category and others mark the boundaries of First Amendment theory. My mistake, on the other hand, was that in an effort to generalize Meiklejohn's theory beyond the

---

[18] Ibid., p. 12.

category of political speech, I took what were in effect features peculiar to this category and presented them, under the heading of autonomy, as a priori constraints on justifications of legitimate authority.

In order to avoid such mistakes it is useful to distinguish several different levels of argument. At one extreme is what might be called the "level of policy," at which we might consider the overall desirability or undesirability of a particular action or policy, e.g. an ordinance affecting expression. At the other extreme is what might be called the "foundational level." Argument at this level is concerned with identifying the ultimate sources of justification relevant to the subject at hand. In the case of expression, these are the relevant participant, audience, and bystander interests and the requirements of distributive justice applicable to their satisfaction. Intermediate between these levels is the "level of rights."[19] The question at this level is what limitations and requirements, if any, must be imposed on policy decisions if we are to avoid results that would be unacceptable with respect to the considerations that are defined at the fundamental level? To claim that something is a right, then, is to claim that some limit or requirement on policy decisions is *necessary* if unacceptable results are to be avoided, and that this particular limit or requirement is a *feasible* one, that is, that its acceptance provides adequate protection against such results and does so at tolerable cost to other interests. Thus, for example, to claim that a particular restriction on searches and seizures is part of a right of privacy would be to claim that it is a feasible form of necessary protection for our important and legitimate interests in being free from unwanted observation and intrusion. What rights there are in a given social setting at a given time depends on which judgments of necessity and feasibility are true at that place and time.[20] This will depend on the nature of the main threats to the interests in question, on the presence or absence of factors tending to promote unequal distribution of the means to their satisfaction, and particularly on the characteristics of the agents (private individuals or governments) who make the relevant policy decisions: what power do they have, and how are they likely to use this power in the absence of constraints?

Most of us believe that freedom of expression is a right. That is, we believe that limits on the power of governments to regulate expression are necessary

---

[19] For a presentation of this view at greater length, see Scanlon, "Rights, Goals, and Fairness" (1978), in this volume, essay 2.

[20] Of course there may be multiple solutions to the problem; that is, different ways in which a right might be defined to give adequate protection to the interests in question. In such a case what there is a right to initially is *some* protection of the relevant kind. At this point the right is incompletely defined. Once one adequate form of protection becomes established as a constraint on policy making, the other alternatives are no longer *necessary* in the relevant sense. In this respect our rights are partly determined by convention.

to protect our central interests as audiences and participants, and we believe that such limits are not incompatible with a healthy society and a stable political order. Hundreds of years of political history support these beliefs. There is less agreement as to exactly how this right is to be understood – what limits and requirements on decision-making authority are necessary and feasible as ways of protecting central participant and audience interests and ensuring the required equity in the access to means of expression. This is less than surprising, particularly given the fact that the answer to this question changes, sometimes rapidly, as conditions change. Some threats are constant – for example the tendency of governments to block the expression of critical views – and these correspond to points of general agreement in the definition of the right. But as new threats arise – from, for example, changes in the form or ownership of dominant means of communication – it may be unclear, and a matter subject to reasonable disagreement, how best to refine the right in order to provide the relevant kinds of protection at a tolerable cost. This disagreement is partly empirical – a disagreement about what is likely to happen if certain powers are or are not granted to governments. It is also in part a disagreement at the foundational level over the nature and importance of audience and participant interests and, especially, over what constitutes a sufficiently equal distribution of the means to their satisfaction. The main role of a philosophical theory of freedom of expression, in addition to clarifying what it is we are arguing about, is to attempt to resolve these foundational issues.

What reasons are there for taking this view of rights in general and of freedom of expression in particular? One reason is that it can account for much of what we in fact believe about rights and can explain what we do in the process of defending and interpreting them. A second reason is that its account of the bases of rights appears to exhaust the relevant concerns: if a form of regulation of expression presents no threat to the interests I have enumerated, nor to the equitable distribution of the means to their satisfaction, what further ground might there be to reject it as violating freedom of expression? Beyond these two reasons, all I can do in defense of my view is to ask, what else? If rights are not instrumental in the way I have described, what are they and what are the reasons for taking them seriously?

IV. CATEGORIES

Let me distinguish two ways in which arguments about freedom of expression may involve distinctions between categories of expression. First, not every participant or audience interest is capable of exerting the same upward pressure on the costs freedom of expression requires us to bear. Freedom of expression often requires that a particular form of expression – leafletting or demonstrations near public buildings – be allowed despite high bystander costs because important participant or audience interests would otherwise be inadequately or unequally served. Such arguments are clearly category-dependent: their force depends on the importance of the particular participant or audience interests in question. But, once it is concluded on the basis of such an argument that a given mode of expression must be permitted, there is the further question whether its use must be permitted for any form of expression or whether it may be restricted to those types of expression whose value was the basis for claiming that this mode of expression must be allowed. If the latter, then not only will categories of interests be assigned different weights in arguments about the content of the right of freedom of expression, but the application of this right to particular cases will also involve determining the category to which the acts in question belong. I will refer to these two forms of categorization as, respectively, categories of interests and categories of acts.

This distinction can be illustrated by considering the ways in which "political speech" can serve as a category. For the purposes of this discussion, I will assume that "political" is to be interpreted narrowly as meaning, roughly, "having to do with the electoral process and the activities of government." We can distinguish a category of interests in expression that are political in this sense, including both participant interests in taking part in the political process and audience (and bystander) interests in the spread of information and discussion about political topics. As a category of acts, on the other hand, "political speech" might be distinguished[21] either by participant intent – expression with a political purpose – or by content and effect – expression that concerns political issues or contributes to the understanding of political issues. These two definitions correspond, roughly, to the two sets of interests just mentioned. I will assume for the moment that the category of political speech is to be understood to include acts falling under either of these definitions.

While the political interests in expression are not uniquely important, the fact that they are inadequately or very unequally served constitutes a strong reason for enlarging or improving available modes of expression. Their particular importance as a source of upward pressure is something that rational argument about freedom of expression must recognize. Must

---

[21] Distinguished, that is, from other forms of protected expression. I am concerned here only with what marks speech as political. A full definition of "political speech" (i.e. permissible political expression) would, in order to exclude such things as bombings, take into account features other than those mentioned here. See note 4 above.

"political speech" be recognized as a category of acts as well? That is, can the fact that an act of expression has the relevant political intent or content exempt it from regulation that would otherwise be compatible with freedom of expression?

Special standards for defamation applicable to expression concerning "public officials," "public figures," or "public issues"[22] indicate that something like "political speech" does function as a category of acts in the current legal understanding of freedom of expression. Reflection on the *Skokie* case may also suggest that "political speech" has a special place in our intuitive understanding of this right. It seems unlikely that expression so deeply offensive to bystanders would be deemed to be protected by freedom of expression if it did not have a political character – if, for example, its purpose had been merely to provide entertainment or to promote commerce. But I do not see how this interpretation of freedom of expression can be defended, at least unless "political" is understood in a very broad sense in which any important and controversial question counts as a "political issue." Expression that is political in the narrow sense is both important and in need of protection, but it is not unique in either respect. Furthermore, even if "political" is understood broadly, the idea that access to a mode of expression can be made to depend on official determination of the "political" nature of one's purposes or one's message does not sit comfortably with the basic ideas of freedom of expression.

This suggests a second, more plausible analysis of the *Skokie* case, one which relies more heavily on categories of interests and less on categories of acts. The judgment that the Nazi march is protected may reflect the view that no[23] ordinance giving local authorities the power to ban such a march could give adequate protection to central interests in political expression. This argument avoids any judgment as to whether the content and purposes of this particular march were "genuinely political." It relies instead on the judgment that such a march could not be effectively and reliably distinguished from political expression that it is essential to protect.

The distinction between categories of interests and categories of acts can be used to explain some of the ambivalence about categories noted at

---

[22] See the line of cases following *New York Times Co.* v. *Sullivan*, 376 U.S. 254 (1964). See, e.g., *Curtis Publishing Co.* v. *Butts*, 388 U.S. 130 (1967); *Gertz* v. *Robert Welch, Inc.*, 418 U.S. 323 (1974); *Herbert* v. *Lando*, 99 S. Ct. 1635 (1979); *Hutchinson* v. *Proxmire*, 99 S. Ct. 2675 (1979).

[23] Of course an actual decision need only find a particular ordinance unconstitutional. I take it, however, that an intuitive judgment that an action is protected by freedom of expression is broader than this and implies that *no* acceptable ordinance could restrict that action.

the beginning of this article. Reference to categories of interests is both important and unavoidable in arguments about freedom of expression. Categories of acts may also be unavoidable – "expression" is itself such a category, and assault, for example, is distinguished from it on the basis of participant intent – but there are good reasons for being wary of categories of acts and for keeping their use to a minimum. Even where there is agreement on the relative importance of various interests in expression, the purposes and content of a given expressive act can be a matter of controversy and likely misinterpretation, particularly in those situations of intense conflict and mistrust in which freedom of expression is most important. (Well-known difficulties in the application of laws against incitement are a good illustration of this point.) Thus the belief that the fundamental principles of freedom of expression must transcend categories derives in part from the recognition that categories of acts rest on distinctions – of intent and content – that a partisan of freedom of expression will instinctively view with suspicion. Nonetheless, in interpreting freedom of expression, we are constantly drawn toward categories of acts as we search for ways of protecting central interests in expression while avoiding unacceptable costs. The current struggle to define the scope of special standards of defamation[24] is a good example of this process. Identifying the categories of acts that can actually be relied upon to give the protection we want is a matter of practical and strategic judgment, not of philosophical theory.

I have mentioned the possibility of official misapplication as one reason for avoiding categories of acts, but this is not the only problem. A second difficulty is the fact that it is extremely difficult to regulate one category of speech without restricting others as well. Here the recent campaign financing law is an instructive example.[25] The basic aim of restricting money spent during a campaign in order to increase the fairness of this particular competition is entirely compatible with freedom of expression. The problem is that in order to regulate spending effectively, it was deemed necessary to make campaign funds flow through a single committee for each candidate. In order to do this a low limit was placed on the amount any private person or group could spend on expression to influence the campaign. But since spending on expression to influence a campaign cannot be clearly separated from expression on political topics generally, the limit on private spending

---

[24] See cases cited in note 22 above.
[25] *Buckley* v. *Valeo*, 424 U.S. 1 (1976). Federal Election Campaign Act of 1971, Pub. L. No. 92–225, 86 Stat. 3 (1972), *as amended by* Federal Election Campaign Act Amendments of 1974, Pub. L. No. 93–443, 88 Stat. 1263 (1974), *as amended by* Federal Election Campaign Act Amendments of 1976, Pub. L. No. 94–283, 90 Stat. 475 (1976).

constituted an unacceptable restriction on expression. Limits on spending for "campaign speech" are in principle as compatible with freedom of expression as limits on the length of speeches in a town meeting: both are acceptable when they enhance the fairness of the proceedings. Unlike a town meeting, however, "campaign speech" is not easily separated from other expression on political topics, hence not easily regulated in a way that leaves this other expression unaffected.

In addition to the difficulty of regulating one category without affecting others, there is the further problem that the categories within which special regulation is held to be permissible may themselves suffer from dangerous overbreadth. I believe that this is true, for example, of the category of commercial speech. Presumably "commercial speech" is to be defined with reference to participant intent: expression by a participant in the market for the purpose of attracting buyers or sellers. It is not identical with advertising, which can serve a wide variety of expressive purposes, and it cannot be defined by its subject matter: *Consumer Reports* has the same subject matter as much commercial speech, but it is entitled to "full" First Amendment protection. Why, then, would anyone take commercial speech to be subject to restrictions that would not be acceptable if applied to other forms of expression? This view is widely held, or has been until recently,[26] and it appears to be supported by the acceptability of laws against false or deceptive advertising, the regulation of cigarette advertising and restriction on the form of classified advertisements of employment opportunities. One reason for this attitude may be that the participant and audience interests at stake in commercial speech – promoting one's business, learning what is available in the market – are not generally perceived as standing in much danger from overrestriction. There is, we are inclined to think, plenty of opportunity for advertising, and we are in no danger of being deprived of needed information if advertising is restricted. In fact, the relevant audience interests are in much more danger from excessive exposure to advertising, and from false and deceptive advertising. In addition, laws against such advertising seem acceptable in a way that analogous laws against false or deceptive political or religious claims would not be, first because there are reasonably clear and objective criteria of truth in this area, and second, we regard the government as much less partisan in the competition between commercial firms than in the struggle between religious or political views.

[26] See *Bates* v. *State Bar of Arizona*, 433 U.S. 350 (1977) *reh. denied* 434 U.S. 881 (1977); *Virginia State Pharmacy Board* v. *Virginia Consumer Council*, 425 U.S. 748 (1976).

Much of this is no doubt true, but it does not support the generalization that commercial speech as a category is subject to less stringent requirements of freedom of expression. The restrictions I have mentioned, where they seem justified, can be supported by arguments that are applicable in principle to other forms of expression (for example, by appeals to qualified paternalism, or to the advantages for audiences of protection against an excessive volume of expression). It is a mistake to think that these arguments are applicable only to commercial speech or that all commercial speech is especially vulnerable to them. In particular, if, as I believe, the assumption that governments are relatively neutral and trustworthy in this area is one reason for our complacent attitude toward regulation of commercial speech, this assumption should be made explicit and treated with care. There are many cases that clearly count as commercial speech in which our traditional suspicions of governmental regulation of expression are as fully justified as they are elsewhere. One such example might be an advertising battle between established energy companies and antiestablishment commercial enterprises promoting alternative energy sources.[27]

V. PORNOGRAPHY

In this final section I will consider the category of pornography. This example will illustrate both the problems of categories just discussed and some of the problems concerning participant and audience interests that were discussed in section II above.

The question to ask about pornography is, why restrict it? I will consider two answers. The first appeals to the interest people have in not being unwillingly exposed to offensive material. By offense, I do not mean a reaction grounded in disapproval but an immediate discomfort analogous to pain, fear, or acute embarrassment. I am willing to assume for purposes of argument that many people do have such a reaction to some sexual material, and that we should take seriously their interest in being protected against it. I also agree that what offends most people will differ from place to place depending on experience and custom. Therefore the appropriate standards of protection may also vary. But if this were the only reason for restricting

---

[27] It might be claimed that insofar as this example has the character I mention it is an instance of political, not merely commercial, speech. Certainly it does have a political element. Nonetheless, the intentions of the participants (and the interests of audiences) may be thoroughly commercial. The political element of the controversy triggers First Amendment reactions because it raises the threat of partisan regulation, not because the interests at stake, on the part of either participants or audience, are political.

pornography the problem would have an easy solution: restrict what can be displayed on the public streets or otherwise forced on an unwilling audience but place no restrictions whatever on what can be shown in theaters, printed in books, or sent through the mails in plain brown wrappers. The only further requirement is that the inconvenience occasioned by the need to separate the two groups should be fairly shared between them.

The idea that this solution should be acceptable to all concerned rests on specific assumptions about the interests involved. It is assumed that consumers of pornography desire private enjoyment, that sellers want to profit from selling to those who have this desire, and that other people want to avoid being forced to see or hear what they regard as offensive. Rarely will one find three sets of interests that are so easily made compatible. There are of course certain other interests which are left out of this account. Perhaps some people want to enjoy pornography in public; their pleasure depends on the knowledge that they are disturbing other people. Also, sellers may want to reach a larger audience in order to increase profits, so they would like to use more stimulating advertisements. Finally, those who wish to restrict pornography may be offended not only by the sight of it but even by the knowledge that some people are enjoying it out of their sight; they will be undisturbed only if it is stopped. But none of these interests has significant weight. There is, to be sure, a general problem of explaining what makes some interests important and others, like these, less significant; but this is not a problem peculiar to freedom of expression.

Unfortunately, offense is not the only reason to restrict pornography. The main reason, I think, is the belief that the availability, enjoyment and even the legality of pornography will contribute to undesirable changes in our attitudes toward sex and in our sexual mores. We all care deeply about the character of the society in which we will live and raise our children. This interest cannot be simply dismissed as trivial or illegitimate. Nor can we dismiss as empirically implausible the belief that the evolution of sexual attitudes and mores is strongly influenced by the books and movies that are generally available and widely discussed, in the way that we can dismiss the belief that pornography leads to rape. Of course, expression is not the only thing that can influence society in these ways. This argument against pornography has essentially the same form as well-known arguments in favor of restricting nonstandard sexual conduct.[28] If the interest to which these arguments appeal is, as I have conceded, a legitimate one, how can the arguments be answered?

---

[28] See Patrick Devlin, *The Enforcement of Morals* (Oxford: Oxford University Press, 1965).

I think that transactions "between consenting adults" can sometimes legitimately be restricted on the ground that, were such transactions to take place freely, social expectations would change, people's motives would be altered and valued social practices would as a result become unstable and decline. I think, for example, that some commercial transactions might legitimately be restricted on such grounds. Thus Richard Titmuss,[29] opposing legalization of blood sales in Britain, claims that the availability of blood on a commercial basis weakens people's sense of interdependence and leads to a general decline in altruistic motivation. Assuming for the purposes of argument that this empirical claim is correct, I am inclined to think that there is no objection to admitting this as *a* reason for making the sale of blood illegal. To ban blood sales for this reason seems at first to be objectionable because it represents an attempt by the state to maintain a certain state of mind in the population. What is objectionable about many such attempts, which violate freedom of expression, is that they seek to prevent changes of mind by preventing people from considering and weighing possible reasons for changing their minds. Such interventions run contrary to important audience interests. As far as I can see, however, the presence of a market in blood does not put us in a better position to decide how altruistic we wish to be.

There are of course other objections to outlawing the sale of blood, objections based simply on the value of the opportunity that is foreclosed. Being deprived of the opportunity to sell one's blood does not seem to me much of a loss. In the case of proposed restrictions on deviant sexual conduct, however, the analogous costs to the individuals who would be restricted are severe – too severe to be justified by the considerations advanced on the other side. In fact, the argument for restriction seems virtually self-contradictory on this score. What is the legitimate interest that people have in the way their social mores evolve? It is in large part the legitimate interest they have in not being under pressure to conform to practices they find repugnant under pain of being thought odd and perhaps treated as an outcast. But just this interest is violated in an even more direct way by laws against homosexual conduct.

The case for restricting pornography might be answered in part by a similar argument, but there is also a further issue, more intrinsic to the question of freedom of expression. Once it is conceded that we all have legitimate and conflicting interests in the evolution of social attitudes and

---

[29] R. Titmuss, *The Gift Relationship* (New York: Random House, 1971), chs. 13–15. See also Singer, "Altruism and Commerce," *Philosophy and Public Affairs* 2 (1973), 312.

mores, the question arises how this conflict can fairly be resolved. In particular, is majority vote a fair solution? Can the majority be empowered to preserve attitudes they like by restricting expression that would promote change? The answer to this question is clearly no. One reason is that, as Meiklejohn would emphasize, the legitimacy of majoritarian political processes themselves depends upon the assumption that the voters have free access to information and are free to attempt to persuade and convince each other. Another reason is that, unlike a decision where to build a road, this is an issue that need not be resolved by a clear decision at any one time. There is hence no justification for allowing a majority to squeeze out and silence a minority. A fair alternative procedure is available: a continuing process of "informal politics" in which the opposing groups attempt to alter or to preserve the social consensus through persuasion and example.

This response to the argument for restricting pornography has several consequences. First, since it rests upon viewing public interaction under conditions of freedom of expression as an informal political process that is preferable to majority voting as a way of deciding certain important questions, the response is convincing only if we can argue that this process is in fact fair. It will not be if, for example, access to the main means of expression, and hence the ability to have an influence on the course of public debate, are very unequally distributed in the society. Thus, equity in the satisfaction of participant interests, discussed above as one goal of freedom of expression, arises here in a new way as part of a defense of freedom of expression against majority control.

A second consequence of the argument is that time, place, and manner restrictions on obscene material, which at first seemed a satisfactory solution to the problem of offense, are no longer so obviously satisfactory. Their appeal as a solution rested on the supposition that, since the interests of consumers and sellers of pronography were either purely private or simply commercial, unwilling audiences were entitled to virtually complete protection, the only residual problem being the relatively trivial one of how to apportion fairly the inconvenience resulting from the need to shield the two groups from each other. But if what the partisans of pornography are entitled to (and what the restrictors are trying to deny them) is a fair opportunity to influence the sexual mores of the society, then it seems that they, like participants in political speech in the narrow sense,[30] are entitled to at least a certain degree of access even to unwilling audiences. I do not find

---

[30] Perhaps Meiklejohn would defend "offensive" discussion of sexual topics in a similar fashion, construing it as a form of political speech. Several differences should be noted, however. First, my argument appeals to participant interests rather than to the audience interests Meiklejohn emphasizes. Second,

this conclusion a particularly welcome one, but it seems to me difficult to avoid once the most important arguments against pornography are taken seriously. Let me conclude by considering several possible responses.

The argument I have presented starts from the high value to be assigned to the participant interest in being able to influence the evolution of attitudes and mores in one's society. But while some publishers of "obscene" materials have this kind of crusading intent, undoubtedly many others do not. Perhaps the proper conclusion of my argument is not that any attempt to publish and disseminate offensive sexual material is entitled to full First Amendment protection but, at most, that such protection can be claimed where the participant's intent is of the relevant "political" character. This would construe "pornography" as a category of acts in the sense defined above: sexually offensive expression in the public forum need not be allowed where the intent is merely that of the pornographer – who aims only to appeal to a prurient interest in sex – but must be allowed where the participant has a "serious" interest in changing society. To take "the obscene" as a category of acts subject to extraordinary regulation would involve, on this view, the same kind of overbreadth that is involved when "commercial speech" is seen as such a category. In each case features typical of at most some instances are taken to justify special treatment of the category as a whole.

As I indicated in section IV above, distinctions based on participant intent cannot be avoided altogether in the application of the right of freedom of expression, but they are nearly always suspect. This is particularly so in the present case; expression dealing with sex is particularly likely to be characterized, by those who disapprove of it, as frivolous, unserious and of interest only to dirty minds. To allow expression in this area to be regulated on the basis of participant intent would be to set aside a normal caution without, as far as I can see, any ground for doing so.

The conclusion that unwilling audiences cannot be fully protected against offensive expression might be avoided in a second way. Even if the "political interest" in expression on sexual topics is an important interest,

the politics I am concerned with here is an informal process distinct from the formal democratic institutions he seems to have in mind. Participation in this informal process is not important merely as a preliminary to making decisions in one's official capacity as a citizen. But even if Meiklejohn would not construe the political role of citizens this narrowly, a further difference remains. Having an influence on the evolving mores of one's society is, in my view, only one important participant interest among many, and I would not make the validity of all First Amendment claims depend on their importance for our role in politics of either the formal or the informal sort. It is true, however, that those ideas controversial enough to be in greatest need of First Amendment protection are likely also to be the subject of politics in one or both of these senses. See note 27 above.

and even if it supports a right of access to unwilling audiences, there is a further question whether this interest requires the presentation of "offensive" material. Perhaps it would be enough to be entitled to present material that "deals with" the question of sexual mores in a sober and nonoffensive manner. Perhaps Larry Flynt and Ralph Ginzburg should, on the one hand, be free to sell as much pornography as they wish for private consumption, and they should on the other hand be free to write newspaper editorials and books, make speeches, or go on television as much as they can to crusade for a sexually liberated society. But the latter activity, insofar as it presses itself on people's attention without warning, is subject to the requirement that it not involve offense.

On the other side, it can be claimed that this argument rests on an overly cognitive and rationalistic idea of how people's attitudes change. Earnest treatises on the virtues of a sexually liberated society can be reliably predicted to have no effect on prevailing attitudes towards sex. What is more likely to have such an effect is for people to discover that they find exciting and attractive portrayals of sex which they formerly thought offensive or, vice versa, that they find boring and offensive what they had expected to find exciting and liberating. How can partisans of sexual change be given a fair chance to make this happen except through a relaxation of restrictions on what can be publicly displayed? I do not assume that the factual claims behind this argument are correct. My question rather is, if they were correct what would follow? From the fact that frequent exposure to material previously thought offensive is a likely way to promote a change in people's attitudes, it does not follow that partisans of change are entitled to use this means. Proponents of a change in attitude are not entitled to use just *any* expressive means to effect their aim even if the given means is the only one that would actually have the effect they desire: audience interests must also be considered. It must be asked whether exposure to these means leads to changes in one's tastes and preferences through a process that is, like subliminal advertising, both outside of one's rational control and quite independent of the relevant grounds for preference, or whether, on the contrary, the exposure to such influences is in fact part of the best way to discover what one really has reason to prefer. I think that a crucial question regarding the regulation of pornography and other forms of allegedly corrupting activity lies here.

It is often extremely difficult to distinguish influences whose force is related to relevant grounds for the attitudes they produce from influences that are the work of irrelevant factors. Making this distinction requires, in many cases, a clearer understanding than we have both of the psychological processes through which our attitudes are altered and of the relevant grounds for holding the attitudes in question. The nature of these grounds, in particular, is often a matter of too much controversy to be relied upon in defining a right of freedom of expression. The power to restrict the presentation of "irrelevant influences" seems threatening because it is too easily extended to restrict any expression likely to mislead.

Subliminal advertising is in this respect an unusual case, from which it is hard to generalize. A law against subliminal advertising could be acceptable on First Amendment grounds because it could be framed as a prohibition simply of certain techniques – the use of hidden words or images – thus avoiding controversial distinctions between relevant and irrelevant influences. Where we are concerned with the apparent – as opposed to the hidden – content of expression, however, things become more controversial (even though it is true that what is clearly seen or heard may influence us, and be designed to do so, in ways that we are quite unaware of).

The case for protecting unwilling audiences against influence varies considerably from one kind of offensive expression to another, even within the class of what is generally called pornography. The separation between the way one's attitudes are affected by unwanted exposure to expression and the relevant grounds for forming such attitudes is clearest in the case of pornography involving violence or torture. The reasons for being opposed to, and revolted by, these forms of behavior are quite independent of the question whether one might, after repeated exposure, come to find them exciting and attractive. This makes it plausible to consider such changes in attitude produced by unchosen exposure to scenes of violence as a kind of harm that an unwilling audience is entitled to protection against.[31] The question is whether this protection can be given without unacceptably restricting other persuasive activity involving scenes of violence, such as protests against war.

The argument for protection of unwilling audiences is much weaker where what is portrayed are mildly unconventional sexual attitudes or practices, not involving violence or domination. Here it is more plausible to say that discovering how one feels about such matters when accustomed to them is the best way of discovering what attitude towards them one has reason to hold. The lack of independent grounds for appraising these attitudes makes it harder to conceive of changes produced by expression as a kind of harm or corruption. Even here there are some independent grounds for

---

[31] Prohibiting the display of such scenes for willing audiences is a separate question. So is their presentation to children. Here and throughout this article I am concerned only with adults.

appraisal, however.[32] Attitudes towards sex involve attitudes towards other people, and the reasons for or against holding *these* attitudes may be quite independent of one's reactions to portrayals of sex, which are, typically, highly impersonal. I believe that there are such grounds for regarding as undesirable changes in our attitudes towards sex produced by pornography, or for that matter by advertising, and for wanting to be able to avoid them. But, in addition to the problem of separability, just mentioned with regard to portrayals of violence, these grounds may be too close to the substantive issues in dispute to be an acceptable basis for the regulation of expression.

It seems, then, that an argument based on the need to protect unwilling audiences against being influenced could justify restriction of at most some forms of offensive expression. This leaves us with the residual question of how much offense must be tolerated in order for persuasion and debate regarding sexual mores to go forward. Here the clearest arguments are by comparison with other categories of expression. The costs that audiences and bystanders are required to bear in order to provide for free political debate are generally quite high. These include very significant psychological costs, as the *Skokie* case indicates. Why should psychological costs of the particular kind occasioned by obscenity be treated differently (or given a particularly high value)? A low cost threshold would be understandable if the issues at stake were trivial ones, but by the would-be restrictors' own account this is not so. I do not find the prospect of increased exposure to offensive expression attractive, but it is difficult to construct a principled argument for restriction that is consistent with our policy towards other forms of expression and takes the most important arguments against pornography seriously.

---

[32] Here the moral status of attitudes and practices may become relevant. Moral considerations have been surprisingly absent from the main arguments for restricting pornography considered in this section: the notion of offense quite explicitly abstracts from moral appraisal, and the importance of being able to influence the future mores of one's society does not depend on the assumption that one's concern with these mores is based in morality. A person can have a serious and legitimate interest in preserving (or eliminating) certain customs even if these are matters of no *moral* significance. But morality is relevant to the argument for audience protection since, if sexual attitudes are a matter of morality, this indicates that they can be appraised on grounds that are independent of subjective reaction, thus providing a possible basis for claiming that a person who has come to have a certain attitude (and to be content with having it) has been made worse off.

6

Human rights as a neutral concern

The thesis that human rights should be an important determinant of foreign policy derives support from certain ideas about what human rights are like. These include the following. Human rights, it is held, are a particularly important class of moral considerations. Their gross and systematic violation represents not just the failure to meet some ideal but rather a case of falling below *minimum* standards required of political institutions. Second, human rights are of *broad application*. They apply not only to countries that have recognized these rights in their legal institutions, and not merely to countries that are "like us" in their political traditions or in their economic development, but to virtually all countries. Human rights are not controversial in the way that other political and economic issues are. This is not to say that everyone respects them or that there is full agreement about what they entail. But the central human rights are recognized, for example, in the constitutions of countries whose political principles are otherwise quite divergent. This normal acceptance, and the fact that violations of human rights are not confined to governments of any particular ideological stripe but occur both on the left and on the right, lend support to the idea that concern for human rights is a ground for action that is neutral with respect to the main political and economic divisions in the world. Thus, whatever our other political commitments may be, we have reason to be opposed to violations of human rights whether they are carried out by regimes of the right or of the left; whether these regimes are parliamentary democracies, military dictatorships, or monarchies. In addition to having this *ideological neutrality*, it is often held, or at least thought, that human rights are *practically separable* from partisan political issues. Thus, in particular, to advocate a cessation of human rights violations in a country does not involve advocating a change in regime. One can oppose what the government is doing without opposing the government, or supporting the opposition.

The first of these ideas – the minimal character of human rights – is important to the positive case for making human rights a determinant of foreign policy. The others – broad applicability, ideological neutrality, and practical separability – are important in overcoming natural objections to giving human rights such a role. These objections turn, for example, on the assertion that human rights are ideal considerations that one cannot hope to see realized, or on the assertion that they are applicable only to countries like our own, or that they are parochial concerns peculiar to our political tradition, not shared by others, or on the assertion that to combat human rights violations in other countries represents an unwarranted intrusion into their domestic affairs, an attempt to impose on them our conception of the government they should have.

In the following brief discussion I will examine some of these claims, specifically, the claims that human rights are ideologically neutral and practically separable from partisan political disputes. I will also consider, on the other side, the charge that it is intrusive to bring pressure on other countries to end human rights violations when these countries may have different political traditions from ours and may not share these values. First, however, I want to say something about what I take rights to be and what kind of foundation I see them as having.

I

It sometimes seems that to invoke a right, particularly one in our familiar pantheon of civil and political liberties, is to appeal to a discrete moral principle whose validity can be apprehended just by thinking about it, without recourse to complicated reasoning or to the calculation of the costs and benefits flowing from a given course of action. But this impression fades when we discover that it is extremely difficult even to give a coherent statement of any of our familiar rights. For example, while we feel that we know what religious persecution is, and that it violates a right, it is not easy to state what this right is. Freedom of religion is violated when there is an established religion; that is, when everyone is required by law to observe the dictates of a particular faith or when membership in a particular religion is made a condition for the possession of other political and legal rights. Freedom of religion is also violated when particular religions are forbidden to hold ceremonies and gatherings or when the publication and dissemination of their tracts and religious materials are proscribed. At least freedom of religion is infringed when these things are done *for certain reasons* – roughly speaking, for reasons concerned with the religious views involved. Not just any restriction on the practice of one's religion infringes freedom of religion. Religion is not a heading under which everything becomes legally permitted. It is compatible with freedom of religion to outlaw the torture of animals in religious rituals, though it would not be so compatible to outlaw it in Baptist rites but allow it for Episcopalians.

What lies behind the claim that the complex of elements I have briefly described here represents a *right*? This claim is supported, first, by the idea that religious belief is important, and important in a particular way. Its primary importance is seen to rest in the value for an individual of remaining true to his or her conscience (and in fact the right in question is often referred to as "freedom of conscience"). The interest in bringing other people's actions into conformity with one's own religious beliefs is seen as having lesser value. But a second element in the case for the right of religious freedom is the belief, drawn from historical experience, that the tendency to look down on other religious groups, to try to drive them out or to force them to convert, is strong and pervasive. Experience strongly suggests that when governments have the power to act in the ways forbidden by the right as described above they will frequently use this power, at great cost to those who find themselves in the minority. Finally, a third element in the case for the right of freedom of religion is the belief that a pluralistic society incorporating the form of religious toleration that this right describes is both possible and desirable. The belief that this is so – that the losses involved in tolerating other beliefs are outweighed by the gains in social harmony, decreased risk of persecution, and so on – depends on the particular view of the importance of religion mentioned above.

I believe that other rights have this same structure.[1] That is to say, first, that to assert a right is not merely to assert the value of some goal or the great disvalue of having a certain harm befall one. Rather, it is either to deny that governments or individuals have the authority to act in certain ways, or to assert that they have an affirmative duty to act in certain other ways, for example, to render assistance of a specified kind. Often, the assertions embodied in rights involve complexes of these positive and negative elements. The backing for a right lies in an empirical judgment that the restrictions on authority or assignments of affirmative permission or duty that the right embodies are both necessary and efficacious. They are necessary because, given the nature of social life and political institutions of the type we are familiar with, when the restrictions or requirements that the right embodies are absent, governments and individuals can be expected to behave in ways that lead to intolerable results. They are efficacious in that recognition of

---

[1] Here I outline a view of rights presented at greater length in "Rights, Goals, and Fairness" (1978), in this volume, essay 2.

the right will provide a significant degree of protection against these results at tolerable cost. Rights do not promise to bring the millennium, and not just any way of improving things gives rise to a right. Rather, rights arise as responses to specific serious threats and generally, though not always, embody specific strategies for dealing with these threats.

The empirical judgments on which rights are based presuppose certain background conditions. The claim that a right is necessary is not a claim about what would happen in a "state of nature" but rather a claim about what we expect to happen in societies of the kind we are familiar with in the absence of a right of the kind in question. The threats that rights are supposed to help meet are generally ones that arise because of the distribution of power and the patterns of motivation typically found in such societies. These conditions are not universal, though in the case of most rights commonly listed as "human rights" they are sufficiently widespread to be considered universal for all practical purposes.

The judgment that a right is efficacious also depends on a view of "how things work." Religious freedom depends on the belief that people can and will develop the patterns of motivation necessary to make a pluralistic society work. Similarly, a belief in the right to due process depends on the belief in the possibility of an independent judiciary or, minimally, on the belief that the need to defend a charge publicly and with reference to a known law serves as a significant, though far from infallible, check on the arbitrary use of power. Commonly claimed rights vary in the degree to which they involve specific institutional strategies of this kind. What are sometimes called welfare or humanitarian rights differ from traditional civil or personal rights in this respect. For example, when people speak of "the right to a decent diet," they are not just saying that it is a very bad thing for people to be without adequate food. They are also, I believe, expressing the judgment that political institutions must take responsibility in this area: institutions that do not take reasonable steps to avert starvation for their citizens (and, one might add, for others) are not meeting minimum conditions of legitimacy. It is this connection with institutional authority and responsibility that makes it appropriate to speak here of a *right*. What differentiates this claim of a right from the rights embodied in our Constitution, however, is in part that it does not focus on any particular institutional mechanisms that would count as "reasonable" protections against the threat in question.

Even among traditional civil rights, and among those commonly called "rights of the person," there are some involving only minimal commitment to institutional mechanisms. Thus, for example, the right against torture, or cruel and unusual punishment, has less such commitment than the rights to due process or various political rights. This lack of dependence makes these rights the most clearly exportable, since it frees them from the limitation of being applicable only where the relevant institutional mechanisms can be expected to work.

Even those human rights involving the least commitment to specific institutional remedies retain a political character that differentiates them from mere goals. To condemn torture as a gross violation of human rights is not simply to deplore pain, suffering, cruelty, and degradation. These things are great evils, but the condemnation of torture involves the invocation of a human right because torture is an evil to which political authorities are particularly prone. Torture, as a violation of a human right, is a political act – political in being carried out by agents of the state and political in its aims, which are typically to crush opposition through the spread of fear. The recognition of a human right against the use of torture reflects the judgment that the temptation to rule in this manner is a recurrent threat and that the power to use torture is a power whose real potential for misuse is so clear as to render it indefensible.[2]

I believe that the view of rights just sketched supports the claims, mentioned at the outset, that human rights are minimal requirements on social and political institutions and that they have broad application. These rights embody fixed points in our judgment of what tolerable institutions must be like. While not literally universal in application, they apply very broadly. In particular, they are not limited to those countries in which they are generally recognized or where they are embodied in law. If they were so limited then much of their critical point would be lost. To hold that there is a certain right is to hold that when people complain of being treated in this way their complaints are justified, whether the perpetrators grant this or not.

II

I turn now to the question of acting in defense of human rights. The moral case for such action is an instance of the general case for aiding a victim of wrongful harm and for doing what one can to stop, or at least not to aid, the person who is wrongfully harming him. Given the minimal character of human rights, gross violations of these rights represent particularly strong instances of the moral requirement to aid a victim and not aid his aggressor. Of course there is also a presupposition against interfering in the affairs of

---

[2] See Henry Shue, "Torture," *Philosophy and Public Affairs* 7 (Winter 1978).

another country, which applies in these cases as well. But this presupposition can be overridden. To argue by analogy, there is a generally strong presupposition against interference in the affairs of another family, but this presupposition does not preclude intervening to protect a battered wife. Now it may seem that there is a clear disanalogy here. No one would suggest that the wife's only recourse is to her husband as protector, but it is more plausible to claim that the political institutions of a country are singled out as the source of protection for citizens. Intervention gains plausibility in the domestic case because here the state stands as an authority outside the family with a duty to protect all of its citizens, including battered wives. But in the international case, while multinational bodies exist, their claim to have this kind of special responsibility and authority is a matter of dispute. Other states and private citizens, on the other hand, have the status of neighbors, on a par with one or another of the disputes.

I do not accept this response. Even in the domestic case, private parties with no special authority can be justified in bringing pressure to bear to protect the wife and even, I think, in intervening physically to protect her if all else fails. People who know well what is going on but do nothing are justly criticized for failure to aid. And the duties of third parties are not limited to cases of physical cruelty. The person who grossly neglects his family is appropriately subject to social pressure as well as to the force of law. I don't know exactly what kinds of pressure third parties are entitled or required to use in such cases, but surely they are required at least not to make things worse. The neighbor who gets a man into debt by selling him expensive cars and hunting rifles when he knows that the man's family is already suffering is clearly morally blameworthy. This suggests that, if the analogy I have been working with holds at all, humanitarian rights too can give rise to moral requirements on third parties.

III

I should say clearly that this analogy has its problems. One of these is simply the fact of scale: attempts by one state to affect the internal affairs of another are fraught with incomparably greater dangers than are analogous interventions between individuals. But the main argument that I want to consider against acting to defend human rights is quite different. This argument, which I have often heard, holds that while human rights have a special place in "our" moral and political tradition they are not universally shared. Many countries have different notions of political morality, and it is therefore inappropriate for us to bring pressure to bear on them to conform to our conception of human rights. To do so is a kind of moral imperialism.

I believe this argument to be seriously mistaken. It puts itself forward as a kind of enlightened and tolerant relativism, but this masks what is in fact an attitude of moral and cultural superiority. Like many forms of relativism, this argument rests on the attribution to "them" of a unanimity that does not in fact exist. "They" are said to be different from us and to live by different rules. Such stereotypes are seldom accurate, and the attribution of unanimity is particularly implausible in the case of human rights violations. These actions have victims who generally resent what is done to them and who would rarely concede that, because such behavior is common in their country, their tormentors are acting quite properly. But even if the victims did take the view that they have no rights against what is done to them, would this settle the issue? Couldn't they be wrong in thinking this? Isn't this what we would say in the case of the battered wife who protests that of course her husband beats her every week, that's what any woman has to expect? (Does our reaction here depend on what we assume to be the customs of the surrounding society? Do we feel differently if we suppose ourselves to be considering a foreign culture in which wife beating is much more common than here and people expect it?) The question here is the following: which is the more objectionable form of cultural superiority, to refuse to aid a victim on the ground that "they live like that – they don't recognize rights as we know them," or to attempt to protect the defenseless even when they themselves feel that suffering is their lot and they have no basis to complain of it?

I admit that we may answer this question differently in different cases. We may feel differently, for example, if the victims are in fact recent perpetrators, and show every intention of becoming perpetrators again when they have the chance. Perhaps we are moved here by retributionist sentiments. But I believe that an important variable is the kind and degree of intervention that would be required to achieve a significant effect. It is one thing to bring diplomatic pressure to bear, to decline to make military assistance agreement, or to use economic pressure in order to bring about an end to a specific series of acts. It would be something else to continue to exert such pressure over a long period of time in order to bring about a general change in people's outlook and in the operation of their political institutions. Such action might in some cases be justified, but it raises obvious and severe problems. I believe that appeals to cultural differences have their main force not by way of a relativism of values but rather through the fact that such differences may greatly increase the scale of any intervention that could hope to be successful, and decrease the chances that any intervention would actually succeed. If people are very different from us in their attitude toward human rights, this doesn't make what they do *right*, but it may mean that there is little we can do about it short of remaking their whole society, and this may be something we are neither required nor even able to do.

I believe that this problem can be a genuine one. Nonetheless, it does not seem to be an important factor in the cases we have actually considered. Despite some mention of the problem of the parochiality of rights in our discussions, none of these cases seems to be an example of a society marked by a complete lack of concern for rights, where implanting such concern would be a major exercise in cultural change.

IV

This brings me to my last question, that of separability. As I mentioned earlier, I think that some support for human rights as a foreign policy objective is aided by the belief that one can oppose human rights violations in a country without taking a stand on domestic political questions such as the question of who is to rule. Thus, support for steps to halt torture or religious discrimination in foreign countries draws its particular strength not only from our strong feelings of revulsion at these practices but also from the view that they are discrete evils whose persistence is separable from that of the prevailing government, whose policies we may or may not agree with but which we would not think it proper for us to attempt directly to alter.

Perhaps no one holds this view. It once played a role in my thinking about human rights, at least, but I now think it mistaken. In those cases in which they raise the most serious problems, the practices just mentioned are engaged in because they are seen as serving important political purposes. These perceptions can, of course, be incorrect, but I see no reason to think that they generally are. A regime may have good reasons to believe that it can remain in power only by quelling opposition through terror, or only by exploiting and catering to religious differences in the country. When such beliefs are correct, ending human rights violations will involve, as a consequence, bringing down the regime. But even though they are practically linked, these two events remain intellectually separable, and the doctrine of separability may persist in a revised form. The fall of the government may be only an unintended consequence of our action, the purpose of which was merely to bring an end to violations of human rights. This distinction may be important; perhaps such an action is less of an objectionable intrusion than an action whose purpose is to bring about a change in government.

This may seem more plausible if it is put in the following way. It is intrusive in an objectionable sense to attempt to bring about a change in government in another country to suit one's own interests. But, as argued above, human rights violations may be a serious enough matter to justify, indeed even to require, outsiders to do what they can to protect and aid the victims. And this may be true even if the result of this aid is internal political change. The force of this argument may lead us to reverse our original question: when a regime engages in serious violations of basic human rights is it even permissible to refrain from taking action on the ground that any successful defense of human rights would lead to undesirable political change?

If by "undesirable" we mean unfavorable to our own country's interests, it seems that the answer to this question will generally be "no," unless the unfavorable results are of major proportions. There is a limit to the sacrifices one is required to make to aid innocent victims, but it is surely corrupt to stand by while someone is beaten up because the aggressor is a customer of yours and you want to keep his business.

Suppose, alternatively, that the undesirable consequences of a change in government would accrue to the people whose government is engaging in human rights violations. It seems that this is, for most people, a more difficult case. Most people are reluctant to take steps to oppose human rights violations when they see the regime in question as basically a good one, but unstable, and likely to be replaced by one that would be much worse from the point of view of most people in the country. Their view seems to be that in situations of political instability a decision whether to bring pressure to end human rights violations has to be made on the basis of a full assessment of the political situation in the country in question. Human rights are one important element in this assessment, but not the only consideration.

This position strikes me as too lenient. While I would not take the extreme position that human rights may never be violated no matter what the consequences, I do want to say that the situations in which their violation could be justified would have to be very extreme indeed. To make my position clearer let me consider a particular problem of separability. It is sometimes asserted that many countries face a choice between adherence to human rights and economic development. The belief that there is such a conflict seems to represent a common ground between people who take it as a justification for suspension of human rights and others who take it as part of a case against economic development for these countries. I say "economic development" here, though of course what is at issue is a particular path of economic development pursued at a particular rate. The two groups just mentioned may be divided over whether what conflicts with human rights is the only path of economic development possible for these countries or whether it is just the particular path favored by outside financial interests.

If this conflict, in either form, is a real one for a society, then a successful defense of human rights there would not only affect the stability of a particular government but also affect and perhaps settle an important question of national policy. This problem might be brought within the account of rights offered earlier in this chapter in the following way. I have said that to claim that there is a right of a particular sort one must, among other things, claim that a society recognizing such a right is feasible – that the right avoids the harms to which it is addressed at tolerable cost. But what costs are "tolerable"? In particular, what sacrifices in economic progress are an acceptable price to pay for the benefits of a society in which civil liberties are observed? Surely, it may be said, different societies may legitimately give different answers to this question, and also to the related question of which forms of development are to be preferred. Isn't it therefore inappropriate for us, as outsiders, to impose our judgment of these matters on another society? Aren't these questions ones that each society is best left to answer for itself?

But here it is important to ask what one means by "letting a society decide for itself." How does a conflict between human rights and the pursuit of economic development (or some other social policy) arise? Most often it arises because there is considerable opposition to the policy in question and human rights must be violated to prevent this opposition from becoming politically effective. In such a situation there is likely to be no consensus on the question of the relative value to be attached to the success of this policy and to human rights. In deciding whether to act in support of human rights in such a society, then, there is no way to escape the need for an independent judgment of the case for these rights in comparison to the competing goals. This judgment should take into account special features of the society – its particular needs, level of development, and so on – which determine the options open to it and affect their desirability. The need for a judgment cannot, however, be finessed by appealing to a supposed consensus in the society in question.

I might summarize this argument by saying that the goal of "letting a society decide for itself" counts more in favor of support for human rights than in favor of a policy of careful neutrality. I believe this to be generally true, particularly in those contemporary cases cited as examples of the conflict between human rights and economic development. But this belief does depend on some conception of the process through which a social decision would be reached in the absence of human rights violations: it depends on the claim that this process could be called one through which the society decides for itself. Perhaps one can imagine cases where this claim would be hard to make; for example, cases where the goal in question is not economic development but political democratization, and the method of decision that will operate if human rights are not violated will allow the traditional oligarchy to preserve its power.[3] But such examples are special in that the goal that is at stake is itself a matter of human rights. The question then becomes whether some human rights may be violated in order that other rights can be secured. Surely this question can *sometimes* be answered positively; it depends on the rights of issue and on the nature of the violations.

I have discussed the practical inseparability of human rights from internal political issues as a problem affecting the arguments for and against action by outsiders in defense of human rights. But this inseparability is an important fact to recognize for another reason as well: it indicates what one is up against in fighting human rights violations. If these violations represent not isolated outbreaks of cruelty and prejudice but, rather, strategic moves in an earnest political struggle, then they will not easily be given up. Moral suasion and the pressure of world opinion, or even the canceling of a few contracts, cannot be expected to carry much weight against considerations of political survival. Those who are serious about human rights must be prepared for a long, hard fight.

[3] For a good discussion of this problem see part III of Charles Beitz, "Political Theory and International Relations" (unpublished doctoral dissertation, Princeton University, 1977).

7

Contractualism and utilitarianism

Utilitarianism occupies a central place in the moral philosophy of our time. It is not the view which most people hold; certainly there are very few who would claim to be act utilitarians. But for a much wider range of people it is the view towards which they find themselves pressed when they try to give a theoretical account of their moral beliefs. Within moral philosophy it represents a position one must struggle against if one wishes to avoid it. This is so in spite of the fact that the implications of act utilitarianism are wildly at variance with firmly held moral convictions, while rule utilitarianism, the most common alternative formulation, strikes most people as an unstable compromise.

The wide appeal of utilitarianism is due, I think, to philosophical considerations of a more or less sophisticated kind which pull us in a quite different direction than our first-order moral beliefs. In particular, utilitarianism derives much of its appeal from alleged difficulties about the foundations of rival views. What a successful alternative to utilitarianism must do, first and foremost, is to sap this source of strength by providing a clear account of the foundations of nonutilitarian moral reasoning. In what follows I will first describe the problem in more detail by setting out the questions which a philosophical account of the foundations of morality must answer. I will then put forward a version of contractualism which, I will argue, offers a better set of responses to these questions than that supplied by straightforward versions of utilitarianism. Finally I will explain why contractualism, as I understand it, does not lead back to some utilitarian formula as its normative outcome.

I am greatly indebted to Derek Parfit for patient criticism and enormously helpful discussion of many earlier versions of this paper. Thanks are due also to the many audiences who have heard parts of those versions delivered as lectures and kindly responded with helpful comments. In particular, I am indebted to Marshall Cohen, Ronald Dworkin, Owen Fiss, and Thomas Nagel for valuable criticism.

Contractualism has been proposed as the alternative to utilitarianism before, notably by John Rawls in *A Theory of Justice.*[1] Despite the wide discussion which this book has received, however, I think that the appeal of contractualism as a foundational view has been underrated. In particular, it has not been sufficiently appreciated that contractualism offers a particularly plausible account of moral motivation. The version of contractualism that I shall present differs from Rawls's in a number of respects. In particular, it makes no use, or only a different and more limited kind of use, of his notion of choice from behind a veil of ignorance. One result of this difference is to make the contrast between contractualism and utilitarianism stand out more clearly.

I

There is such a subject as moral philosophy for much the same reason that there is such a subject as the philosophy of mathematics. In moral judgments, as in mathematical ones, we have a set of putatively objective beliefs in which we are inclined to invest a certain degree of confidence and importance. Yet on reflection it is not at all obvious what, if anything, these judgments can be about, in virtue of which some can be said to be correct or defensible and others not. This question of subject matter, or the grounds of truth, is the first philosophical question about both morality and mathematics. Second, in both morality and mathematics it seems to be possible to discover the truth simply by thinking or reasoning about it. Experience and observation may be helpful, but observation in the normal sense is not the standard means of discovery in either subject. So, given any positive answer to the first question – any specification of the subject matter or ground of truth in mathematics or morality – we need some compatible epistemology explaining how it is possible to discover the facts about this subject matter through something like the means we seem to use.

Given this similarity in the questions giving rise to moral philosophy and to the philosophy of mathematics, it is not surprising that the answers commonly given fall into similar general types. If we were to interview students in a freshman mathematics course many of them would, I think, declare themselves for some kind of conventionalism. They would hold that mathematics proceeds from definitions and principles that are either arbitrary

---

[1] John Rawls, *A Theory of Justice* (Cambridge, MA: Harvard University Press, 1971).

or instrumentally justified, and that mathematical reasoning consists in perceiving what follows from these definitions and principles. A few others, perhaps, would be realists or platonists according to whom mathematical truths are a special kind of nonempirical fact that we can perceive through some form of intuition. Others might be naturalists who hold that mathematics, properly understood, is just the most abstract empirical science. Finally there are, though perhaps not in an average freshman course, those who hold that there are no mathematical facts in the world "outside of us," but that the truths of mathematics are objective truths about the mental constructions of which we are capable. Kant held that pure mathematics was a realm of objective mind-dependent truths, and Brouwer's mathematical Intuitionism is another theory of this type (with the important difference that it offers grounds for the warranted assertability of mathematical judgments rather than for their truth in the classical sense). All of these positions have natural correlates in moral philosophy. Intuitionism of the sort espoused by W. D. Ross is perhaps the closest analogue to mathematical platonism, and Kant's theory is the most familiar version of the thesis that morality is a sphere of objective, mind-dependent truths.

All of the views I have mentioned (with some qualification in the case of conventionalism) give positive (i.e. nonskeptical) answers to the first philosophical question about mathematics. Each identifies some objective, or at least intersubjective, ground of truth for mathematical judgments. Outright skepticism and subjective versions of mind-dependence (analogues of emotivism or prescriptivism) are less appealing as philosophies of mathematics than as moral philosophies. This is so in part simply because of the greater degree of intersubjective agreement in mathematical judgment. But it is also due to the difference in the further questions that philosophical accounts of the two fields must answer.

Neither mathematics nor morality can be taken to describe a realm of facts existing in isolation from the rest of reality. Each is supposed to be connected with other things. Mathematical judgments give rise to predictions about those realms to which mathematics is applied. This connection is something that a philosophical account of mathematical truth must explain, but the fact that we can observe and learn from the correctness of such predictions also gives support to our belief in objective mathematical truth. In the case of morality the main connection is, or is generally supposed to be, with the will. Given any candidate for the role of subject matter of morality we must explain why anyone should care about it, and the need to answer this question of motivation has given strong support to subjectivist views.

But what must an adequate philosophical theory of morality say about moral motivation? It need not, I think, show that the moral truth gives anyone who knows it a reason to act which appeals to that person's present desires or to the advancement of his or her interests. I find it entirely intelligible that a moral requirement might correctly apply to a person even though that person had no reason of either of these kinds for complying with it. Whether moral requirements give those to whom they apply reasons for compliance of some third kind is a disputed question which I shall set aside. But what an adequate moral philosophy must do, I think, is to make clearer to us the nature of the reasons that morality does provide, at least to those who are concerned with it. A philosophical theory of morality must offer an account of these reasons that is, on the one hand, compatible with its account of moral truth and moral reasoning and, on the other, supported by a plausible analysis of moral experience. A satisfactory moral philosophy will not leave concern with morality as a simple special preference, like a fetish or a special taste, which some people just happen to have. It must make it understandable why moral reasons are ones that people can take seriously, and why they strike those who are moved by them as reasons of a special stringency and inescapability.

There is also a further question whether susceptibility to such reasons is compatible with a person's good or whether it is, as Nietzsche argued, a psychological disaster for the person who has it. If one is to defend morality one must show that it is not disastrous in this way, but I will not pursue this second motivational question here. I mention it only to distinguish it from the first question, which is my present concern.

The task of giving a philosophical explanation of the subject matter of morality differs both from the task of analyzing the meaning of moral terms and from that of finding the most coherent formulation of our first-order moral beliefs. A maximally coherent ordering of our first-order moral beliefs could provide us with a valuable kind of explanation: it would make clear how various, apparently disparate moral notions, precepts, and judgments are related to one another, thus indicating to what degree conflicts between them are fundamental and to what degree, on the other hand, they can be resolved or explained away. But philosophical inquiry into the subject matter of morality takes a more external view. It seeks to explain what kind of truths moral truths are by describing them in relation to other things in the world and in relation to our particular concerns. An explanation of how we can come to know the truth about morality must be based on such an external explanation of the kind of things moral truths are rather than on a list of particular moral truths, even a maximally coherent list. This seems to be true as well about explanations of how moral beliefs can give one a reason to act.[2]

Coherence among our first-order moral beliefs – what Rawls has called narrow reflective equilibrium[3] – seems unsatisfying[4] as an account of moral truth or as an account of the basis of justification in ethics just because, taken by itself, a maximally coherent account of our moral beliefs need not provide us with what I have called a philosophical explanation of the subject matter of morality. However internally coherent our moral beliefs may be rendered, the nagging doubt may remain that there is nothing to them at all. They may be merely a set of socially inculcated reactions, mutually consistent perhaps but not judgments of a kind which can properly be said to be correct or incorrect. A philosophical theory of the nature of morality can contribute to our confidence in our first-order moral beliefs chiefly by allaying these natural doubts about the subject. Insofar as it includes an account of moral epistemology, such a theory may guide us towards new forms of moral argument, but it need not do this. Moral argument of more or less the kind we have been familiar with may remain as the only form of justification in ethics. But whether or not it leads to revision in our modes of justification, what a good philosophical theory should do is to give us a clearer understanding of what the best forms of moral argument amount to and what kind of truth it is that they can be a way of arriving at. (Much the same can be said, I believe, about the contribution which philosophy of mathematics makes to our confidence in particular mathematical judgments and particular forms of mathematical reasoning.)

Like any thesis about morality, a philosophical account of the subject matter of morality must have some connection with the meaning of moral terms: it must be plausible to claim that the subject matter described is in fact what these terms refer to at least in much of their normal use. But the current meaning of moral terms is the product of many different moral beliefs held by past and present speakers of the language, and this meaning is

---

[2] Though here the ties between the nature of morality and its content are more important. It is not clear that an account of the nature of morality which left its content *entirely* open could be the basis for a plausible account of moral motivation.

[3] See John Rawls, "The Independence of Moral Theory," *Proceedings and Adresses of the American Philosophical Association* 47 (1974–5), p. 8; and Norman Daniels, "Wide Reflective Equilibrium and Theory Acceptance in Ethics," *Journal of Philosophy* 76 (1979), 256–82, pp. 257–8. How closely the process of what I am calling philosophical explanation will coincide with the search for "wide reflective equilibrium" as this is understood by Rawls and by Daniels is a further question which I cannot take up here.

[4] For expression of this dissatisfaction see Peter Singer, "Sidgwick and Reflective Equilibrium," *The Monist* 58 (1974), 490–517, and R. B. Brandt, *A Theory of the Good and the Right* (Oxford: Oxford University Press, 1979), pp. 16–21.

surely compatible with a variety of moral views and with a variety of views about the nature of morality. After all, moral terms are used to express many different views of these kinds, and people who express these views are not using moral terms incorrectly, even though what some of them say must be mistaken. Like a first-order moral judgment, a philosophical characterization of the subject matter of morality is a substantive claim about morality, albeit a claim of a different kind.

While a philosophical characterization of morality makes a kind of claim that differs from a first-order moral judgment, this does not mean that a philosophical theory of morality will be neutral between competing normative doctrines. The adoption of a philosophical thesis about the nature of morality will almost always have some effect on the plausibility of particular moral claims, but philosophical theories of morality vary widely in the extent and directness of their normative implications. At one extreme is intuitionism, understood as the philosophical thesis that morality is concerned with certain non-natural properties. Rightness, for example, is held by Ross[5] to be the property of "fittingness" or "moral suitability." Intuitionism holds that we can identify occurrences of these properties, and that we can recognize as self-evident certain general truths about them, but that they cannot be further analyzed or explained in terms of other notions. So understood, intuitionism is in principle compatible with a wide variety of normative positions. One could, for example, be an intuitionistic utilitarian or an intuitionistic believer in moral rights, depending on the general truths about the property of moral rightness which one took to be self-evident.

The other extreme is represented by philosophical utilitarianism. The term "utilitarianism" is generally used to refer to a family of specific normative doctrines – doctrines which might be held on the basis of a number of different philosophical theses about the nature of morality. In this sense of the term one might, for example, be a utilitarian on intuitionist or on contractualist grounds. But what I will call "philosophical utilitarianism" is a particular philosophical thesis about the subject matter of morality, namely the thesis that the only fundamental moral facts are facts about individual well-being.[6] I believe that this thesis has a great deal of plausibility for many people, and that, while some people are utilitarians for other reasons, it is the attractiveness of philosophical utilitarianism which accounts for the widespread influence of utilitarian principles.

[5] W. D. Ross, *Foundations of Ethics* (Oxford: Oxford University Press, 1939), pp. 52–4, 315.
[6] For purposes of this discussion I leave open the important questions of which individuals are to count and how "well-being" is to be understood. Philosophical utilitarianism will retain the appeal I am concerned with under many different answers to these questions.

It seems evident to people that there is such a thing as individuals' being made better or worse off. Such facts have an obvious motivational force; it is quite understandable that people should be moved by them in much the way that they are supposed to be moved by moral considerations. Further, these facts are clearly relevant to morality as we now understand it. Claims about individual well-being are one class of valid starting points for moral argument. But many people find it much harder to see how there could be any other, independent starting points. Substantive moral requirements independent of individual well-being strike people as intuitionist in an objectionable sense. They would represent "moral facts" of a kind it would be difficult to explain. There is no problem about recognizing it as a fact that a certain act is, say, an instance of lying or of promise breaking. And a utilitarian can acknowledge that such facts as these often have (derivative) moral significance: they are morally significant because of their consequences for individual well-being. The problems, and the charge of "intuitionism," arise when it is claimed that such acts are wrong in a sense that is not reducible to the fact that they decrease individual well-being. How could this independent property of moral wrongness be understood in a way that would give it the kind of importance and motivational force which moral considerations have been taken to have? If one accepts the idea that there are no moral properties having this kind of intrinsic significance, then philosophical utilitarianism may seem to be the only tenable account of morality. And once philosophical utilitarianism is accepted, some form of normative utilitarianism seems to be forced on us as the correct first-order moral theory. Utilitarianism thus has, for many people, something like the status which Hilbert's Formalism and Brouwer's Intuitionism have for their believers. It is a view which seems to be forced on us by the need to give a philosophically defensible account of the subject. But it leaves us with a hard choice: we can either abandon many of our previous first-order beliefs or try to salvage them by showing that they can be obtained as derived truths or explained away as useful and harmless fictions.

It may seem that the appeal of philosophical utilitarianism as I have described it is spurious, since this theory must amount either to a form of intuitionism (differing from others only in that it involves just one appeal to intuition) or else to definitional naturalism of a kind refuted by Moore and others long ago. But I do not think that the doctrine can be disposed of so easily. Philosophical utilitarianism is a philosophical thesis about the nature of morality. As such, it is on a par with intuitionism or with the form of contractualism which I will defend later in this paper.

None of these theses need claim to be true as a matter of definition; if one of them is true it does not follow that a person who denies it is misusing the words "right," "wrong," and "ought." Nor are all these theses forms of intuitionism, if intuitionism is understood as the view that moral facts concern special non-natural properties, which we can apprehend by intuitive insight but which do not need or admit of any further analysis. Both contractualism and philosophical utilitarianism are specifically incompatible with this claim. Like other philosophical theses about the nature of morality (including, I would say, intuitionism itself), contractualism and philosophical utilitarianism are to be appraised on the basis of their success in giving an account of moral belief, moral argument, and moral motivation that is compatible with our general beliefs about the world: our beliefs about what kinds of things there are in the world, what kinds of observation and reasoning we are capable of, and what kinds of reasons we have for action. A judgment as to which account of the nature of morality (or of mathematics) is most plausible in this general sense is just that: a judgment of overall plausibility. It is not usefully described as an insight into concepts or as a special intuitive insight of some other kind.

If philosophical utilitarianism is accepted then some form of utilitarianism appears to be forced upon us as a normative doctrine, but further argument is required to determine which form we should accept. If all that counts morally is the well-being of individuals, no one of whom is singled out as counting for more than the others, and if all that matters in the case of each individual is the degree to which his or her well-being is affected, then it would seem to follow that the basis of moral appraisal is the goal of maximizing the *sum*[7] of individual well-being. Whether this standard is to be applied to the criticism of individual actions, or to the selection of rules or policies, or to the inculcation of habits and dispositions to act is a further question, as is the question of how "well-being" itself is to be understood. Thus the hypothesis that much of the appeal of utilitarianism as a normative doctrine derives from the attractiveness of philosophical utilitarianism explains how people can be convinced that some form of utilitarianism must be correct while yet being quite uncertain as to which form it is, whether it is "direct" or "act" utilitarianism or some form of indirect "rule" or "motive" utilitarianism. What these views have in common, despite their differing normative consequences, is the identification of the same class of fundamental moral facts.

---

[7] "Average Utilitarianism" is most plausibly arrived at through quite a different form of argument, one more akin to contractualism. I discuss one such argument in section IV below.

II

If what I have said about the appeal of utilitarianism is correct, then what a rival theory must do is to provide an alternative to philosophical utilitarianism as a conception of the subject matter of morality. This is what the theory which I shall call contractualism seeks to do. Even if it succeeds in this, however, and is judged superior to philosophical utilitarianism as an account of the nature of morality, normative utilitarianism will not have been refuted. The possibility will remain that normative utilitarianism can be established on other grounds, for example as the normative outcome of contractualism itself. But one direct and, I think, influential argument for normative utilitarianism will have been set aside.

To give an example of what I mean by contractualism, a contractualist account of the nature of moral wrongness might be stated as follows.

An act is wrong if its performance under the circumstances would be disallowed by any system of rules for the general regulation of behavior which no one could reasonably reject as a basis for informed, unforced general agreement.

This is intended as a characterization of the kind of property which moral wrongness is. Like philosophical utilitarianism, it will have normative consequences, but it is not my present purpose to explore these in detail. As a contractualist account of one moral notion, what I have set out here is only an approximation, which may need to be modified considerably. Here I can offer a few remarks by way of clarification.

The idea of "informed agreement" is meant to exclude agreement based on superstition or false belief about the consequences of actions, even if these beliefs are ones which it would be reasonable for the person in question to have. The intended force of the qualification "reasonably," on the other hand, is to exclude rejections that would be unreasonable *given* the aim of finding principles which could be the basis of informed, unforced general agreement. Given this aim, it would be unreasonable, for example, to reject a principle because it imposed a burden on you when every alternative principle would impose much greater burdens on others. I will have more to say about grounds for rejection later in the paper.

The requirement that the hypothetical agreement which is the subject of moral argument be unforced is meant not only to rule out coercion, but also to exclude being forced to accept an agreement by being in a weak bargaining position, for example because others are able to hold out longer and hence to insist on better terms. Moral argument abstracts from such considerations. The only relevant pressure for agreement comes from the desire to find and agree on principles which no one who had this desire could reasonably reject. According to contractualism, moral argument concerns the possibility of agreement among persons who are all moved by this desire, and moved by it to the same degree. But this counter-factual assumption characterizes only the agreement with which morality is concerned, not the world to which moral principles are to apply. Those who are concerned with morality look for principles for application to their imperfect world which they could not reasonably reject, and which others in this world, who are not now moved by the desire for agreement, could not reasonably reject should they come to be so moved.[8]

The contractualist account of moral wrongness refers to principles "which no one could reasonably reject" rather than to principles "which everyone could reasonably accept" for the following reason.[9] Consider a principle under which some people will suffer severe hardships, and suppose that these hardships are avoidable. That is, there are alternative principles under which no one would have to bear comparable burdens. It might happen, however, that the people on whom these hardships fall are particularly self-sacrificing, and are willing to accept these burdens for the sake of what they see as the greater good of all. We would not say, I think, that it would be unreasonable of them to do this. On the other hand, it might not be unreasonable for them to refuse these burdens, and, hence, not unreasonable for someone to reject a principle requiring him to bear them. If this rejection would be reasonable, then the principle imposing these burdens is put in doubt, despite the fact that some particularly self-sacrificing people could (reasonably) accept it. Thus it is the reasonableness of rejecting a principle, rather than the reasonableness of accepting it, on which moral argument turns.

It seems likely that many nonequivalent sets of principles will pass the test of nonrejectability. This is suggested, for example, by the fact that there are many different ways of defining important duties, no one of which is more or less "rejectable" than the others. There are, for example, many different systems of agreement-making and many different ways of assigning responsibility to care for others. It does not follow, however, that any action allowed by at least one of these sets of principles cannot be morally wrong according to contractualism. If it is important for us to have *some* duty of a given kind (some duty of fidelity to agreements, or some duty of mutual aid) of which there are many morally acceptable forms, then

---

[8] Here I am indebted to Gilbert Harman for comments which have helped me to clarify my statement of contractualism.

[9] A point I owe to Derek Parfit.

one of these forms needs to be established by convention. In a setting in which one of these forms *is* conventionally established, acts disallowed by it will be wrong in the sense of the definition given. For, given the need for such conventions, one thing that could not be generally agreed to would be a set of principles allowing one to disregard conventionally established (and morally acceptable) definitions of important duties. This dependence on convention introduces a degree of cultural relativity into contractualist morality. In addition, what a person can reasonably reject will depend on the aims and conditions that are important in his life, and these will also depend on the society in which he lives. The definition given above allows for variation of both of these kinds by making the wrongness of an action depend on the circumstances in which it is performed.

The partial statement of contractualism which I have given has the abstract character appropriate in an account of the subject matter of morality. On its face, it involves no specific claim as to which principles could be agreed to or even whether there is a unique set of principles which could be the basis of agreement. One way, though not the only way, for a contractualist to arrive at substantive moral claims would be to give a technical definition of the relevant notion of agreement, e.g. by specifying the conditions under which agreement is to be reached, the parties to this agreement and the criteria of reasonableness to be employed. Different contractualists have done this in different ways. What must be claimed for such a definition is that (under the circumstances in which it is to apply) what it describes is indeed the kind of unforced, reasonable agreement at which moral argument aims. But contractualism can also be understood as an informal description of the subject matter of morality on the basis of which ordinary forms of moral reasoning can be understood and appraised without proceeding via a technical notion of agreement.

Who is to be included in the general agreement to which contractualism refers? The scope of morality is a difficult question of substantive morality, but a philosophical theory of the nature of morality should provide some basis for answering it. What an adequate theory should do is to provide a framework within which what seem to be relevant arguments for and against particular interpretations of the moral boundary can be carried out. It is often thought that contractualism can provide no plausible basis for an answer to this question. Critics charge either that contractualism provides no answer at all, because it must begin with some set of contracting parties taken as given, or that contractualism suggests an answer which is obviously too restrictive, since a contract requires parties who are able to make and keep agreements and who are each able to offer the others some benefit in return for their cooperation. Neither of these objections applies to the version of contractualism that I am defending. The general specification of the scope of morality which it implies seems to me to be this: morality applies to a being if the notion of justification to a being of that kind makes sense. What is required in order for this to be the case? Here I can only suggest some necessary conditions. The first is that the being have a good, that is, that there be a clear sense in which things can be said to go better or worse for that being. This gives partial sense to the idea of what it would be reasonable for a trustee to accept on the being's behalf. It would be reasonable for a trustee to accept at least those things that are good, or not bad, for the being in question. Using this idea of trusteeship we can extend the notion of acceptance to apply to beings that are incapable of literally agreeing to anything. But this minimal notion of trusteeship is too weak to provide a basis for morality, according to contractualism. Contractualist morality relies on notions of what it would be reasonable to accept, or reasonable to reject, which are essentially comparative. Whether it would be unreasonable for me to reject a certain principle, given the aim of finding principles which no one with this aim could reasonably reject, depends not only on how much actions allowed by that principle might hurt me in absolute terms but also on how that potential loss compares with other potential losses to others under this principle and alternatives to it. Thus, in order for a being to stand in moral relations with us it is not enough that it have a good, it is also necessary that its good be sufficiently similar to our own to provide a basis for some system of comparability. Only on the basis of such a system can we give the proper kind of sense to the notion of what a trustee could reasonably reject on a being's behalf.

But the range of possible trusteeship is broader than that of morality. One could act as a trustee for a tomato plant, a forest or an ant colony, and such entities are not included in morality. Perhaps this can be explained by appeal to the requirement of comparability: while these entities have a good, it is not comparable to our own in a way that provides a basis for moral argument. Beyond this, however, there is in these cases insufficient foothold for the notion of justification *to* a being. One further minimum requirement for this notion is that the being constitute a point of view; that is, that there be such a thing as what it is like to be that being, such a thing as what the world seems like to it. Without this, we do not stand in a relation to the being that makes even hypothetical justification *to it* appropriate.

On the basis of what I have said so far contractualism can explain why the capacity to feel pain should have seemed to many to count in favor of moral status: a being which has this capacity seems also to satisfy the three conditions I have just mentioned as necessary for the idea of justification to it to make sense. If a being can feel pain, then it constitutes a centre of consciousness to which justification can be addressed. Feeling pain is a clear way in which the being can be worse off; having its pain alleviated a way in which it can be benefited; and these are forms of weal and woe which seem directly comparable to our own.

It is not clear that the three conditions I have listed as necessary are also sufficient for the idea of justification to a being to make sense. Whether they are, and, if they are not, what more may be required, are difficult and disputed questions. Some would restrict the moral sphere to those to whom justifications could in principle be communicated, or to those who can actually agree to something, or to those who have the capacity to understand moral argument. Contractualism as I have stated it does not settle these issues at once. All I claim is that it provides a basis for argument about them which is at least as plausible as that offered by rival accounts of the nature of morality. These proposed restrictions on the scope of morality are naturally understood as debatable claims about the conditions under which the relevant notion of justification makes sense, and the arguments commonly offered for and against them can also be plausibly understood on this basis.

Some other possible restrictions on the scope of morality are more evidently rejectable. Morality might be restricted to those who have the capacity to observe its constraints, or to those who are able to confer some reciprocal benefit on other participants. But it is extremely implausible to suppose that the beings excluded by these requirements fall entirely outside the protection of morality. Contractualism as I have formulated it[10] can explain why this is so: the absence of these capacities alone does nothing to undermine the possibility of justification to a being. What it may do in some cases, however, is to alter the justifications which are relevant. I suggest that whatever importance the capacities for deliberative control and reciprocal benefit may have is as factors altering the duties which beings

---

[10] On this view (as contrasted with some others in which the notion of a contract is employed) what is fundamental to morality is the desire for reasonable agreement, not the pursuit of mutual advantage. See section v below. It should be clear that this version of contractualism can account for the moral standing of future persons who will be better or worse off as a result of what we do now. It is less clear how it can deal with the problem presented by future people who would not have been born but for actions of ours which also made the conditions in which they live worse. Do such people have reason to reject principles allowing these actions to be performed? This difficult problem, which I cannot explore here, is raised by Derek Parfit in "On Doing the Best for Our Children," in M. Bayles, ed., *Ethics and Population* (Cambridge, MA: Schenkman Publishing Co. Inc., 1976), pp. 100–15.

have and the duties others have towards them, not as conditions whose absence suspends the moral framework altogether.

III

I have so far said little about the normative content of contractualism. For all I have said, the act utilitarian formula might turn out to be a theorem of contractualism. I do not think that this is the case, but my main thesis is that whatever the normative implications of contractualism may be it still has distinctive content as a philosophical thesis about the nature of morality. This content – the difference, for example, between being a utilitarian because the utilitarian formula is the basis of general agreement and being a utilitarian on other grounds – is shown most clearly in the answer that a contractualist gives to the first motivational question.

Philosophical utilitarianism is a plausible view partly because the facts which it identifies as fundamental to morality – facts about individual well-being – have obvious motivational force. Moral facts can motivate us, on this view, because of our sympathetic identification with the good of others. But as we move from philosophical utilitarianism to a specific utilitarian formula as the standard of right action, the form of motivation that utilitarianism appeals to becomes more abstract. If classical utilitarianism is the correct normative doctrine then the natural source of moral motivation will be a tendency to be moved by changes in aggregate well-being, however these may be composed. We must be moved in the same way by an aggregate gain of the same magnitude whether it is obtained by relieving the acute suffering of a few people or by bringing tiny benefits to a vast number, perhaps at the expense of moderate discomfort for a few. This is very different from sympathy of the familiar kind toward particular individuals, but a utilitarian may argue that this more abstract desire is what natural sympathy becomes when it is corrected by rational reflection. This desire has the same content as sympathy – it is a concern for the good of others – but it is not partial or selective in its choice of objects.

Leaving aside the psychological plausibility of this even-handed sympathy, how good a candidate is it for the role of moral motivation? Certainly sympathy of the usual kind is one of the many motives that can sometimes impel one to do the right thing. It may be the dominant motive, for example, when I run to the aid of a suffering child. But when I feel convinced by Peter Singer's article[11] on famine, and find myself crushed by

---

[11] Peter Singer, "Famine, Affluence and Morality," *Philosophy and Public Affairs* 1 (1972), 229–43.

the recognition of what seems a clear moral requirement, there is something else at work. In addition to the thought of how much good I could do for people in drought-stricken lands, I am overwhelmed by the further, seemingly distinct thought that it would be wrong for me to fail to aid them when I could do so at so little cost to myself. A utilitarian may respond that his account of moral motivation cannot be faulted for not capturing this aspect of moral experience, since it is just a reflection of our nonutilitarian moral upbringing. Moreover, it must be groundless. For what kind of fact could this supposed further fact of moral wrongness be, and how could it give us a further, special reason for acting? The question for contractualism, then, is whether it can provide a satisfactory answer to this challenge.

According to contractualism, the source of motivation that is directly triggered by the belief that an action is wrong is the desire to be able to justify one's actions to others on grounds they could not reasonably[12] reject. I find this an extremely plausible account of moral motivation – a better account of at least my moral experience than the natural utilitarian alternative – and it seems to me to constitute a strong point for the contractualist view. We all might like to be in actual agreement with the people around us, but the desire which contractualism identifies as basic to morality does not lead us simply to conform to the standards accepted by others whatever these may be. The desire to be able to justify one's actions to others on grounds they could not reasonably reject will be satisfied when we know that there is adequate justification for our action even though others in fact refuse to accept it (perhaps because they have no interest in finding principles which we and others could not reasonably reject). Similarly, a person moved by this desire will not be satisfied by the fact that others accept a justification for his action if he regards this justification as spurious.

One rough test of whether you regard a justification as sufficient is whether you would accept that justification if you were in another person's position. This connection between the idea of "changing places" and the motivation which underlies morality explains the frequent occurrence of "Golden Rule" arguments within different systems of morality and in the teachings of various religions. But the thought experiment of changing places is only a rough guide; the fundamental question is what would it be unreasonable to reject as a basis for informed, unforced, general agreement? As Kant observed,[13] our different individual points of view, taken as they are,

---

[12] Reasonably, that is, given the desire to find principles which others similarly motivated could not reasonably reject.

[13] *Grundlegung zur Metaphysik der Sitten* (1785), trans. H. J. Paton as *The Moral Law* (London: Hutchinson, 1948), section 2, footnote 14.

may in general be simply irreconcilable. "Judgmental harmony" requires the construction of a genuinely interpersonal form of justification which is nonetheless something that each individual could agree to. From this interpersonal standpoint, a certain amount of how things look from another person's point of view, like a certain amount of how they look from my own, will be counted as bias.

I am not claiming that the desire to be able to justify one's actions to others on grounds they could not reasonably reject is universal or "natural." "Moral education" seems to me plausibly understood as a process of cultivating this desire and shaping it, largely by learning what justifications others are in fact willing to accept, by finding which ones you yourself find acceptable as you confront them from a variety of perspectives, and by appraising your own and others' acceptance or rejection of these justifications in the light of greater experience.

In fact it seems to me that the desire to be able to justify one's actions (and institutions) on grounds one takes to be acceptable is quite strong in most people. People are willing to go to considerable lengths, involving quite heavy sacrifices, in order to avoid admitting the unjustifiability of their actions and institutions. The notorious insufficiency of moral motivation as a way of getting people to do the right thing is not due to simple weakness of the underlying motive, but rather to the fact that it is easily deflected by self-interest and self-deception.

It could reasonably be objected here that the source of motivation I have described is not tied exclusively to the contractualist notion of moral truth. The account of moral motivation which I have offered refers to the idea of a justification which it would be unreasonable to reject, and this idea is potentially broader than the contractualist notion of agreement. For let M be some noncontractualist account of moral truth. According to M, we may suppose, the wrongness of an action is simply a moral characteristic of that action in virtue of which it ought not to be done. An act which has this characteristic, according to M, has it quite independently of any tendency of informed persons to come to agreement about it. However, since informed persons are presumably in a position to recognize the wrongness of a type of action, it would seem to follow that if an action is wrong then such persons would agree that it is not to be performed. Similarly, if an act is not morally wrong, and there is adequate moral justification to perform it, then there will presumably be a moral justification for it which an informed person would be unreasonable to reject. Thus, even if M, and not contractualism, is the correct account of moral truth, the desire to be able to justify my actions to others on grounds they could not reasonably reject could still serve as a basis for moral motivation.

What this shows is that the appeal of contractualism, like that of utilitarianism, rests in part on a qualified skepticism. A noncontractualist theory of morality can make use of the source of motivation to which contractualism appeals. But a moral argument will trigger this source of motivation only in virtue of being a good justification for acting in a certain way, a justification which others would be unreasonable not to accept. So a noncontractualist theory must claim that there are moral properties which have justificatory force quite independent of their recognition in any ideal agreement. These would represent what John Mackie has called instances of intrinsic "to-be-doneness" and "not-to-be-doneness."[14] Part of contractualism's appeal rests on the view that, as Mackie puts it, it is puzzling how there could be such properties "in the world." By contrast, contractualism seeks to explain the justificatory status of moral properties, as well as their motivational force, in terms of the notion of reasonable agreement. In some cases the moral properties are themselves to be understood in terms of this notion. This is so, for example, in the case of the property of moral wrongness, considered above. But there are also right- and wrong-making properties which are themselves independent of the contractualist notion of agreement. I take the property of being an act of killing for the pleasure of doing so to be a wrong-making property of this kind. Such properties are wrong-making because it would be reasonable to reject any set of principles which permitted the acts they characterize. Thus, while there are morally relevant properties "in the world" which are independent of the contractualist notion of agreement, these do not constitute instances of intrinsic "to-be-doneness" and "not-to-be-doneness": their moral relevance – their force in justifications as well as their link with motivation – is to be explained on contractualist grounds.

In particular, contractualism can account for the apparent moral significance of facts about individual well-being, which utilitarianism takes to be fundamental. Individual well-being will be morally significant, according to contractualism, not because it is intrinsically valuable or because promoting it is self-evidently a right-making characteristic, but simply because an individual could reasonably reject a form of argument that gave his well-being no weight. This claim of moral significance is, however, only approximate, since it is a further difficult question exactly how "well-being" is to be understood and in what ways we are required to take account of the well-being of others in deciding what to do. It does not follow from this claim, for example, that a given desire will always and everywhere have the

---

[14] J. L. Mackie, *Ethics: Inventing Right and Wrong* (Harmondsworth: Pelican, 1977), p. 42.

same weight in determining the rightness of an action that would promote its satisfaction, a weight proportional to its strength or "intensity." The right-making force of a person's desires is specified by what might be called a conception of morally legitimate interests. Such a conception is a product of moral argument; it is not given, as the notion of individual well-being may be, simply by the idea of what it is rational for an individual to desire. Not everything for which I have a rational desire will be something in which others need concede me to have a legitimate interest which they undertake to weigh in deciding what to do. The range of things which may be objects of my rational desires is very wide indeed, and the range of claims which others could not reasonably refuse to recognize will almost certainly be narrower than this. There will be a tendency for interests to conform to rational desire – for those conditions making it rational to desire something also to establish a legitimate interest in it – but the two will not always coincide.

One effect of contractualism, then, is to break down the sharp distinction, which arguments for utilitarianism appeal to, between the status of individual well-being and that of other moral notions. A framework of moral argument is required to define our legitimate interests and to account for their moral force. This same contractualist framework can also account for the force of other moral notions such as rights, individual responsibility, and procedural fairness.

IV

It seems unlikely that act utilitarianism will be a theorem of the version of contractualism which I have described. The positive moral significance of individual interests is a direct reflection of the contractualist requirement that actions be defensible to each person on grounds he could not reasonably reject. But it is a long step from here to the conclusion that each individual must agree to deliberate always from the point of view of maximum aggregate benefit and to accept justifications appealing to this consideration alone. It is quite possible that, according to contractualism, *some* moral questions may be properly settled by appeal to maximum aggregate well-being, even though this is not the sole or ultimate standard of justification.

What seems less improbable is that contractualism should turn out to coincide with some form of "two-level" utilitarianism. I cannot fully assess this possibility here. Contractualism does share with these theories the important features that the defense of individual actions must proceed via a defense of principles that would allow those acts. But contractualism differs from *some* forms of two-level utilitarianism in an important way. The role of principles in contractualism is fundamental; they do not enter merely as devices for the promotion of acts that are right according to some other standard. Since it does not establish two potentially conflicting forms of moral reasoning, contractualism avoids the instability which often plagues rule utilitarianism.

The fundamental question here, however, is whether the principles to which contractualism leads must be ones whose general adoption (either ideally or under some more realistic conditions) would promote maximum aggregate well-being. It has seemed to many that this must be the case. To indicate why I do not agree I will consider one of the best-known arguments for this conclusion and explain why I do not think it is successful. This will also provide an opportunity to examine the relation between the version of contractualism I have advocated here and the version set forth by Rawls.

The argument I will consider, which is familiar from the writings of Harsanyi[15] and others, proceeds via an interpretation of the contractualist notion of acceptance and leads to the principle of maximum average utility. To think of a principle as a candidate for unanimous agreement I must think of it not merely as acceptable to *me* (perhaps in virtue of my particular position, my tastes, etc.) but as acceptable[16] to others as well. To be relevant, my judgment that the principle is acceptable must be impartial. What does this mean? To judge impartially that a principle is acceptable is, one might say, to judge that it is one which you would have reason to accept no matter who you were. That is, and here is the interpretation, to judge that it is a principle which it would be rational to accept if you did not know which person's position you occupied and believed that you had an equal chance of being in any of these positions. ("Being in a person's position" is here understood to mean being in his objective circumstances and evaluating these from the perspective of his tastes and preferences.) But, it is claimed, the principle which it would be rational to prefer under these circumstances – the one which would offer the chooser greatest expected utility – would be that principle under which the average utility of the affected parties would be highest.

[15] See John C. Harsanyi, "Cardinal Welfare, Individualistic Ethics, and Interpersonal Comparisons of Utility," *Journal of Political Economy* 63 (1955), 309–21, section IV. He is there discussing an argument which he presented earlier in Harsanyi, "Cardinal Utility in Welfare Economics and the Theory of Risk-Taking," *Journal of Political Economy* 61 (1953), 434–5.

[16] In discussing Harsanyi and Rawls I will generally follow them in speaking of the acceptability of principles rather than their unrejectability. The difference between these, pointed out above, is important only within the version of contractualism I am presenting; accordingly, I will speak of rejectability only when I am contrasting my own version with theirs.

This argument might be questioned at a number of points, but what concerns me at present is the interpretation of impartiality. The argument can be broken down into three stages. The first of these is the idea that moral principles must be impartially acceptable. The second is the idea of choosing principles in ignorance of one's position (including one's tastes, preferences, etc.). The third is the idea of rational choice under the assumption that one has an equal chance of occupying anyone's position. Let me leave aside for the moment the move from stage two to stage three, and concentrate on the first step, from stage one to stage two. There is a way of making something like this step which is, I think, quite valid, but it does not yield the conclusion needed by the argument. If I believe that a certain principle, *P*, could not reasonably be rejected as a basis for informed, unforced general agreement, then I must believe not only that it is something which it would be reasonable for me to accept but something which it would be reasonable for others to accept as well, insofar as we are all seeking a ground for general agreement. Accordingly, I must believe that I would have reason to accept *P* no matter which social position I were to occupy (though, for reasons mentioned above, I may not believe that I *would* agree to *P* if I were in some of these positions). Now it may be thought that no sense can be attached to the notion of choosing or agreeing to a principle in ignorance of one's social position, especially when this includes ignorance of one's tastes, preferences, etc. But there is at least a minimal sense that might be attached to this notion. If it would be reasonable for everyone to choose or agree to *P*, then my knowledge that I have reason to do so need not depend on my knowledge of my particular position, tastes, preferences, etc. So, insofar as it makes any sense at all to speak of choosing or agreeing to something in the absence of this knowledge, it could be said that I have reason to choose or agree to those things which everyone has reason to choose or agree to (assuming, again, the aim of finding principles on which all could agree). And indeed, this same reasoning can carry us through to a version of stage three. For if I judge *P* to be a principle which everyone has reason to agree to, then it could be said that I would have reason to agree to it if I thought that I had an equal chance of being anybody, or indeed, if I assign any other set of probabilities to being one or another of the people in question.

But it is clear that this is not the conclusion at which the original argument aimed. That conclusion concerned what it would be rational for a self-interested person to choose or agree to under the assumption of ignorance or equal probability of being anyone. The conclusion we have reached appeals to a different notion: the idea of what it would be unreasonable for people to reject given that they are seeking a basis for general agreement.

The direction of explanation in the two arguments is quite different. The original argument sought to explain the notion of impartial acceptability of an ethical principle by appealing to the notion of rational self-interested choice under special conditions, a notion which appears to be a clearer one. My revised argument explains how *a* sense might be attached to the idea of choice or agreement in ignorance of one's position given some idea of what it would be unreasonable for someone to reject as a basis for general agreement. This indicates a problem for my version of contractualism: it may be charged with failure to explain the central notion on which it relies. Here I would reply that my version of contractualism does not seek to explain this notion. It only tries to describe it clearly and to show how other features of morality can be understood in terms of it. In particular, it does not try to explain this notion by reducing it to the idea of what would maximize a person's self-interested expectations if he were choosing from a position of ignorance or under the assumption of equal probability of being anyone.

The initial plausibility of the move from stage one to stage two of the original argument rests on a subtle transition from one of these notions to the other. To believe that a principle is morally correct one must believe that it is one which all could reasonably agree to and none could reasonably reject. But my belief that this is the case may often be distorted by a tendency to take its advantage to me more seriously than its possible costs to others. For this reason, the idea of "putting myself in another's place" is a useful corrective device. The same can be said for the thought experiment of asking what I could agree to in ignorance of my true position. But both of these thought experiments are devices for considering more accurately the question of what *everyone* could reasonably agree to or what no one could reasonably reject. That is, they involve the pattern of reasoning exhibited in my revised form of the three-stage argument, not that of the argument as originally given. The question, what would maximize the expectations of a single self-interested person choosing in ignorance of his true position, is a quite different question. This can be seen by considering the possibility that the distribution with the highest average utility, call it *A*, might involve extremely low utility levels for some people, levels much lower than the minimum anyone would enjoy under a more equal distribution.

Suppose that *A* is a principle which it would be rational for a self-interested chooser with an equal chance of being in anyone's position to select. Does it follow that no one could reasonably reject *A*? It seems evident that this does not follow.[17] Suppose that the situation of those who would

---

[17] The discussion which follows has much in common with the contrast between majority principles and unanimity principles drawn by Thomas Nagel in "Equality," chapter 8 of *Mortal Questions* (Cambridge: Cambridge University Press, 1979). I am indebted to Nagel's discussion of this idea.

fare worst under A, call them the losers, is extremely bad, and that there is an alternative to A, call it E, under which no one's situation would be nearly as bad as this. Prima facie, the losers would seem to have a reasonable ground for complaint against A. Their objection may be rebutted, by appeal to the sacrifices that would be imposed on some other individual by the selection of E rather than A. But the mere fact that A yields higher average utility, which might be due to the fact that many people do very slightly better under A than under E while a very few do much worse, does not settle the matter.

Under contractualism, when we consider a principle our attention is naturally directed first to those who would do worst under it. This is because if anyone has reasonable grounds for objecting to the principle it is *likely* to be them. It does not follow, however, that contractualism always requires us to select the principle under which the expectations of the worse off are highest. The reasonableness of the losers' objection to A is not established simply by the fact that they are worse off under A and no one would be this badly off under E. The force of their complaint depends also on the fact that their position under A is, in absolute terms, very bad, and would be significantly better under E. This complaint must be weighed against those of individuals who would do worse under E. The question to be asked is, is it unreasonable for someone to refuse to put up with the losers' situation under A in order that someone else should be able to enjoy the benefits which he would have to give up under E? As the supposed situation of the Loser under A becomes better, or his gain under E smaller in relation to the sacrifices required to produce it, his case is weakened.

One noteworthy feature of contractualist argument as I have presented it so far is that it is nonaggregative: what are compared are individual gains, losses, and levels of welfare. How aggregative considerations can enter into contractualist argument is a further question too large to be entered into here.

I have been criticizing an argument for average utilitarianism that is generally associated with Harsanyi, and my objections to this argument (leaving aside the last remarks about maximin) have an obvious similarity to objections raised by Rawls.[18] But the objections I have raised apply as well against some features of Rawls's own argument. Rawls accepts the first step of the argument I have described. That is, he believes that the correct principles of justice are those which "rational persons concerned to advance their interests" would accept under the conditions defined by his Original

---

[18] For example, the intuitive argument against utilitarianism on page 14 of Rawls, *A Theory of Justice*, and his repeated remark that we cannot expect some people to accept lower standards of life for the sake of the higher expectations of others.

Position, where they would be ignorant of their own particular talents, their conception of the good, and the social position (or generation) into which they were born. It is the second step of the argument which Rawls rejects, i.e. the claim that it would be rational for persons so situated to choose those principles which would offer them greatest expected utility under the assumption that they have an equal chance of being anyone in the society in question. I believe, however, that a mistake has already been made once the first step is taken.

This can be brought out by considering an ambiguity in the idea of acceptance by persons "concerned to advance their interests." On one reading, this is an essential ingredient in contractual argument; on another it is avoidable and, I think, mistaken. On the first reading, the interests in question are simply those of the members of society to whom the principles of justice are to apply (and by whom those principles must ultimately be accepted). The fact that they have interests which may conflict, and which they are concerned to advance, is what gives substance to questions of justice. On the second reading, the concern "to advance their interests" that is in question is a concern of the parties to Rawls's Original Position, and it is this concern which determines, in the first instance,[19] what principles of justice they will adopt. Unanimous agreement among these parties, each motivated to do as well for himself as he can, is to be achieved by depriving them of any information that could give them reason to choose differently from one another. From behind the veil of ignorance, what offers the best prospects for one will offer the best prospects for all, since no one can tell what would benefit him in particular. Thus the choice of principles can be made, Rawls says, from the point of view of a single rational individual behind the veil of ignorance.

Whatever rules of rational choice this single individual, concerned to advance his own interests as best he can, is said to employ, this reduction of the problem to the case of a single person's self-interested choice should arouse our suspicion. As I indicated in criticizing Harsanyi, it is important to ask whether this single individual is held to accept a principle because he judges that it is one he could not reasonably reject whatever position he turns out to occupy, or whether, on the contrary, it is supposed to be acceptable to a person in any social position because it would be the rational choice for a single self-interested person behind the veil of ignorance. I

---

[19] Though they must then check to see that the principles they have chosen will be stable, not produce intolerable strains of commitment, and so on. As I argue below, these further considerations can be interpreted in a way that brings Rawls's theory closer to the version of contractualism presented here.

have argued above that the argument for average utilitarianism involves a covert transition from the first pattern of reasoning to the second. Rawls's argument also appears to be of this second form; his defense of his two principles of justice relies, at least initially, on claims about what it would be rational for a person, concerned to advance his own interests, to choose behind a veil of ignorance. I would claim, however, that the plausibility of Rawls's arguments favoring his two principles over the principle of average utility is preserved, and in some cases enhanced, when they are interpreted as instances of the first form of contractualist argument.

Some of these arguments are of an informal moral character. I have already mentioned his remark about the unacceptability of imposing lower expectations on some for the sake of the higher expectations of others. More specifically, he says of the parties to the Original Position that they are concerned "to choose principles the consequences of which they are prepared to live with whatever generation they turn out to belong to"[20] or, presumably, whatever their social position turns out to be. This is a clear statement of the first form of contractualist argument. Somewhat later he remarks, in favor of the two principles, that they "are those a person would choose for the design of a society in which his enemy is to assign him a place."[21] Rawls goes on to dismiss this remark, saying that the parties "should not reason from false premises,"[22] but it is worth asking why it seemed a plausible thing to say in the first place. The reason, I take it, is this. In a contractualist argument of the first form, the object of which is to find principles acceptable to each person, assignment by a malevolent opponent is a thought experiment which has a heuristic role like that of a veil of ignorance: it is a way of testing whether one really does judge a principle to be acceptable from all points of view or whether, on the contrary, one is failing to take seriously its effects on people in social positions other than one's own.

But these are all informal remarks, and it is fair to suppose that Rawls's argument, like the argument for average utility, is intended to move from the informal contractualist idea of principles "acceptable to all" to the idea of rational choice behind a veil of ignorance, an idea which is, he hopes, more precise and more capable of yielding definite results. Let me turn then to his more formal arguments for the choice of the Difference Principle by the parties to the Original Position. Rawls cites three features of the decision faced by parties to the Original Position which, he claims, make it rational for them to use the maximin rule and, therefore, to select his

[20] Ibid., p. 137. [21] Ibid., p. 152. [22] Ibid., p. 153.

Difference Principle as a principle of justice. These are (1) the absence of any objective basis for estimating probabilities, (2) the fact that some principles could have consequences for them which "they could hardly accept" while (3) it is possible for them (by following maximin) to ensure themselves of a minimum prospect, advances above which, in comparison, matter very little.[23] The first of these features is slightly puzzling, and I leave it aside. It seems clear, however, that the other considerations mentioned have at least as much force in an informal contractualist argument about what all could reasonably agree to as they do in determining the rational choice of a single person concerned to advance his interests. They express the strength of the objection that the "losers" might have to a scheme that maximized average utility at their expense, as compared with the counter-objections that others might have to a more egalitarian arrangement.

In addition to this argument about rational choice, Rawls invokes among "the main grounds for the two principles" other considerations which, as he says, use the concept of contract to a greater extent.[24] The parties to the Original Position, Rawls says, can agree to principles of justice only if they think that this agreement is one that they will actually be able to live up to. It is, he claims, more plausible to believe this of his two principles than of the principle of average utility, under which the sacrifices demanded ("the strains of commitment") could be much higher. A second, related claim is that the two principles of justice have greater psychological stability than the principle of average utility. It is more plausible to believe, Rawls claims, that in a society in which they were fulfilled people would continue to accept them and to be motivated to act in accordance with them. Continuing acceptance of the principle of average utility, on the other hand, would require an exceptional degree of identification with the good of the whole on the part of those from whom sacrifices were demanded.

These remarks can be understood as claims about the "stability" (in a quite practical sense) of a society founded on Rawls's two principles of justice. But they can also be seen as an attempt to show that a principle arrived at via the second form of contractualist reasoning will also satisfy the requirements of the first form, i.e. that it is something no one could reasonably reject. The question "Is the acceptance of this principle an agreement you could actually live up to?" is, like the idea of assignment by one's worst enemy, a thought experiment through which we can use our own reactions to test our judgment that certain principles are ones that no one could reasonably reject. General principles of human psychology can also be invoked to this same end.

---

[23] Ibid., p. 154.　　[24] Ibid., section 29, pp. 175ff.

Rawls's final argument is that the adoption of his two principles gives public support to the self-respect of individual members of society, and gives "a stronger and more characteristic interpretation of Kant's idea"[25] that people must be treated as ends, not merely as means to the greater collective good. But, whatever difference there may be here between Rawls's two principles of justice and the principle of average utility, there is at least as sharp a contrast between the two patterns of contractualist reasoning distinguished above. The connection with self-respect, and with the Kantian formula, is preserved by the requirement that principles of justice be ones which no member of the society could reasonably reject. This connection is weakened when we shift to the idea of a choice which advances the interests of a single rational individual for whom the various individual lives in a society are just so many different possibilities. This is so whatever decision rule this rational chooser is said to employ. The argument from maximin seems to preserve this connection because it reproduces as a claim about rational choice what is, in slightly different terms, an appealing moral argument.

The "choice situation" that is fundamental to contractualism as I have described it is obtained by beginning with "mutually disinterested" individuals with full knowledge of their situations and adding to this (not, as is sometimes suggested, benevolence but) a desire on each of their parts to find principles which none could reasonably reject insofar as they too have this desire. Rawls several times considers such an idea in passing.[26] He rejects it in favor of his own idea of mutually disinterested choice from behind a veil of ignorance on the ground that only the latter enables us to reach definite results: "if in choosing principles we required unanimity even where there is full information, only a few rather obvious cases could be decided."[27] I believe that this supposed advantage is questionable. Perhaps this is because my expectations for moral argument are more modest than Rawls's. However, as I have argued, almost all of Rawls's own arguments have at least as much force when they are interpreted as arguments within the form of contractualism which I have been proposing. One possible exception is the argument from maximin. If the Difference Principle were taken to be generally applicable to decisions of public policy, then the second form of contractualist reasoning through which it is derived would have more far reaching implications than the looser form of argument by comparison of losses, which I have employed. But these wider applications of the principle are not always plausible, and I do not think that Rawls intends it to be

[25] Ibid., p. 183.
[26] E.g. ibid., pp. 141, 148, although these passages may not clearly distinguish between this alternative and an assumption of benevolence.
[27] Ibid., p. 141.

applied so widely. His intention is that the Difference Principle should be applied only to major inequalities generated by the basic institutions of a society, and this limitation is a reflection of the special conditions under which he holds maximin to be the appropriate basis for rational choice: some choices have outcomes one could hardly accept, while gains above the minimum one can assure oneself matter very little, and so on. It follows, then, that in applying the Difference Principle – in identifying the limits of its applicability – we must fall back on the informal comparison of losses which is central to the form of contractualism I have described.

v

I have described this version of contractualism only in outline. Much more needs to be said to clarify its central notions and to work out its normative implications. I hope that I have said enough to indicate its appeal as a philosophical theory of morality and as an account of moral motivation. I have put forward contractualism as an alternative to utilitarianism, but the characteristic feature of the doctrine can be brought out by contrasting it with a somewhat different view.

It is sometimes said[28] that morality is a device for our mutual protection. According to contractualism, this view is partly true but in an important way incomplete. Our concern to protect our central interests will have an important effect on what we could reasonably agree to. It will thus have an important effect on the content of morality if contractualism is correct. To the degree that this morality is observed, these interests will gain from it. If we had no desire to be able to justify our actions to others on grounds they could reasonably accept, the hope of gaining this protection would give us reason to try to instil this desire in others, perhaps through mass hypnosis or conditioning, even if this also meant acquiring it ourselves. But given that we have this desire already, our concern with morality is less instrumental.

The contrast might be put as follows. On one view, concern with protection is fundamental, and general agreement becomes relevant as a means or a necessary condition for securing this protection. On the other, contractualist view, the desire for protection is an important factor determining the content of morality because it determines what can reasonably be agreed to. But the idea of general agreement does not arise as a means of securing protection. It is, in a more fundamental sense, what morality is about.

---

[28] In different ways by G. J. Warnock in *The Object of Morality* (London: Methuen, 1971), and by J. L. Mackie in *Ethics*. See also Richard Brandt's remarks on justification in *A Theory of the Good and the Right*, ch. 10.

8

Content regulation reconsidered

I. INTRODUCTION

For many years I have thought that there was an important and appealing fundamental truth behind Justice Thurgood Marshall's observation that "above all else, the First Amendment means that government has no power to restrict expression because of its message, its ideas, its subject matter, or its content."[1] As the years have gone by, however, this truth has come to seem more elusive, more limited, and less fundamental than it once did. What follows is an attempt to reexamine the impermissibility of content-based restrictions by regarding it as one element within a larger view of freedom of expression as a right.

The idea that there is something especially bad about government regulation of the content of expression, whether this takes the form of prohibiting some contents or requiring others, has obvious relevance to many questions about the regulation of mass media, ranging from restrictions on advertising of alcohol and tobacco products to the fairness doctrine and statutes mandating a right to reply to political editorials. I shall discuss some of these issues briefly, but I shall not be able to explore any of them in detail. My aim is, rather, to provide a general framework within which they can be discussed in a systematic way.

II. THE STRUCTURE OF RIGHTS

In my view, rights are constraints on discretion to act that we believe to be important means for avoiding morally unacceptable consequences.[2] To claim that a certain action or policy violates a right is to claim: first, that

---

[1] *Police Department of Chicago v. Mosley*, 408 U.S. 92 (1972).

[2] Here and in the following section I summarize a view of rights that I have set out more fully in "Rights, Goals, and Fairness" (1978), in this volume, essay 2. I have applied this view to freedom of expression in "Freedom of Expression and Categories of Expression" (1979), in this volume, essay 5.

unfettered discretion to act in a certain way (whether on the part of private individuals or those occupying institutional roles) leads to unacceptable consequences; second, that certain constraints on this discretion, which either are or ought to be in force in the situation at hand, are a feasible way of preventing these consequences at acceptable cost to other goods; and, third, that the action or policy in question is forbidden by these constraints.

Our thinking about a right can be analyzed into three components: (1) ends – the goals or values relative to which the consequences of unfettered discretion are judged to be unacceptable and the constraints proposed are held to be justified; (2) means – the particular constraints that the right in question is taken to involve; and (3) linking empirical beliefs about the consequences of unfettered discretion and about how these consequences would be altered by the constraints the right proposes. These include beliefs about the motivation of the relevant actors, about the opportunities to act that are available to them, and about the collective results of the decisions they are likely to make. Also relevant here are facts about the institutional background that determine whether a given constraint is "in force."

To illustrate these components of a right, consider the right to privacy. The idea that there is such a right depends, first, on the belief that unfettered discretion to observe us and investigate our affairs would be unacceptable: we need to be able to conduct part of our lives out of public view, as well as to communicate with others without being overheard by third parties. (This belief reflects judgments both about ends and about linking empirical beliefs.) Many different sets of constraints might provide the protection we need here, some more efficiently than others. In order for our privacy rights to be made determinate, we need institutions and conventions that make a selection from among the sets of morally acceptable constraints – institutions and conventions that indicate, for example, when we may and may not be observed, which of our written and electronic communications are protected and which are fair game for others to read or intercept.

Sometimes (as in the case of the often invoked "right to life") appeals to a right leave the constraints that it is supposed to involve almost entirely unspecified. The claim that there is a right is thus reduced to the claim that a certain factor is of great moral value and must be given great weight in deciding what discretion people have to act. Moral argument involving rights of this kind becomes a process of "balancing" rights against one another by comparing their relative "weight." This strikes me as an unedifying form of moral argument. If appeals to rights are to be useful and informative, these rights need to be understood in terms of some specific limitations on discretion to act, limitations that represent a reasonably clear strategy for avoiding the threatened evils at tolerable cost. When a right is understood in this way, the process of applying it will be largely a process of working out what such a strategy requires in a given situation. If, under normal conditions, the strategy really represents a way of avoiding the threatened evil at tolerable cost, the need to "balance" competing rights against one another will be greatly reduced.

The term "rights" can be used in many different ways. Some claims about the rights we have depend directly on particular laws and institutions: my right to return the used car I have recently bought, for example, may derive simply from the "lemon law" the state legislature has passed; and if you have rented half of my garage, the rights you have to park your car there, to drive in and out of my driveway, and so on, depend simply on the law of property and contracts and on the agreement we have made. The origin of such rights is a relatively straightforward matter. But another, more critical use of the notion of rights assumes that rights are not merely the creatures of particular legal systems but also tell us what those systems ought to be like. It is puzzling what the "existence" of such rights could amount to. What does it mean to say that "there is" a right of this kind? When we disagree about the content of these rights, in virtue of what could one of us be correct and the other mistaken?

The analysis I have sketched is meant as a response to these puzzles. It follows from this analysis that the relation between legal rights and more general moral or political rights is complex. On the one hand, legal institutions can incorporate rights that have an independent existence as critical moral ideals. The speech clause of the First Amendment, for example, needs to be understood in the light of a more general moral idea of freedom of expression, which exists independently of that particular amendment and which we can appeal to in appraising institutions other than our own. On the other hand, as I have just suggested, the exact content of such moral rights often depends on an institutional context. Often, more than one system of constraints is capable of providing the protection that a right holds to be necessary, and it may therefore be difficult or impossible to argue simply from first principles that a particular system of constraints is morally required. In these cases the content of people's rights will depend on the institutional strategy in place in their society (assuming, of course, that that strategy actually provides the needed protection).

It is sometimes said, for example, in the context of argument about the First Amendment, that a newspaper or a television station is a "voice" rather than a "forum." There is no necessity about this: one could operate something like a newspaper as a public forum, and some cable television channels are operated in this way. The point of the claim, I take it, is that in our way of achieving the aims of freedom of expression the function of newspapers and many broadcasting stations is to serve as independent voices reflecting the judgment and opinions of those who own them. The force of this claim is partly a matter of property rights and expectations that are independent of freedom of expression. It derives further protection from that right as well, however, insofar as these functions are part of our strategy for achieving a "system of freedom of expression" (and insofar as that strategy is a reasonably successful one).

This qualification points toward another feature of rights, which might be called their "creative instability." First, because rights as I understand them involve a significant empirical component, our understanding of a right can always be upset by evidence that forces a change in these empirical beliefs. Second, at any given time our understanding of the three elements of a right that I have distinguished – the ends, the constraints, and the linking empirical beliefs – may not (indeed, probably will not) form a coherent whole. That is, the constraints we regard as adequate protection for the values underlying the right may not actually be adequate. It may be that they can be thought adequate only if we adopt linking beliefs that are in fact false. This tension gives rights a dynamic quality that can lead to an almost constant process of revision. New situations or changes in our "linking beliefs" can, as just suggested, lead us to conclude that old constraints are inadequate. Similarly, new cases, or reflection on our reactions to old ones, can lead us to enlarge or redefine the set of values in terms of which existing constraints are justified. I do not mean to suggest, however, that these tensions can always be resolved. It may happen that the values presupposed by a right cannot be adequately served without radically departing from that strategy of constraints in terms of which the right is customarily understood. (I will consider one example of this kind of tension in the right of freedom of expression at the end of the next section.)

III. FREEDOM OF EXPRESSION AS A RIGHT

To analyze freedom of expression along the lines I have suggested, we need to identify the values it seeks to protect. I begin with the values attached to satisfying certain widely shared private interests. These include, first, interests that we all have, as potential speakers and writers, in having the opportunity to communicate with those who wish to hear or read us and, especially in political life, to have the opportunity to gain the attention of others who have not specifically chosen to hear or see us. Second, there are our interests, as potential audiences, in having access to expression that we wish to hear or read, and even in being exposed to some degree to expression we have not chosen. These interests are diverse. They include interests in being informed, amused, stimulated in a variety of ways, and even provoked when this leads to reflection and growth. Third, there are our interests as bystanders (that is, not necessarily as either participants in expression or audiences). These include such things as, on the one hand, the benefits of living in a society that enjoys the cultural, political, and technological benefits of free expression and, on the other, the interest we all have in not bearing the costs, such as noise and disorder, that expression can entail.

In addition to these categories of private interest, there are more general moral and political values that freedom of expression is also supposed to protect. Most commonly mentioned here is the value of having fair and effective democratic political institutions. In order for the formal process of democratic politics to confer legitimacy on its outcomes, this process must operate under conditions of free and open public debate, and one of the aims of freedom of expression is to prevent these conditions from being undermined. This important public value gives added support to individuals' interests in having access to means of expression. It also adds an important new element to arguments about freedom of expression because fair democratic politics requires an equality – an equal opportunity to participate – that is not necessarily in the interest of particular individuals.

I have described the goals of freedom of expression very abstractly, in terms of the values attached to various categories of activity and opportunities. Individuals will inevitably disagree about the value of particular acts of expression within these categories – for example, about the merits of the various political doctrines, scientific hypotheses, and theological positions that are expressed. Our views about freedom of expression, however, are based on a measure of agreement about the value of having the opportunity to engage in, and to have access to, expression on these topics, whatever the merits of the particular messages we choose to express or receive may be. There are some participant and audience interests, however – such as the interest in learning how to make bombs or in teaching others how to do so, and the interest in cheating others through fraudulent mail-order schemes – to which no such value is attached; and other interests have values intermediate between these extremes, that is, are capable of asserting intermediate degrees of "upward pressure" on the limits of expression.

These categories of expression make it possible to formulate widely shared judgments of value on which argument in favor of freedom of expression can be based, and they do this by abstracting from more specific value judgments that we use our freedom of expression to argue about. I do not mean to suggest that these categories are entirely uncontroversial or that their relative values cannot be questioned. My aim is merely to point out, first, that they are a way of expressing judgments of relative value and, second, that they provide a way of arguing about expression that sets aside even more controversial questions. The distinction between these two kinds of judgments about the value of expression is important for the question of content regulation, because the idea that expression should not be regulated on the basis of its content amounts in part to the idea that regulation must not be based on evaluation of the more specific and controversial kind just distinguished.

I turn now to what I earlier called "linking empirical beliefs" about the motives and opportunities of various agents that lead us to conclude that in the absence of constraints, the values just listed are seriously at risk. Chief among these are generalizations about how governments generally behave. Governments, whether elected or not, have a settled tendency to try to silence their critics. They also tend to be unsympathetic to ideas, values, and points of view that are unpopular in the society at large. As a result they are often reluctant to bear the burden of ensuring that people speaking for these points of view have an opportunity to be heard. Governments tend to overestimate threats posed to the security of the country and to their own policies. In particular, they tend to overestimate the costs of unrestricted expression, which are visible and dramatic and often seem to be easily foreseeable, and to underestimate its values, which make themselves felt gradually and unpredictably over a long period of time. These faults need not be due to evil intent, but are typical of all governments we know of, those whose structure and policies we otherwise admire as well as those we disapprove of.

The empirical assumptions on which freedom of expression is based are not, however, limited to beliefs about the behavior of governments but also include beliefs about the behavior of private agents that we need protection against. We know, for example, that when people believe they can prevent the expression of ideas they strongly disagree with by threatening a violent response, they are likely to employ this tactic. This leads us to a familiar conclusion about the impermissibility of the "heckler's veto," namely, that governments should not be free to ban expression whenever they believe it may lead to public disorder.

It is extremely difficult to state explicitly the constraints that make up the right of freedom of expression even as these are understood at a given time. Our understanding of these constraints is carried mainly by a series of examples that are taken to illustrate the unacceptable consequences of restrictions violating the right. Application of the right to new cases proceeds by a process of generalization from these examples, guided by our understanding of the values at stake and of the general strategies our responses to these examples are taken to involve.

In saying that the right to freedom of expression is composed of "constraints on discretion to act" I do not suggest that it is what is sometimes called a "negative right," in other words, that it only requires that governments refrain from interfering with expression. As the example of the heckler's veto indicates, freedom of expression also requires governments to take positive action to protect speakers, and it can require other costly actions, for instance, that public spaces be made available for expression even when this interferes significantly with other pursuits. Nor does freedom of expression constrain only governmental agents. Governments are not the only threats to freedom of expression, and they are also not the only agents capable of violating it. Suppose, for example, that a large private corporation were to adopt a policy of firing any employee who took a public stand on some controversial issue – say, abortion – with which the company's directors disagreed. This seems to me to represent a clear violation of the employees' right to freedom of expression because such a use of economic power is a standing threat that clearly needs to be constrained. It is a separate question, however, whether such an action would violate the First Amendment, which states only: "Congress shall make no law . . ."

Just as the First Amendment can be seen as involving a narrower range of constraints than the intuitive moral idea of freedom of expression does, it is also important to see that freedom of expression itself is only one part of a larger family of strategies for protecting the same values. The Freedom of Information Act, for example, promotes many of the audience values just listed, but it is not simply a part of the right of freedom of expression (and not simply a corollary of the First Amendment). Similarly, the idea of academic freedom promotes these same values, by protecting important sources of ideas and information and providing for their dissemination. But this idea, again, is not simply a part of freedom of expression: it is not concerned only with expression or with expression generally. Rather, it applies only to those who work within certain institutions, and it derives its authority from the nature and purposes of those institutions.

The rights described by academic freedom are consequences of the ways in which the control of universities from without, and the authority of deans and boards of trustees within them, must be constrained if the institutions are to fulfill their stated function as centers of thought and inquiry.[3] It might be argued that journalists have analogous rights, reflecting the ways in which the authority not only of the government but also of editors and publishers must be limited if "the press" is to fulfill its function in society. This argument would be more difficult to carry through because "the function and purpose" of publishing and broadcasting companies are less clear. While universities are nonprofit enterprises that are chartered and seek financial support on the basis of their dedication to the aims of scholarship and teaching, publishing and broadcasting companies are in large part commercial enterprises. It might be possible, however, to argue as follows: insofar as these companies claim that their function in society requires special protection from governmental regulation, they open the door also to claims that authority within them must be constrained in the ways that are required in order to ensure that this function will be served. Even if arguments of this kind were to succeed, however, the special journalistic rights they establish would not be part of freedom of expression but, like academic freedom, ancillary to it.[4]

Insofar as freedom of expression involves only a limited range of strategies for protecting the values with which it is concerned, creative instability of the kind mentioned in the previous section is likely to arise, since these means are almost certain to be insufficient for the full realization of these goals. The natural response is that rights do not promise to ensure the full realization of the values with which they are concerned, but only to ward off certain serious threats to these values. The tension remains, however, because this response leaves open the question of why the range of strategies that the right involves should not be extended.

The problem of equality of access provides a clear example of this instability. One aim of freedom of expression is to provide opportunities for the kind of public discussion that is an essential precondition for fair democratic politics. If the political system is to be fair, however, a significantly widespread equality of opportunity to engage in this discussion is required. The familiar idea that leafletting must be permitted because it is "the poor man's printing press" reflects this commitment. But in a society like ours, one cannot achieve a significant degree of equality of access to effective means of expression simply through the strategies that freedom of

---

[3] I have elaborated this view of academic freedom in "Academic Freedom and the Control of Research," in E. Pincoffs, ed., *The Concept of Academic Freedom* (Austin: University of Texas Press, 1975), pp. 237–54.

[4] They would thus not follow from the "speech" clause of the First Amendment. Whether they would be covered by the "press" clause is, of course, a separate question.

expression has traditionally involved (i.e. simply by constraining the power to regulate expression). This generates pressure to find new strategies, but it is not clear where these are to be found.

IV. THE PROBLEM OF CONTENT REGULATION

This brings me to the problem of content regulation. It is common to state the constraints that make up the right of freedom of expression in two parts. Freedom of expression requires, first, that expression not be restricted on the basis of its content, and, second, that it should not be restricted *too much*: any regulation should leave ample opportunity for (at least the valued forms of) expression. Laurence Tribe states this familiar idea with particular clarity by distinguishing between two ways in which government can "abridge speech":

First, government can aim at ideas or information, in the sense of singling out actions for government control or penalty either (a) because of the specific viewpoint such actions express, or (b) because of the effects produced by awareness of the information such actions impart... *Second*, without aiming at ideas or information in either of the above senses, government can constrict the flow of information and ideas while pursuing other goals, either (a) by limiting an activity through which information and ideas might be conveyed, or (b) by enforcing rules compliance with which might discourage the communication of ideas or information.[5]

Tribe summarizes this distinction by saying that "the first form of abridgment may be summarized as encompassing government actions *aimed at communicative impact*; the second, as encompassing government actions *aimed at non-communicative impact* but nonetheless having adverse effects on communicative opportunity."[6]

As Tribe goes on to say, First Amendment theory has regarded these two forms of abridgment in a somewhat different light:

Any government action aimed at communicative impact is presumptively at odds with the first amendment. For if the constitutional guarantee means anything, it means that, ordinarily at least, "government has no power to restrict expression because of its message, its ideas, its subject matter, or its content..." ... Whatever might in theory be said either way, the choice between "the dangers of suppressing information and the dangers of its misuse if it is freely available" is, ultimately, a choice "that the First Amendment makes for us."[7]

---

[5] Laurence Tribe, *American Constitutional Law* (Mineola, NY: Foundation Press, 1978), p. 580.
[6] Ibid.
[7] Ibid., p. 581. The first quoted passage is from *Mosley*; the other, from *Virginia State Pharmacy Board v. Virginia Consumer Council*, 425 U.S. 748 (1976).

On the other hand:

Where government aims at the noncommunicative impact of an act, the correct result in any particular case... reflects some "balancing" of the competing interests; regulatory choices aimed at harms not caused by ideas or information as such are acceptable so long as they do not *unduly* constrict the flow of information and ideas. In such cases the first amendment does not make the choice but instead requires a "thumb" on the scale to assure that the balance struck in any particular situation properly reflects the central position of free expression in the constitutional scheme.[8]

This "two-track" analysis is extremely appealing, and seems to capture a distinction which is an important feature of our ideas about freedom of expression. The interesting question is why the constraints that make up the right of freedom of expression should have this two-part structure. This is particularly puzzling because, as Geoffrey Stone has pointed out,[9] restrictions of expression based on its content are not always more damaging to our interests in expression than content-neutral restrictions: a law banning discussions of abortion on morning television, for example, does no more harm to these interests than a law banning morning television altogether. Stone points out that content-based restrictions often have a "distorting effect" on public debate: A law banning political advertising on billboards except by candidates of the two major parties would in that respect be worse than a statute banning all billboards. Concern with this kind of distortion and unfairness does seem to have something to do with our antipathy to content regulation, but it does not seem to be the central factor, because, as Stone says,[10] content-neutral restrictions can also have distorting effects, and even when they do, the case against them must, on the two-track analysis, be made by balancing competing concerns, while the presumption is that content-based restrictions are ruled out absolutely.

The analysis of rights sketched in the preceding sections suggests the following alternative explanation, at least as a first approximation: our ideas about rights are ideas about the constraints on discretion to act that we regard as both necessary and feasible. These ideas are always incompletely formulated, and our understanding of them depends heavily on the "lessons" of particular historical examples. Prominent among these lessons is the idea that general powers of government censorship, and laws against

---

[8] Tribe, *American Constitutional Law*, pp. 581–2.
[9] Geoffrey R. Stone, "Content Regulation and the First Amendment," *William and Mary Law Review* 25 (Winter 1983), 197.
[10] Ibid., p. 218.

political sedition, are impermissible. These are powers that, I believe, it is not only necessary but also feasible simply to deny to governments. On the other hand, it is clearly not feasible to deny governments all powers to regulate expression; nor does this seem necessary: laws regulating the use of loudspeakers and the placement of billboards, for example, are clearly acceptable. Because the powers it is clearly necessary to constrain and feasible simply to deny involve the regulation of expression on the basis of its content, whereas many of those that it is not feasible and seemingly not necessary to deny are content-neutral, it is natural to draw the conclusion that the power to regulate on the basis of content is prima facie illegitimate.

This would be an overgeneralization, however. Some content-based restrictions, such as restrictions on libel and false advertising, seem clearly permissible even when the harms they protect against are not overwhelming. But at least we can say this: there are some powers to restrict expression on the basis of its content that it is important and feasible simply to deny to governments. These forms of regulation are distinguished not by the greater seriousness of the threat they present but, rather, by the nature of the appropriate response to that threat, which is simply to deny that such powers can legitimately be exercised. Although there may be some powers to regulate on a content-neutral basis that should also simply be denied, such as the power to forbid the publication of any newspapers at all, this is of lesser importance. Such powers are less of a threat to us because they are less likely to be asserted than powers to regulate on the basis of content are, since every government wants to preserve effective means of mass communication, at least for its own favored ideas.

It follows that while the impermissibility of (some forms of) content regulation has a special place on the "surface" of freedom of expression (i.e. in the constraints that make up the practical content of that right), this does not reflect any special objection to such regulation that is apparent at a more fundamental level. But there has often seemed to be something fundamental about the impermissibility of content regulation. It has seemed to many people that at least certain forms of content-based regulation should be opposed because they allow governments to manipulate public discussion of important issues and are therefore a threat to citizens' "autonomy." In an earlier article[11] I myself took this view. I characterized the power that must be denied to governments as the power to restrict expression on the ground that it would cause harms of certain kinds – namely:

[11] T. M. Scanlon, Jr., "A Theory of Freedom of Expression" (1972), in this volume, essay 1.

(a) harms to certain individuals which consist in their coming to have false beliefs as a result of those acts of expression; (b) harmful consequences of acts performed as a result of those acts of expression, where the connection between the acts of expression and the subsequent harmful acts consists merely in the fact that the act of expression led the agents to believe (or increased their tendency to believe) these acts to be worth performing.[12]

The idea that these harms cannot be taken to justify restrictions on expression was what I called the Millian Principle. This principle was not intended as a complete account of freedom of expression. Its function was simply to keep certain considerations "out of the scales" of justification. Further components in my theory specified that participant and audience interests in expression are to receive high value among those elements that can be weighed in assessing the justifiability of restrictions on expression, and that opportunities to enjoy these values must be distributed in such a way that general criteria of distributive justice and the special requirements of rights to political participation are fulfilled.

The two parts of this theory – the Millian Principle, which keeps certain harms out of the "scales of justification" altogether, and the positive values, which place a "thumb on the scales" in the subsequent balancing – correspond roughly to Tribe's two tracks.[13] That is to say, the two theories describe a similar set of constraints. There is, however, a significant difference in the reasoning that the theories offer for these constraints. My theory not only proposed a set of constraints that prevented certain kinds of balancing in the application of the right of freedom of expression but also carried this hostility toward balancing into the theoretical justification for these constraints themselves. Accordingly, I claimed that the Millian Principle was a constraint on the justification of restrictions on expression that arose from the idea of autonomy itself and did not depend on judgments about the relative value of different forms of expression. This claim now seems to me to have been mistaken.

The problem with this appeal to autonomy was that it did not allow for the different degrees to which content-based restrictions of expression represent a threat to our ability to make up our own minds about important matters. Governments have no power to restrict expression on the ground that it would undermine respect for law and government or because it questions the institutions of marriage and the family. Such powers would threaten our "autonomy" – our ability to make up our minds about

---

[12] Ibid., p. 14.

[13] Only roughly, because the range of considerations screened out by my Millian Principle is narrower than what Tribe calls "communicative impact."

important questions through public discussion. On the other hand, penalties attached to false advertising or to expression that defames or invades the privacy of private citizens present no such threat. The Millian Principle allowed for content-based restrictions of the latter kinds, since the harms they are designed to prevent are not of the types that it screens out. (They do not lie simply in the disutility of false belief or in the harmful actions others will be led to take.) But the real difference between these restrictions and impermissible forms of content regulation lies in factors ignored by the argument for the Millian Principle, namely, the different values attached to free public discussion of different topics, and the different degrees of risk involved in authorizing government to regulate the content of these discussions.

The lesson of all this is that we cannot understand or interpret the idea that content-based regulation is impermissible without ourselves drawing distinctions between different forms of expression on the basis of their content (or at least their subject matter) and making judgments about the relative value of these forms of expression.[14] This may be only a superficial irony, but it is instructive. Bearing it in mind, I shall turn in the next section to a more detailed discussion of some forms of content-based regulation. As a basis for that discussion, it will be helpful to review the standards for appraising restrictions on expression that emerge from the preceding analysis.

In discussions of "autonomy" the emphasis is on audience values. It is important to audiences that they have access to "enough" expression (where this level is determined by the value of expression as compared with competing goods) and that the expression to which they have access should not be distorted. Parallel to these on the participant side, but not exactly coincident with them,[15] are the participant interests in having "enough" opportunities for expression and the value of having these opportunities not be unfairly distributed. This unfairness can be of two kinds. The first is unfairness between representatives of opposing positions on the same issue – for example, between competing political parties, labor unions, or religious groups. The second kind of unfairness is between different topics

[14] That is, we must make distinctions between categories of expression of the kind described in the preceding section, even though we may be able to avoid drawing more controversial distinctions between acts of expression within these categories. Tribe is quite clear about the fact that these categorical distinctions convey judgments of relative value. See Tribe, *American Constitutional Law*, p. 583. See also John H. Ely, "Flag Desecration: A Case Study in the Roles of Categorization and Balancing in First Amendment Analysis," *Harvard Law Review* 88 (1975), 1482.

[15] Not coincident because even perfect fairness to all parties can result in a "distorted" discussion if there are important considerations that none of these parties wishes to mention (perhaps because some of them are unaware of these considerations).

of discussion. This occurs when, for example, there are ample opportunities for public discussion of religious and political questions but such opportunities are denied to those who wish to engage in artistic expression or to challenge established scientific views. These types of unfairness are analogous to two forms of "distortion" from the point of view of audiences: distortion of the discussion of particular topics, which can lead to the manipulation of people's attitudes on that question, and distortion that leads to emphasis on some topics and neglect of others. The power to regulate expression on the basis of its content is illegitimate when it poses a serious threat of "distortion" or "unfairness" of either of these two kinds.

But what constitutes "distortion" or "unfairness" of the relevant kinds? It would be unrealistic and even dangerous to grant to legislatures or to judges the power to engage in detailed regulation of expression based on their conceptions of perfectly fair and undistorted discussion. This would be unrealistic because we lack a sufficiently clear and widely shared view of what these ideals come to and because, in any plausible view, actual discussion will always fall short of these ideals. It would also be dangerous insofar as it would involve assigning to actual political institutions, for instance, courts or legislatures, the power to prohibit any expression that falls short of their conception of these ideals. Despite these problems, however, we can identify certain clear examples that would count as unfairness or distortion on any account, and it is such cases that we refer to in determining the shape of the right of freedom of expression. This is one example of a way in which that right is "negative," in other words, aimed at warding off recognized harms rather than at realizing an ideal. It does not follow, however, that it is a "negative right" in the more familiar sense of that term, since the prevention of these harms can require "positive" action, as mentioned in discussing the "heckler's veto."

V. VARIETIES OF CONTENT REGULATION

Let us now consider some specific examples of content regulation in the light of the analysis presented. Statutes allowing for prosecution for false advertising are an instance of content regulation that seems clearly legitimate, and it is easy to see why this should be so. It would be a mistake to deny that "commercial speech" in general serves legitimate and important interests for both participants and audiences. But the participant interest in having the opportunity to try to defraud carries no value, and as long as the standards for what constitutes "falsehood" are sufficiently clear and are not tied up with matters of great political controversy it seems likely that the power to prosecute for false advertising will not become a threat to other participant and audience values.

Restrictions on television advertising of liquor and tobacco are slightly more controversial but still seem justifiable. The participant interest involved is generally regarded as having a greater claim to legitimacy than false advertising does, but it seems clear that no audience interest is threatened. (No one would complain that they have insufficient opportunity to see such advertising.) If there is a worry, it is that there is a greater threat that regulation, if permitted here, might expand into other areas. If advertising can be regulated in this way, why not other aspects of program content? The answer, I believe, is the one just given, namely, that there are few other areas where regulation could be allowed with so little threat to audience interests.

Consider, for example, the power to regulate the portrayal of sex and violence in television programs. Here the problem is not merely one of spillover but of how to define the power itself in a way that does not already threaten important interests of speakers and audiences. This is extremely difficult to do, especially since programs that have the same "amount" of sex or violence can suggest quite different attitudes toward it, and, presumably, have quite different effects on their audiences. It is difficult to see how to frame a power to regulate the worst programming that would not in practice threaten some of the best as well.

I have concentrated so far on what might be called judgmental regulation: regulation that is based on a judgment about what the correct opinions or attitudes are on a given question and is aimed at preventing expression that might mislead or degrade people. I turn now to two forms of content-based regulation that do not have this judgmental character, to consider how the issues they raise are similar to, and how they differ from, those just discussed. These are viewpoint discrimination and subject matter restrictions.

Regulation that discriminates among speakers on the basis of their points of view can reflect the judgment that some of these points of view are mistaken, but it can also have other aims. It can, for example, be aimed simply at favoring speakers who have political power or those whom the governing authorities wish to see prevail in public debate, and this need not reflect any judgment as to the merits of their claims. More benignly, viewpoint-based regulation may be aimed at securing a higher degree of fairness in public discussion by constraining those who already have a great deal of exposure in order to give others a chance to be heard. Our resistance to viewpoint discrimination differs from our resistance to judgmental regulation by having a slightly different empirical basis. It arises from fear of partisanship and partiality rather than fear of paternalism. The speaker and audience interests that are threatened are the same, but because of the nature of the threatening motives our resistance to viewpoint discrimination puts more emphasis on the protection of participant values and the value of fairness.

Unlike the aims that lie behind some judgmental restrictions, motives of partisanship lack even prima facie justificatory weight. They thus present no theoretical problem in our thinking about freedom of expression but only pose a threat to be guarded against. Fairness, however, is a more difficult problem. It seems clearly mistaken to say that freedom of expression never licenses government to restrict the speech of some in order to allow others a better chance to be heard.[16] On the other hand, as I observed in the preceding section, the power to demand what one judges to be a fair and balanced discussion may easily become the power to demand a discussion that leads to what one judges to be the correct outcome (since a discussion that leads to the wrong outcome must fail to give some considerations their due weight). Giving the FCC power to deny license renewal to television stations whose coverage of public affairs it judges to have been "unbalanced" would, for example, be ruled out on this ground. In between these extremes, however, limited powers to prohibit clear and specific forms of unfairness may be compatible with freedom of expression and even required by it. The case for or against such powers must be made out on the basis of their consequences. Statutes requiring that opponents of newspaper or television editorials be given the opportunity to reply are not, on the face of it, inconsistent with the right of freedom of expression. Everything depends on what the consequences of such statutes would be as compared with the likely alternatives. If they pose a serious threat to the relevant interests, they violate that right; otherwise they do not, even though they may be ineffective or otherwise ill-advised. Would they simply discourage controversial editorials and programs and thus diminish the effective "voice" of editors? Or would they provide a chance for other voices to be heard without diminishing the range and liveliness of the debate? It may seem odd to make a question of rights turn on such empirical considerations. But if the role of freedom of expression is simply to safeguard central participant and audience interests how can that right be interpreted without taking these factors into account?

I turn now to subject matter restrictions, which bring me back to the *Mosley* case quoted at the outset. I have stated that it is impossible to argue sensibly about freedom of expression without recognizing the fact

---

[16] As maintained in *Buckley* v. *Valeo*, 424 U.S. 1 (1976), at 48–9.

that some forms of expression are of higher value than others. We need to distinguish between the values assigned to different categories of expression (because of the differing participant and audience values they serve) and the values assigned to particular acts of expression within these categories. It is mainly discrimination of this latter kind that we want to exclude in ruling out judgmental and viewpoint-based restrictions on expression, and our reasons for this exclusion are brought vividly to mind by Justice Marshall's ringing denunciation of the regulation of expression on the basis of "its message, its ideas, its subject matter, or its content." But these words do not seem to fit the issues in the *Mosley* case, which struck down an ordinance prohibiting picketing near schools except for picketing by the parties to labor disputes at that school. This ordinance does distinguish between acts of expression on the basis of their content, but it does not reflect any judgment of the merits of various messages, nor, on the face of it, does it seem to favor some points of view over others with which they are in competition.

This appearance may be misleading, however. Mosley was picketing the school to protest racial segregation. If we suppose, as seems quite plausible, that the ordinance was aimed at silencing him and others with a similar message, then something more like objectionable viewpoint discrimination emerges. But the fact that the ordinance makes an exception for labor pick-eting, thus distinguishing between acts of expression on the basis of their content (in this case their subject matter) is irrelevant to this objection. A blanket prohibition of all picketing near schools would also be objection-able, assuming that it had the same aim and no stronger justification. The relevant criticism of those who passed the Chicago ordinance is thus not that they should not have distinguished between categories of expression on the basis of their content but rather that they should have recognized expression of the kind that Mosley was engaged in as having a particu-larly high value – at least as high as that of labor picketing. Armed with that judgment, we can explain why both the blanket prohibition and the selective one are to be rejected.

What the selective nature of the prohibition does, however, is to offer the court the opening for an ad hominem argument through which it can avoid the need to balance the value of opportunities for various kinds of expression against the value of preserving a peaceful atmosphere near schools. The city council has already determined that the latter value does not outweigh the importance of opportunities for labor picketing, so the court, assuming only that political protest is at least as important, can conclude that there is insufficient justification for denying Mosley the right to picket.

A second way to look at *Mosley* is to see it as raising the question of fair distribution of a scarce resource. If it would be too disruptive to allow anyone who likes to picket near a school, the question is, who, if anyone, is to be allowed this opportunity? This brings out both a similarity to and a difference from central cases of content-based regulation. The similarity lies in the fact that we are concerned with the question of fairness to participants and with the threat of favoritism on the part of political authorities. (It is reasonable to suppose that the exception for labor picketing in the *Mosley* ordinance reflected the political power of labor unions.) The Chicago ordinance does seem unfair, but it is not clear that fairness rules out drawing distinctions between participants on the basis of the subject matter with which they are concerned. It would not seem unfair, for example, if picketing near schools must be restricted, to limit it to those whose message is concerned in some way with school policy.

VI. CONCLUSION

Does the restriction of expression on the basis of its content represent a particularly clear or particularly serious violation of freedom of expression? The idea that it does seems to me to have two sources. First, our thinking about rights is strongly influenced by a few leading examples, and some of the clearest examples of unacceptable regulation of expression involve regulation on the basis of content. But great care has to be exercised in generalizing from these examples. Second, in contrast to other decisions, which involve messy balancing of competing interests, the conclusion that a form of regulation is illegitimate because it involves distinguishing between acts of expression on the basis of their content has the clear ring of principle. This makes them appealing to the theorist, who likes sharp distinctions, as well as to the judge, who may prefer decisions that do not involve large and obvious elements of value judgment. But this clearness may be an illusion. Distinguishing permissible from impermissible forms of content-based regulation requires us to weigh the value of different categories of expression, and this element of balancing should not be ignored.

The impermissibility of certain forms of content-based regulation plays a prominent role in the constraints that define freedom of expression. This fact is important, but the clarity of this prohibition should not be taken to represent something more fundamental. Like all judgments about rights, it rests on judgments of strategy about the constraints we need to protect us against those outcomes which we have most reason to avoid.

9

Value, desire, and quality of life

I

The notion of the quality of life suffers from an embarrassing richness of possibilities. First, there are a number of related but distinct questions with which this notion might be associated. What kinds of circumstances provide good conditions under which to live? What makes a life a good one for the person who lives it? What makes a life a valuable one (a good thing, as Sidgwick put it, "from the point of view of the universe")? Second, each of these questions admits of different interpretations and a number of possible answers. Finally, there are a number of different standpoints from which the question of what makes a person's life better, in any one of these senses, might be asked. It might be asked from the point of view of that person herself, who is trying to decide how to live. It might be asked from the point of view of a benevolent third party, a friend or parent, who wants to make the person's life better. It might be asked, in a more general sense, from the point of view of a conscientious administrator, whose duty it is to act in the interest of some group of people. It might be asked, again in this more general sense, by a conscientious voter who is trying to decide which policy to vote for and defend in public debate and wants to support the policy which will improve the quality of life in her society. Finally, the question of what makes a person's life better also arises in the course of moral argument about what our duties and obligations are, since these duties and obligations are surely determined, at least to some extent, by what is needed to make people's lives better or, at least, to prevent them from being made worse.

It is important to keep in mind not only the question we are asking but also the point of view from which it is being asked, since the plausibility of various answers can be strongly influenced by the point of view of the

I am grateful to Sissela Bok and James Griffin for their helpful comments on the version of this paper presented at the Helsinki conference.

question, and unnoticed shifts in point of view can drive us back and forth between different answers. I assume that in discussing the quality of life our main concern is with the second question listed above, "What makes a life a good one for the person who lives it?" and perhaps with the closely related question "What circumstances constitute good conditions under which to live?" These questions have priority in so far as we see improvement in the quality of people's lives as morally and politically important because of the benefit it brings *to them*.

I have mentioned the third question, the question of value, primarily to distinguish it from these two, with the intention of then leaving it aside. This question admits of several interpretations, each of which is somewhat tangential to what I take to be our present concern. One might be moved to improve the quality of a person's life by the thought that one would thereby make it more valuable – that the world containing this life would become a better world. But this aim seems, to me at least, to depart from the concern with what we owe *to the person* which lies at the heart of morality and justice. An individual might try to make her own life more valuable, in a slightly different sense, by making herself a morally better person or by aiming at other things that she takes to be worthwhile. This is certainly a laudable aim, but making people's lives more valuable in this sense does not seem to me to be part of the concern with others which lies behind our inquiry into the quality of life. (That it is not is a consequence of the point of view from which the question is normally asked, a matter I will discuss in section II.)

Several answers – or, rather, several types of answer – to the question of what makes a life good for the person who lives it have become established in the literature as the standard alternatives to be considered. Derek Parfit,[1] for example, distinguishes hedonistic theories, desire theories, and objective list theories. The defining mark of hedonistic theories is what James Griffin[2] has called the "experience requirement," that is, the thesis that nothing can affect the quality of a life except by affecting the experience of living that life. A hedonistic theory needs to be filled out by specifying how the quality of this experience is to be judged. This has normally been done by specifying certain states (such as pleasure or happiness, understood in a particular way) as the ones which make a life better or worse. An alternative is to adopt the view that the experience of living a life is made better by the presence in it of those mental states, whatever they may be, which the

---

[1] *Reasons and Persons* (Oxford: Oxford University Press, 1984), app. I.
[2] *Well Being* (Oxford: Oxford University Press, 1986), p. 13.

person living the life wants to have, and is made worse by containing those states which that person would prefer to avoid. Parfit calls this alternative view "preference hedonism."

Desire theories reject the experience requirement and allow that a person's life can be made better and worse not only by changes in that person's states of consciousness but also by occurrences elsewhere in the world which fulfil that person's preferences. The most general view of this kind – it might be called the "unrestricted actual desire theory" – holds that the quality of a person's life at a given time[3] is measured by the degree to which the preferences which he or she has at that time are fulfilled. Since a person can in principle have preferences about anything whatever – about the number of moons the planet Uranus has, about the colour of Frank Sinatra's eyes, or about the sexual mores of people whom they will never see – this theory makes the determinants of the quality of a person's life very wide indeed. Other forms of desire theory restrict the range of these determinants. Sometimes this is done by restricting the objects which the relevant preferences can have. What Parfit calls the "success theory," for example, counts only preferences which are, intuitively, "about the person's own life."[4] Other forms of desire theory restrict attention to preferences which have a certain sort of basis. Harsanyi,[5] for example, excludes preferences based on a person's moral beliefs, as well as what he calls "anti-social" preferences, and Griffin proposes what he calls an "informed desire theory," which would make the quality of people's lives depend only on the fulfillment of those desires that they would have if they "appreciated the true nature" of the objects of those desires.[6]

What is the rationale for these departures from the unrestricted actual desire theory? Parfit's success theory might be proposed simply as a way of bringing the desire theory closer to the ordinary meaning of the phrase "quality of a person's life." It sounds odd to say that if I happen to have a desire that Uranus should have six moons, then my life will be better if it turns out that this is in fact the case. (Assuming, of course, that I am not an astronomer and have not invested any effort in trying to determine

---

[3] I set aside here the problem of how this view can be extended into an account of the quality of a person's life as a whole which allows for the fact that preferences change over time. The difficulty of making this extension has been emphasized by Richard Brandt. See Richard Brandt, *A Theory of the Good and the Right* (Oxford: Oxford University Press, 1979), ch. 13.

[4] *Reasons and Persons*, p. 494. For a similar proposal see Griffin, *Well Being*, p. 13.

[5] See John C. Harsanyi, "Morality and the Theory of Rational Behaviour," in Amartya Sen and Bernard Williams, eds., *Utilitarianism and Beyond* (Cambridge: Cambridge University Press, 1982), pp. 39–62, here p. 56.

[6] Griffin, *Well Being*, p. 11.

how many moons Uranus has or in developing cosmological theories which would be confirmed or disconfirmed by such a fact.)

A second reason for such restrictions is provided by the aim of describing a concept of well-being which preserves the idea that any improvement in a person's well-being has positive ethical value. The unrestricted actual desire theory fails to preserve this idea, since there are many preferences whose fulfillment appears to have no weight in determining what others should do. If, for example, I were to have a strong preference about how people quite remote from me in time and space lead their personal lives, this preference would give rise to no reason at all – not even a reason which is outweighed by other considerations – why they should behave in the way that I prefer. So the unrestricted actual desire theory must be scaled back if the direct ethical significance of well-being is to be preserved, and I believe that most modifications of the desire theory are motivated by similar ethical concerns.[7]

The appeal of desire theories also derives in large part from ethical ideas. Harsanyi, for example, bases his preference utilitarianism on what he calls the "principle of preference autonomy," "the principle that, in deciding what is good and what is bad for a given individual, the ultimate criterion can only be his own wants and his own preferences."[8] Some of the modified desire theories mentioned above involve departures from this principle, however. The exclusion of preferences based on moral beliefs may not be such a departure: since a person who wants a certain thing to happen because he considers it morally right is unlikely to take its happening as a benefit *to him*, the preferences excluded by this restriction may not represent a person's view about "what is good and bad for him." The same may be true of the preferences excluded by the success theory. But the informed desire theory is in stronger tension with the principle of preference autonomy, since it allows us to say that some of a person's firmly held preferences about his life are simply mistaken. For this reason and some others, I believe that the informed desire theory should probably not be counted as a form of desire theory at all but assigned instead to Parfit's third category, which he calls objective list theories. I will return to this question after I have discussed that category in more detail.

Of the three categories listed by Parfit, the category of objective list theories is least closely tied to a specific and well-known view of what makes

---

[7] I argue elsewhere that this is true of the modifications which Harsanyi proposes. See Scanlon, "The Moral Basis of Interpersonal Comparisons," in Jon Elster and John Roemer, eds., *Interpersonal Comparisons of Well-Being* (Cambridge: Cambridge University Press, 1991).

[8] Harsanyi, "Morality and the Theory of Rational Behaviour," p. 55.

a life go better. (There is no familiar theory of which it is the generalization in the way that the category of mental state theories is a generalization of hedonism.) None the less, this category seems to me to contain all the most plausible candidates for an account of what makes a life better. The name, "objective list theory," is doubly unfortunate. The term "list" suggests a kind of arbitrariness (just what its critics would charge), and "objective" suggests a kind of rigidity (as if the same things must be valuable for everyone), as well as inviting a host of difficult questions about the various forms of objectivity and the possibility of values being objective in any of these senses. One might think the name had been coined by opponents of views of this kind.[9]

But while its name may seem to imply a controversial claim to objectivity, this is not what is essential to the category as I understand it. What is essential is that these are theories according to which an assessment of a person's well-being involves a substantive judgment about what things make life better, a judgment which may conflict with that of the person whose well-being is in question. This is in contrast to the central idea of desire theories, according to which substantive questions about which things are actually good are (at least within limits) deferred to the judgment of the person whose well-being is being assessed. According to the unrestricted actual desire theory, for example, if a person cares as much about *A* as about *B* then *A* contributes as much to that person's well-being as *B* does, and if a person cares more about *A* than about *B* then *A* contributes more to that person's well-being. Other desire theories depart from this principle in some cases, but it remains the central touchstone of theories of this type. Since this seems to amount to the claim that standards of well-being are subjective, it is tempting to apply the contrasting term "objective" to any view which rejects this principle. But this now seems to me a mistake.[10] I am not sure what the best label is for theories in Parfit's third category, but I suggest that we call them "substantive good theories" since, unlike desire theories, they are based on substantive claims about what goods, conditions, and opportunities make life better.

[9] Though Parfit is not such an opponent, and I myself bear some responsibility here since I have also used the term "objective" in arguing for the necessity of a view of this kind. See Scanlon, "Preference and Urgency" (1975), in this volume, essay 4.

[10] In ibid., p. 658, I wrote, "By an objective criterion I mean a criterion which provides a basis for appraisal of a person's well-being which is independent of that person's tastes and interests." This formulation now seems unfortunate in several respects. As I have said, the term "objective" was not apt. In addition, I should have made it clearer that by "independent of" I meant "not wholly dependent on." I did not mean to suggest that a criterion of the kind I had in mind would always ignore differences in individual tastes and interests, but only that it did not have to be governed by them.

Hedonism in its classical form,[11] according to which pleasure is the only thing which contributes to the quality of a life, counts as a substantive good theory on the definition I have offered. This may seem odd. Hedonism may seem more akin to desire theories because it bases well-being in certain mental states and because it introduces an important element of subjectivity into the determination of well-being since different people receive pleasure from, and are made happy by, different things. But both of these reasons for associating the two views with one another are mistaken. Both views involve "mental states," but they do so in very different ways. Hedonism takes certain mental states to be the only things of ultimate value. Desire theories count things as valuable if they are the objects of the appropriate "mental states" or attitudes, but the things valued need not be mental states and the attitudes which confer value need not themselves be valuable.

The mistake underlying the second reason for linking hedonism and desire theories is, for present purposes, more important. What Parfit calls objective list theories of well-being, and I am calling substantive good theories, have often been accused of excessive rigidity, as if they had to prescribe the same goods for everyone without regard for individual differences. Griffin, for example, cites "flexibility" as an important advantage of his informed desire theory, and as his main reason for classifying it as a form of *desire* theory:

The informed-desire account can allow that the values on the list (enjoyment, accomplishment, autonomy, etc.) are values for everyone, but it also allows that there may be very special persons for whom any value on the list (say, accomplishment), though valuable for them as for everybody, conflicts enough with another value (say, freedom from anxiety) for it not, all things considered, to be valuable for them to have.[12]

As Griffin goes on to acknowledge, however, substantive good theories can also allow for this kind of variation. They can count various kinds of enjoyment among those things that can make a life better, and can also recognize that different people experience these forms of enjoyment under different circumstances, and are capable of experiencing them to

---

[11] "Preference hedonism" may seem a different case since, while it retains the experience requirement, it leaves the qualities of experience which make life better to be determined by each individual's own preferences. It could thus be classed as a restricted desire theory. But the restriction in question – excluding everything other than the quality of a person's experience – is sufficiently strong that I would count preference hedonism too as a substantive good theory. Note that it could be arrived at from the informed desire theory only by adding a strong claim about what it is in fact rational to desire.

[12] Griffin, *Well Being*, p. 33.

different degrees and at different costs. Consequently, a substantive good theory can allow for the fact that the best lives for different people may contain quite different ingredients. Griffin observes that a substantive good theory of this kind becomes "very hard to distinguish from the informed-desire approach."[13] As he also suggests, a decision about how to classify the resulting theory is apt to turn on the question of priority between value and desire. As I see it, according to a desire theory, when something makes life better this is always because that thing satisfies some desire. Substantive good theories can allow for the fact that this is sometimes the case – it is sometimes a good thing simply to be getting what you want – but according to these theories being an object of desire is not in general what makes things valuable.

Someone who accepts a substantive good theory, according to which certain goods make a life better, will no doubt also believe that these goods are the objects of informed desire – that they would be desired by people who fully appreciated their nature and the nature of life. But the order of explanation here is likely to be from the belief that these things are genuine goods to the conclusion that people will, if informed, come to desire them. The fact that certain things are the object of desires which are, as far as we can tell, informed desires, can be a reason for believing these things to be goods. But "reason" here is a matter of evidence – of reason for believing – not a ground of value of the sort which the original desire theory was, I am assuming, supposed to supply.

This assumption raises a general question about what a philosophical theory of well-being is supposed to do. One objective of such a theory is to describe a class of things which make lives better, perhaps also offering some account of the kind of case that can be made for the claim that a thing belongs to this class. A second, more ambitious objective is to give a general account of the ground of this kind of value – a general account of what it is that makes a life a good life. I take it that classical hedonism was supposed to do both of these things, and I have been assuming that the unrestricted actual desire theory also aimed at the second of these objectives at least as much as the first; that is, that it sought to explain what makes things valuable at least as much as to identify any particular group of things as desirable.

If I am right about this then the introduction of the adjective "informed," which looks like a small qualification, in fact represents a significant departure. Informed desires are desires which are responsive to the relevant

13 Ibid.

features of their objects. By acknowledging the importance of these features in making the objects good (and making the desires for them appropriate rather than mistaken), this theory parts company sharply with the unrestricted actual desire theory, according to which it was the *satisfaction of desire* which made things good.[14]

A substantive good theory could have both of the theoretical objectives mentioned above, but the most plausible theories of this kind aim only at the first. Such a theory claims that certain diverse goods make a life better, and it will be prepared to defend this claim by offering reasons (possibly different in each case) about why these things are desirable. But it may offer no unified account of what makes things good. It seems to me unlikely that there is any such account to be had, since it is unlikely that there are any good-making properties which are common to all good things. If this is correct, then there will be no general theory of goodness in between, on the one hand, a purely formal analysis of "good" such as "answers to certain interests" or "has the properties it is rational to want in a thing of that kind"[15] and, on the other hand, diverse arguments about why various properties of particular objects make those objects good.

II

Let me turn now to a consideration of the various points of view which I have distinguished above. I have long been skeptical about desire theories as an account of well-being appropriate for moral theory, but I have supposed that there is more to be said for them as an account appropriate for individual decision making. This seems to me to be a mistake, and I now believe that desire theories should also be rejected as accounts of well-being appropriate to the first-person point of view. I will argue against such theories in the following way. The fact that an outcome would improve a person's well-being ("make his or her life go better") provides that person with a reason (other things being equal) for wanting that outcome to occur. If a desire theory were correct as an account of well-being, then, the fact that a certain outcome would fulfil a person's desire would be a basic reason for that person to want that thing to come about. But desires do not provide basic reasons of this sort, at least not in nontrivial cases. The fact that we prefer a certain outcome can provide us with a serious reason for bringing it about

---

[14] Compare Gilbert Harman's observation about the tendency of emotivism to evolve into ideal observer theory in Harman, *The Nature of Morality* (New York: Oxford University Press, 1977), ch. 4.

[15] Analyses such as those offered in Paul Ziff, *Semantic Analysis* (Ithaca: Cornell University Press, 1960), ch. 6, and John Rawls, *A Theory of Justice* (Cambridge, MA: Harvard University Press, 1971), ch. 7.

"for our own sake." But when it does, this reason is either a reason of the sort described by a mental state view such as hedonism or a reason based on some other notion of substantive good rather than a reason grounded simply in the fact of desire, in the way that desire theories would require. To see this we need to consider each of these cases in a little more detail.

In many cases, the fact that I desire a certain outcome provides me with a reason for trying to bring it about because the presence of that desire indicates that the outcome will be pleasant or enjoyable for me. I can have reasons of this kind, for example, for ordering fish rather than tortellini, for climbing to the top of a hill, or for wearing a particular necktie. The end sought in these cases is the experience or mental state which the object or activity in question is expected to produce, and the desire is an indication that this state is likely to be forthcoming (as well as, perhaps, a factor in producing it).

In other cases, my desire that a certain state of affairs should obtain reflects my judgment that that state of affairs is desirable for some reason other than the mere fact that I prefer it: it may reflect, for example, my judgment that that state of affairs is morally good, or that it is in my overall interest, or that it is a good thing of its kind. This represents, I believe, the most common kind of case in which preferences are cited as reasons for action; the fact that I prefer a certain outcome *is* a reason for action in such a case, but not a fundamental one. My preferences are not the source of reasons but reflect conclusions based on reasons of other kinds. There are, of course, other cases in which I might say that the only reason I have for doing or choosing something is simply that "I prefer it." But these cases are trivial ones rather than examples of the typical form of rational decision making.

My conclusion, then, is that when statements of preference or desire represent serious reasons for action they can be understood in one of the two ways just described: either as stating reasons which are at base hedonistic or as stating judgments of desirability reached on other grounds. What convinces me of this conclusion is chiefly the fact that I am unable to think of any clear cases in which preferences provide nontrivial reasons for action which are not of these two kinds.

Additional support for this conclusion is provided by its ability to explain the familiar fact, emphasized by Richard Brandt, that past desires do not in general provide reasons for action and that their fulfillment does not in itself contribute to a person's well-being. Brandt[16] gives the example of a

---

[16] Brandt, *A Theory of the Good and the Right*, ch. 13.

man who, as a child, desired intensely that he go for a roller-coaster ride on his fiftieth birthday. As the date approaches, however, the man finds that he no longer enjoys roller-coaster rides and that there are many other things he would rather do to celebrate his birthday. Surely, Brandt claims, the fact that he once had this desire gives the man no reason to take a roller-coaster ride which he will not enjoy, nor would taking the ride contribute towards making his life better on the whole just because it is something which he once desired.

Brandt's conclusion is that the desire theory should be rejected as an account of what makes a person's life go better, and that a mental state theory should be adopted instead. But these examples provide no reason to move to a mental state theory rather than a substantive good theory, particularly when we bear in mind the fact that any plausible substantive good theory will count agreeable mental states among the things which can make a life better. If some such theory is correct, then the conclusion arrived at above – namely that the reason-giving force of preferences always depends either on the pleasure which their fulfillment will bring or on the truth of the substantive judgments of desirability which they reflect – provides a systematic explanation of the phenomenon which Brandt describes.

On the one hand, the fulfillment of desires that are no longer held brings no pleasure of satisfaction. On the other, in so far as the reason-giving force of past preferences depends on substantive judgments of desirability, they obviously lose this force when those judgments are rejected. That is to say, the agent will no longer regard these preferences as providing reasons for action. Of course it may be that the agent's original judgment of desirability was correct, and he or she is therefore wrong to reject it. In that case the fulfillment of the original preference might indeed make the agent's life better and so, in a sense, he or she may have reason to seek its fulfillment. But the force of that reason, if it is one, has nothing to do with the fact that the agent once had this preference.

Similar remarks apply to future preferences. When one agrees with the judgment of desirability that a future preference will express, one will believe that one has reason now to promote the fulfillment of that preference. So, for example, a person who believes that in ten years she will have children for whom she will want to provide a good education, and who believes now that educating one's children is very important, will believe that she now has a reason to promote that future goal. But the future preference itself is doing little work in such cases; what matters is the underlying judgment of desirability. The cases in which the fact of future preference is itself most clearly fundamental fit the hedonistic (or, more broadly, experiential) model: our concern in these cases is to bring ourselves the pleasant experience of having these preferences fulfilled or to spare ourselves the unpleasant experience of having them frustrated. For example, a 19-year-old who cares nothing for old family photographs but believes that in thirty years he will feel quite different about such things has reason to save them simply in order to bring himself pleasure, and avoid sadness, in the future.

It is difficult to come up with a plausible example in which future preferences which one does not now have none the less provide one with direct reasons for action that are independent of experiential or other indirect effects and independent of the merits of the judgments on which those preferences are based. My belief is that if such an example were offered, it would turn out on examination to be better understood as an instance of a quasi-moral obligation to respect the autonomy of one's future self rather than as a case of regard for one's overall well-being (identified with one's level of preference satisfaction). For it is hard to see how a concern for one's *well-being* could be the motive for promoting the fulfillment of a future preference if one regards that preference as mistaken (i.e. believes that its object is inferior to other alternatives) and if one's concern is not with the quality of one's future experience.

Nothing that I have said here in criticizing the desire theory as an account of an individual's view of his or her own well-being is incompatible with the thesis that it is rational to act in such a way as to maximize one's expected utility. This thesis does not assert that people should take utility maximization to be their most basic reason for action. It is not a thesis about the reasons people have for acting but rather a thesis about the structure which the preferences of a rational individual will have (whatever the content or ground of these preferences may be). The thesis asserts that the preferences of a rational person will satisfy certain axioms and that when this is the case there will be a mathematical measure of expected preference satisfaction such that the individual will always prefer the alternative to which this measure assigns the greater number. In short, it asserts that a rational individual will choose in such a way as to maximize utility, but does not claim that utility is a quantity which (like pleasure) supplies the reasons for these choices.[17]

[17] It should also be noted that the most plausible version of the utility maximization thesis is one in which the relevant notion of utility is based on *all* of a person's preferences, no matter what the objects of these preferences may be. For the reasons noted in the previous section, the breadth of this notion of utility makes it an implausible account of well-being, whatever merits it may have as a description of what a rational individual would aim at.

Let me turn now to consider the point of view of a benevolent third party, such as a friend or parent, who wants to promote a person's well-being. What concept of well-being is appropriate here? Harsanyi has suggested that the relevant notion is fulfillment of the preferences of the intended beneficiary, and he points out that this is what we aim at when we are selecting a gift for a friend.[18] Brandt, on the other hand, has argued, citing psychological evidence, that what benevolent individuals in fact aim at is the happiness of their intended beneficiaries rather than the fulfillment of their desires, and he defends this aim as rational.[19] It seems to me that Brandt offers the correct account of Harsanyi's examples. Preferences are important when we are selecting a gift, baking a birthday cake, or deciding where to take a friend to dinner because what we are aiming at in such cases is a person's happiness. What we want is to please them, and preferences play a double role here. First, they indicate what gift is likely to bring pleasure. In addition, a person can be pleased simply by the fact that we have taken care to discern what his preferences are and to find a gift that fulfils them. But, contrary to Brandt's suggestion, it is not clear that pleasure is what we should always aim at *qua* benefactors. Surely there are cases in which a true benefactor will aim at a person's overall good at the expense of what would be pleasing (or will at least be torn between these two objectives). If this is correct, then a benefactor's conception of well-being must include a notion of the substantive good of the beneficiary which can diverge from the idea of what the beneficiary will find pleasing. But in so far as the idea of pure desire satisfaction diverges from these two it seems to play little role in the thinking of a rational benefactor.

This idea gets greater weight, however, when we shift from the role of benefactor to that of agent or representative. A person who is acting for a friend (or son or daughter) may be constrained by that person's preferences, in so far as these are known, in a way that a benefactor is not. (Certainly this is the view that my own children take!) Whatever view children may take, however, the role of parents is not merely to be the *agents* of their children. They are not bound always to take their children's preferences as definitive of their good, and need to be able to form an independent judgment about that good. But it is when we focus on people whose role is solely that of agents for other adults that the desire theory has its greatest plausibility. That view owes much of its influence to its wide acceptance among economists, and it seems likely that this acceptance is in turn based

---

[18] Harsanyi, "Can the Maximin Principle Serve as a Basis for Morality? A Critique of John Rawls's Theory," *American Political Science Review* 69 (1975), 594–606, here pp. 600–1.

[19] Brandt, *A Theory of the Good and the Right*, pp. 147–8.

on the idea that officials who must choose social policies for a society should think of themselves as agents of the members of that society, and therefore as bound to promote the fulfillment of the members' preferences.

It is no objection here that from the point of view of the members themselves the reason-giving force of these preferences depends on other factors, in the way I have argued above. These preferences can count as ultimate sources of reasons from the point of view of the decision maker whatever their standing may be for the individuals whose preferences they are. Official responsibility can be defined in many different ways, but it is natural to suppose that an official could be conceived both to be acting for the good of a group and to be bound to accept the expressed judgment of members of that group as to where that good lies. Here, then, is a natural home for desire theories.

What makes such theories seem appropriate to questions of social policy is not the nature of the questions at issue. If the same policy questions were to be decided by referendum then each individual voter would be free to consider what he or she thinks would be best, and not bound to take the idea of what is "best" as defined by the expressed preferences of all the members of society. The appeal of desire theories arises rather from the constraints which we have taken to apply to the decision maker, and the point to be made is that these constraints, which may in context be quite appealing, are also quite special. The question is how broadly they apply. Do they, for example, apply to each of us when we adopt the attitude of impartiality which is appropriate to moral argument? I will turn next to that question.

III

Any discussion of the role of well-being in moral argument takes place against the background of utilitarianism, which assigns this concept such a fundamental role. Even in nonutilitarian theories, however, the justification of rights and principles must refer at least in part to the importance of the interests which they promote and protect, and any such theory must therefore face the questions of how these interests are to be characterized and how their claims to moral importance are to be justified.

Answers to these questions depend on a view of the nature of moral judgment and moral argument. I will discuss the answers which seem to me to be supported by my own contractualist moral theory.[20] According to

[20] As outlined in Scanlon, "Contractualism and Utilitarianism" (1982), in this volume, essay 7.

this theory, the basic motive behind morality is the desire to be able to justify one's actions to others on grounds that they have reason to accept if they are also concerned with mutual justification. The theory holds that when we address a question of right and wrong the question we are addressing is whether the proposed action would be allowed by principles of conduct which people moved by this desire could not reasonably reject.

When can a principle be reasonably rejected by someone who is motivated in this way? This is a difficult question which I cannot answer fully, but I think that at least the following is true. A person can reasonably reject a principle if (1) general acceptance of that principle in a world like the one we are familiar with would cause that person serious hardship, and (2) there are alternative principles, the general acceptance of which would not entail comparable burdens for anyone. In order, then, to decide whether a given principle can reasonably be rejected we will need some interpretation of the terms "serious hardship" and "comparable burden." This is how the notion of individual well-being makes its fundamental appearance in contractualist moral argument.

Note that the context of moral argument as contractualism describes it differs in two important respects from the situation of the social decision maker discussed at the end of the preceding section. First, that decision maker was assumed to be dealing with a given set of specific individuals whose preferences had been expressed. But when we are trying to work out what is right we are concerned with the choice of general principles of action, which will apply to an indefinite range of individuals whose particular preferences there is no way of knowing in detail (though we do know general facts about the kinds of preference most people have). Second, while the task of the official is to reach a decision by amalgamating the stated preferences of the members of the group, a person considering a moral question is (according to contractualism) trying to work out the terms of a hypothetical agreement among these people. The imagined role of the members of the group is thus quite different in the two cases: in one case all they are taken to have done is to submit their personal preferences, while in the other they are thought of, hypothetically, as reacting to one another, trying to find principles that they can all accept. These two features, the generality of moral argument and the central place within it of the aim of agreement, are important in determining the relevant notions of individual benefit and burden.

I argued above that individuals' choices, and their conceptions of their own well-being, are guided by their ideas of substantive good, which typically include but are not limited to the experiential goods of various "desirable states of consciousness." Such a conception of substantive goods will provide an individual with a basis for deciding what a good life is, but it may also go beyond that, since the things which an individual recognizes as substantive goods may include some which lie outside his or her "life" in the ordinary sense.

An individual will thus have *a* reason for wanting to reject a principle if the results of its general acceptance would be very bad from the point of view of that person's conception of substantive good. Suppose, however, that the person is moved to find and act on principles which no one could reasonably reject. How could his or her rejection of this principle be shown to be reasonable? What the person must do to show this is to put the reasons for that rejection in terms that others must recognize as important, terms that they would want to employ themselves to reject principles which burden them and that they are therefore prepared to recognize as generally compelling.

It is easiest to claim this status for substantive bads which everyone recognizes as serious: such things as loss of life, intense physical pain, and mental or physical disability. In general, losses of what Sen[21] calls "functionings" will be good candidates for this list. But the things that are important to an individual will go beyond these basic functionings, and there will normally be less agreement about the nature and relative value of these further goods. Different individuals may enjoy different pursuits, follow different religions, and find different aims worth pursuing.

There are several ways to find agreement despite this diversity. First, there may be agreement on the importance of those goods and opportunities which are the main means to these diverse ends. Rawlsian "primary social goods" such as income, wealth, and socially protected opportunities for self-expression would be examples of such means. The value that we can agree to assign to these resources need not be "fetishistic" in the sense criticized by Sen[22] as long as it is acknowledged that their moral importance depends on their strategic role in the pursuit of diverse individual aims. Even if they are of only instrumental value, however, it might be claimed that these resources are none the less *morally* basic measures of well-being because their importance to life can be the object of the kind of consensus required to confer moral status, whereas there may be no consensus on the value of the particular pursuits to which they are the means (no agreement, for

---

[21] In, for example, Amartya K. Sen, "Well-being, Agency and Freedom," *Journal of Philosophy* 82 (1984), 161–221, here pp. 197 ff.

[22] See Amartya K. Sen, "Equality of What?" in Sen, *Choice, Welfare and Measurement* (Cambridge, MA: MIT Press, 1980), p. 366.

example, on the value of the particular forms of expression which various individuals want to engage in).

It is unlikely, however, that particular resources will be morally basic in this sense.[23] Lying behind such primary goods will be broad categories of good and harm which carry specific weight in moral argument. People can agree, for example, on the importance of having opportunities for self-expression (the exact form of these opportunities being as yet unspecified) even though they disagree sharply over the merits of particular speeches, plays, demonstrations, etc. Similarly, people who hold very different and conflicting beliefs may still be able to agree that "being able to follow one's religion" is (for those who have one) an important part of life, and consequently a personal value which must be given significant weight in moral argument. The formulation of such abstract categories of good and harm is one of the main means through which a common set of moral values is developed. Moral argument clearly requires values of this kind which are intermediate between specific resources on the one hand and particular individual aims on the other, since the adequacy of specific resources, such as specific legally defined rights of freedom of expression or freedom of religion, can always be questioned, and these rights may need to be redefined as conditions change. In order to argue about such matters we need a moral vocabulary in which we can express the moral importance of the underlying individual interests.

What emerges, then, as a basis for arguing about the acceptability or unacceptability of particular moral principles is a heterogeneous collection of conditions, goods, and categories of activity[24] to which certain moral weights are assigned. Let me call this a system of moral goods and bads. The process of thought through which one arrives at such a system includes a mixture of "fact" and "value" elements. One begins with one's own view of the substantive goods which, in general, make life better and with a knowledge of how other individuals differ in their circumstances and in their views about what is substantively good.[25] The pressure to formulate a system of common values is then provided by the moral aim of finding a way of evaluating principles of action which all these individuals could accept despite their differences.

[23] This is not an objection to Rawls since he does not present "primary social goods" as the most fundamental moral measures of well-being but rather as an index of distributive shares to be used for the purposes of assessing the justice of basic economic and political institutions. Their adequacy for this more specialized purpose is a separate question from the one I am discussing.
[24] Sen's notion of "functionings" may be broad enough to encompass all of these.
[25] See Griffin, *Well Being*, p. 114, for an excellent statement of this starting point.

I argued in section II that individuals themselves, and benevolent third parties, assess well-being in terms of substantive goods rather than in terms of the satisfaction of desires. In moral thinking as well, what we should (and, I believe, normally do) appeal to is our best estimate of what is important to making our lives and the lives of others good (recognizing that, in view of our differences, this will not always be the same). But the aim of finding a mode of argument that others could not reasonably refuse to accept forces us to consider not only what *we* take to be important goods for other people (what we think they would recognize as good if they were fully informed and rational) but also what it would be unreasonable of them, under normal conditions, not to recognize as important goods. The aim then is to develop a set of goods and bads which we all, in so far as we are trying to find a common vocabulary of justification, have reason to accept as covering the most important ways in which life can be made better or worse.

The system of moral goods and bads which emerges from such a search for common standards of evaluation may include some elements, such as the importance of avoiding physical pain and bodily harm, which are common to almost every individual's list of substantive goods. But because it must be the object of a consensus, the system of moral goods and bads may not assign these goods and bads the same relative values which they receive in some individual outlooks. In addition, it may contain some elements which have no analogous role in individuals' views of the good. The category of religion can be seen as an example of this. For a believer, the abstract category of religion may be of little interest since it groups her own most important beliefs together with other systems of thought which may strike her as, at best, objects of curiosity. The importance of this category lies either in sociological reflection or, more relevant for present purposes, in liberal morality. In the former, it groups together disparate practices and systems of belief in virtue of similarities in the role they play in the lives of different groups of people. In the latter, it serves to express a willingness to equate, *for the purposes of moral argument*, beliefs and practices which have a similar importance in the lives of different people but which are, from the point of view of any one such person, of very different value. The moral aim of finding forms of justification which others can also accept pushes us to develop such categories and to give them a central role in our thinking.

In so far as a system of moral goods and bads differs in these ways from individual conceptions of well-being, it could be said to be "not subjective," that is, not an expression of any individual's preferences. As I mentioned earlier in this essay, however, it does not follow that such a system is "objective." For one thing, there is the question of the objectivity of the judgment that a particular system of values of this kind represents a standard which it is reasonable to employ, given the existing diversity of individual points of view. Second, the process I have described, through which such a system is arrived at and defended, can be expected to yield different outcomes in different social settings, since the activities and pursuits which are important to individual lives will vary from society to society. Even the relative importance of various physical and mental capacities will vary depending on the kind of life that people have the opportunity to live. Whether these considerations undermine the "objectivity" of a system of moral goods and bads, and how, if at all, that matters, are difficult questions which it seems best to leave aside for the present.

For the purposes of argument about which principles it is reasonable to reject, a system of moral goods and bads does not need to provide a very complete ordering of levels of well-being. It is enough to distinguish between those "very severe" losses which count as grounds for reasonable rejection and those gains and losses which are not of comparable severity. If we were to accept a principle requiring the equalization of well-being (as defined by such a system of moral goods and bads) then the level of completeness demanded would be much stronger. My own view is that such a global principle of equality is not very plausible: the ideas of equality which are most significant and morally compelling deal with a narrower range of goods. But that is a larger issue which I will leave for another occasion.

10

The difficulty of tolerance

I. WHAT IS TOLERANCE?

Tolerance requires us to accept people and permit their practices even when we strongly disapprove of them. Tolerance thus involves an attitude that is intermediate between wholehearted acceptance and unrestrained opposition.[1] This intermediate status makes tolerance a puzzling attitude. There are certain things, such as murder, that ought not be tolerated. There are limits to what we are able to do to prevent these things from happening, but we need not restrain ourselves out of tolerance for these actions as expressions of the perpetrators' values. In other cases, where our feelings of opposition or disapproval should properly be reined in, it would be better if we were to get rid of these feelings altogether. If we are moved by racial or ethnic prejudice, for example, the preferred remedy is not merely to tolerate those whom we abhor but to stop abhorring people just because they look different or come from a different background.

Perhaps everything would, ideally, fall into one or the other of these two classes. Except where wholehearted disapproval and opposition are appropriate, as in the case of murder, it would be best if the feelings that generate conflict and disagreement could be eliminated altogether. Tolerance, as an attitude that requires us to hold in check certain feelings of opposition and disapproval, would then be just a second best – a way of dealing with attitudes that we would be better off without but that are, unfortunately, ineliminable. To say this would not be to condemn tolerance. Even if it is, in this sense, a second best, the widespread adoption of tolerant attitudes would be a vast improvement over the sectarian blood-shed that we hear of every day, in many parts of the globe. Stemming this violence would be no mean feat.

I am grateful to Joshua Cohen and Will Kymlicka for their helpful comments on earlier drafts of this paper.

[1] As John Horton points out in "Toleration as a Virtue" in David Heyd, ed., *Toleration: An Elusive Virtue* (Princeton: Princeton University Press, 1996), pp. 28–43.

Still, it seems to me that there are pure cases of tolerance, in which it is not merely an expedient for dealing with the imperfections of human nature. These would be cases in which persisting conflict and disagreement are to be expected and are, unlike racial prejudice, quite compatible with full respect for those with whom we disagree. But while respect for each other does not require us to abandon our disagreement, it does place limits on how this conflict can be pursued. In this essay, I want to investigate the possibility of pure tolerance of this kind, with the aim of better understanding our idea of tolerance and the difficulty of achieving it. Because I particularly want to see more clearly why it is a difficult attitude and practice to sustain, I will try to concentrate on cases in which I myself find tolerance difficult. I begin with the familiar example of religious toleration, which provides the model for most of our thinking about toleration of other kinds.

Widespread acceptance of the idea of religious toleration is, at least in North America and Europe, a historical legacy of the European Wars of Religion. Today, religious toleration is widely acknowledged as an ideal, even though there are many places in the world where, even as we speak, blood is being spilled over what are at least partly religious divisions.

As a person for whom religion is a matter of no personal importance whatever, it seems easy for me, at least at the outset, to endorse religious toleration. At least this is so when toleration is understood in terms of the twin principles of the First Amendment to the Constitution of the United States: "Congress shall make no law respecting an establishment of religion, or prohibiting the free exercise thereof." Accepting these principles seems to be all benefit and no cost from my point of view. Why should I want to interfere with other people's religious practice, provided that they are not able to impose that practice on me? If religious toleration has costs, I am inclined to say, they are borne by others, not by me.

So it seems at first (although I will later argue that this is a mistake) that for me religious toleration lacks the tension I just described: I do not feel the opposition it tells me to hold in check. Why should I want to tell others what religion to practice, or to have one established as our official creed? On the other hand, for those who do want these things, religious toleration seems to demand a great deal: if I thought it terribly important that everyone worship in the correct way, how could I accept toleration except as an uneasy truce, acceptable as an alternative to perpetual bloodshed, but even so a necessity that is to be regretted? Pure toleration seems to have escaped us.

I want to argue that this view of things is mistaken. Tolerance involves costs and dangers for all of us, but it is nonetheless an attitude that we all have reason to value.

II. WHAT DOES TOLERATION REQUIRE?

This is a difficult question to answer, in part because there is more than one equally good answer, in part because any good answer will be vague in important respects. Part of any answer is legal and political. Tolerance requires that people who fall on the "wrong" side of the differences I have mentioned should not, for that reason, be denied legal and political rights: the right to vote, to hold office, to benefit from the central public goods that are otherwise open to all, such as education, public safety, the protections of the legal system, health care, and access to "public accommodations." In addition, it requires that the state not give preference to one group over another in the distribution of privileges and benefits.

It is this part of the answer that seems to me to admit of more than one version. For example, in the United States, the requirement that each religious group is equally entitled to the protections and benefits conferred by the state is interpreted to mean that the state may not support, financially or otherwise, any religious organization. The main exception, not an insignificant one, is that any religious organization can qualify for tax-exempt status. So even our idea of "nonestablishment" represents a mixed strategy: some forms of support are prohibited for *any* religion, others are allowed provided they are available for *all* religions. This mixture strikes me more as a particular political compromise than as a solution uniquely required by the idea of religious toleration. A society in which there was a religious qualification for holding public office could not be accounted tolerant or just. But I would not say the same about just any form of state support for religious practice. In Great Britain, for example, there is an established church, and the state supports denominational as well as nondenominational schools. In my view, the range of these schools is too narrow to reflect the religious diversity of contemporary Britain, but I do not see that just any system of this kind is to be faulted as lacking in toleration. Even if it would be intolerant to give one religion certain special forms of support, there are many different acceptable mixtures of what is denied to every religion and what is available to all. The particular mixture that is now accepted in the United States is not the only just solution.

This indeterminacy extends even to the area of freedom of expression, which will be particularly important in what follows. Any just and tolerant society must protect freedom of expression. This does not mean merely that censorship is ruled out, but requires as well that individuals and groups have some effective means for bringing their views before the public. There are, however, many ways of doing this.[2] There are, for example, many ways of defining and regulating a "public forum," and no one of these is specifically required. Permitted and protected modes of expression need not be the same everywhere.

Let me now move from the most clearly institutional aspects of toleration to the less institutional and more attitudinal, thereby moving from the indeterminate to the vague. I have said that toleration involves "accepting as equals" those who differ from us. In what I have said so far, this equality has meant equal possession of fundamental legal and political rights, but the ideal of equality that toleration involves goes beyond these particular rights. It might be stated as follows: all members of society are equally entitled to be taken into account in defining what our society is and equally entitled to participate in determining what it will become in the future. This idea is unavoidably vague and difficult to accept. It is difficult to accept insofar as it applies to those who differ from us or disagree with us, and who would make our society something other than what we want it to be. It is vague because of the difficulty of saying exactly what this "equal entitlement" involves. One mode of participation is, of course, through the formal politics of voting, running for office, and trying to enlist votes for the laws and policies that one favors. But what I now want to stress is the way in which the requirements of toleration go beyond this realm of formal politics into what might be called the informal politics of social life.

The competition among religious groups is a clear example of this informal politics, but it is only one example. Other groups and individuals engage in the same political struggle all the time: we set and follow examples, seek to be recognized or have our standard-bearers recognized in every aspect of cultural and popular life. A tolerant society, I want to say, is one that is democratic in its informal politics. This democracy is a matter of law and institutions (a matter, for example, of the regulation of expression). But it is also, importantly and irreducibly, a matter of attitude. Toleration of this kind is not easy to accept – it is risky and frightening – and it is not easy to achieve, even in one's own attitudes, let alone in society as a whole.

To explain what I have in mind, it is easiest to begin with some familiar controversies over freedom of expression and over "the enforcement of morals." The desire to prevent those with whom one disagrees from

---

[2] More exactly, there are many ways of trying to do it. I believe that our ideas of freedom of expression must be understood in terms of a commitment both to certain goals and to the idea of certain institutional arrangements as crucial means to those goals. But the means are never fully adequate to the goals, which drive their constant evolution. I discuss this "creative instability" in "Content Regulation Reconsidered" in (1991) this volume, essay 8.

influencing the evolution of one's society has been a main motive for restricting expression – for example, for restricting religious proselytizing and
for restricting the sale of publications dealing with sex, even when these
are not sold or used in a way that forces others to see them. This motive
supports not only censorship but also the kind of regulation of private
conduct that raises the issue of "the enforcement of morals." Sexual relations between consenting adults in the privacy of their bedrooms are not
"expression," but it is no mistake to see attempts to regulate such conduct
and attempts to regulate expression as closely related. In both cases, what
the enforcers want is to prevent the spread of certain forms of behavior
and attitude both by deterring it and, at least as important, by using the
criminal law to make an authoritative statement of social disapproval.

One form of liberal response has been to deny the legitimacy of any
interest in "protecting society" from certain forms of change. (The analog
of declaring religion to be purely a private matter.) This response seems
to me to be mistaken.[3] We all have a profound interest in how prevailing
customs and practices evolve. Certainly, I myself have such an interest,
and I do not regard it as illegitimate. I do not care whether other people,
individually, go swimming in the nude or not, but I do not want my society
to become one in which nude bathing becomes so much the norm that
I cannot wear a suit without attracting stares and feeling embarrassed. I
have no desire to dictate what others, individually, in couples or in groups,
do in their bedrooms, but I would much prefer to live in a society in
which sexuality and sexual attractiveness, of whatever kind, was given less
importance than it is in our society today. I do not care what others read
and listen to, but I would like my society to be one in which there are
at least a significant number of people who know and admire the same
literature and music that I do, so that that music will be generally available, and so that there will be others to share my sense of its value.

Considered in this light, religious toleration has much greater risks
for me than I suggested at the beginning of this essay: I am content to
leave others to the religious practices of their choice provided that they
leave me free to enjoy none. But I will be very unhappy if this leads in
time to my society becoming one in which almost everyone is, in one
way or another, deeply religious, and in which religion plays a central
part in all public discourse. Moreover, I would feel this way even if I
would continue to enjoy the firm protection of the First Amendment.

---

[3] Here I draw on points made in section v of my essay, "Freedom of Expression and Categories of
Expression" (1979) in this volume, essay 5.

What I fear is not merely the legal enforcement of religion but its social predominance.

So I see nothing mistaken or illegitimate about at least some of the *concerns* that have moved those who advocate the legal enforcement of morals or who seek to restrict expression in order to prevent what they see as the deterioration of their society. I might disagree with them in substance, but I would not say that concerns of this kind are ones that anyone should or could avoid having. What is objectionable about the "legal enforcement of morals" is the attempt to restrict individuals' personal lives as a way of controlling the evolution of mores. Legal moralism is an example of intolerance, for example, when it uses the criminal law to deny that homosexuals are legitimate participants in the informal politics of society.

I have not tried to say how this informal politics might be regulated. My aims have been, rather, to illustrate what I mean by informal politics, to point out what I take to be its great importance to all of us, and to suggest that for this reason toleration is, for all of us, a risky matter, a practice with high stakes.

III. THE VALUE OF TOLERANCE

Why, then, value tolerance? The answer lies, I believe, in the relation with one's fellow citizens that tolerance makes possible. It is easy to see that a tolerant person and an intolerant one have different attitudes toward those in society with whom they disagree. The tolerant person's attitude is this: "Even though we disagree, they are as fully members of society as I am. They are as entitled as I am to the protections of the law, as entitled as I am to live as they choose to live. In addition (and this is the hard part) neither their way of living nor mine is uniquely *the* way of our society. These are merely two among the potentially many different outlooks that our society can include, each of which is equally entitled to be expressed in living as one mode of life that others can adopt. If one view is at any moment numerically or culturally predominant, this should be determined by, and dependent on, the accumulated choices of individual members of the society at large."

Intolerant individuals deny this. They claim a special place for their own values and way of life. Those who live in a different way – Turks in Germany, for example, Muslims in India, and homosexuals in some parts of the United States – are, in their view, not full members of their society, and the intolerant claim the right to suppress these other ways of living in the name of protecting their society and "its" values. They seek to do this either by the force of criminal law or by denying forms of public support that other groups enjoy, such as public subsidies for the arts.

What I have just provided is description, not argument. But the first way of making the case for tolerance is simply to point out, on the basis of this description, that tolerance involves a more attractive and appealing relation between opposing groups within a society. Any society, no matter how homogeneous, will include people who disagree about how to live and about what they want their society to be like. (And the disagreements within a relatively homogeneous culture can be more intense than those within a society founded on diversity, like the United States.) Given that there must be disagreements, and that those who disagree must somehow live together, is it not better, if possible, to have these disagreements contained within a framework of mutual respect? The alternative, it seems, is to be always in conflict, even at the deepest level, with a large number of one's fellow citizens. The qualification "even at the deepest level" is crucial here. I am assuming that in any society there will over time be conflicts, serious ones, about the nature and direction of the society. What tolerance expresses is a recognition of common membership that is deeper than these conflicts, a recognition of others as just as entitled as we are to contribute to the definition of our society. Without this, we are just rival groups contending over the same territory. The fact that each of us, for good historical and personal reasons, regards it as *our* territory and *our* tradition just makes the conflict all the deeper.

Whether or not one accepts it as sufficient justification for tolerance, the difference that tolerance makes in one's relation to those who are "different" is easy to see. What is less obvious, but at least as important, is the difference tolerance makes in one's relation with those to whom one is closest. One's children provide the clearest case. As my children, they are as fully members of our society as I am. It is their society just as much as it is mine. What one learns as a parent, however, is that there is no guarantee that the society they will want is the same one that I want. Intolerance implies that their right to live as they choose and to influence others to do so is conditional on their agreement with me about what the right way to live is. If I believe that others, insofar as they disagree with me, are not as entitled as I am to shape the mores of our common society, then I must think this of my children as well, should they join this opposition. Perhaps I hold that simply being *my children* gives them special political standing. But this seems to me unlikely. More likely, I think, is that this example brings out the fact that intolerance involves a denial of the full membership of "the others." What is special about one's children is, in this case, just that their membership is impossible to deny. But intolerance forces one to deny it, by making it conditional on substantive agreement with one's own values.

My argument so far is that the case for tolerance lies in the fact that rejecting it involves a form of alienation from one's fellow citizens. It is important to recognize, however, that the strength of this argument depends on the fact that we are talking about membership in "society" as a political unit. This can be brought out by considering how the argument for tolerance would apply within a private association, such as a church or political movement.[4] Disagreements are bound to arise within any such group about how their shared values are to be understood. Is it then intolerant to want to exclude from the group those with divergent views, to deny them the right to participate in meetings and run for office under the party label, to deny them the sacraments, or stop inviting them to meetings? It might be said that this also involves the kind of alienation I have described, by making others' standing as members conditional on agreement with our values. But surely groups of this kind have good reason to exclude those who disagree. Religious groups and political movements would lose their point if they had to include just anyone.

In at least one sense, the ideas of tolerance and intolerance that I have been describing do apply to private associations. As I have said, disagreements are bound to arise within such groups, and when they do it is intolerant to attempt to deny those with whom one disagrees the opportunity to persuade others to adopt their interpretation of the group's values and mission. Tolerance of this kind is required by the very idea of an association founded on a commitment to "shared values." In what sense would these values be "shared" unless there were some process – like the formal and informal politics to which I have referred – through which they evolve and agreement on them is sustained?[5] But there are limits. The very meaning of the goods in question – the sacraments, the party label – requires that they be conditional on certain beliefs. So it is not intolerant for the group as a whole, after due deliberation, to deny these goods to those who clearly lack these beliefs.

Tolerance at the level of political society is a different matter. The goods at stake here, such as the right to vote, to hold office, and to participate in

---

4 Here I am indebted to very helpful questions raised by Will Kymlicka. I do not know whether he would agree with my way of answering them.

5 As Michael Walzer has written, addressing a similar question, "When people disagree about the meaning of social goods, when understandings are controversial, then justice requires that the society be faithful to the disagreements, providing institutional channels for their expression, adjudicative mechanisms, and alternative distributions." *Spheres of Justice* (New York: Basic Books, 1984), p. 313.

the public forum, do not lose their meaning if they are extended to people with whom we disagree about the kind of society we would like to have, or even to those who reject its most basic tenets. One can become a member of society, hence entitled to these goods, just by being born into it (as well as in other ways), and one is required to obey its laws and institutions as long as one remains within its territory. The argument for tolerance that I have been describing is based on this idea of society and on the idea that the relation of "fellow citizen" that it involves is one we have reason to value. The form of alienation I have mentioned occurs when the terms of this relation are violated: when we deny others, who are just as much members of our society as we are, the right to their part in defining and shaping it.[6]

As I have said, something similar can occur when we deny fellow members of a private association their rightful share in shaping it. But the relation of "fellow member" that is violated is different from the relation of "fellow citizen," and it is to be valued for different reasons. In particular, the reasons for valuing such a relation often entail limits on the range of its application. It would be absurd, for example, for Presbyterians to consider everyone born within the fifty United States a member of their church, and it would therefore not be intolerant to deny some of them the right to participate in the evolution of this institution. But the relation of "fellow citizen" is supposed to link at least everyone born into a society and remaining within its borders. So it does not entail, and is in fact incompatible with, any narrower limits.

IV. THE DIFFICULTY OF TOLERANCE

Examples of intolerance are all around us. To cite a few recent examples from the United States, there are the referenda against gay rights in Oregon and Colorado, attempts by Senator Jesse Helms and others to prevent the National Endowment for the Arts and the National Endowment for the Humanities from supporting projects of which they (Helms et al.) disapprove, recent statements by the governor of Mississippi that "America is a Christian nation," and similar statements in the speeches at the 1992 Republican National Convention by representatives of the Christian right.

But it is easy to see intolerance in one's opponents and harder to avoid it oneself. I am thinking here, for example, of my reactions to recurrent

---

[6] Intolerance can also be manifested when we deny others the opportunity to *become* members on racial or cultural grounds. But it would take me too far afield to discuss here the limits on just immigration and naturalization policies.

controversies in the United States over the teaching of evolution and "creation science" in public schools and to the proposal to amend the Constitution if necessary in order to allow organized prayer in public schools. I firmly believe that "creation science" is bogus and that science classes should not present scientific theory and religious doctrine as alternatives with similar and equal claim to the same kind of assent. I therefore do not think that it is intolerant per se to oppose the creationists. But I confess to feeling a certain sense of partisan zeal in such cases, a sense of superiority over the people who propose such things and a desire not to let them win a point even if it did not cost anyone very much. In the case of science teaching, there is a cost, as there is in the case of school prayer. But I am also inclined to support removing "In God We Trust" from our coinage and to favor discontinuing the practice of prayer at public events.

These changes appeal to me because they would make the official symbolism of our country more thoroughly secular, hence more in line with my own outlook, and I can also claim that they represent a more consistent adherence to the constitutional principle of "nonestablishment" of religion. Others see these two reasons as inconsistent. In their view, I am not simply removing a partisan statement from our official symbolism, but at the same time replacing it with another; I am not making our public practice neutral as between secularism and religiosity but asking for an official step that would further enthrone secularism (which is already "officially endorsed" in many other ways, they would say) as our national outlook. I have to admit that, whatever the right answer to the constitutional question might be (and it might be indeterminate), this response has more than a little truth to it when taken as an account of my motives, which are strongly partisan.

But why should they not be partisan? It might seem that here I am going too far, bending over backwards in the characteristically liberal way. After all, the argument that in asking to have this slogan removed from our money I am asking for the official endorsement of *ir*religiosity is at best indirect and not really very persuasive. Whereas the slogan itself does have that aggressively inclusive, hence potentially exclusive "we": "In God *We* Trust." (Who do you mean "we"?)

Does this mean that in a truly tolerant society there could be no public declarations of this kind, no advocacy or enforcement by the state of any particular doctrine? Not even tolerance itself? This seems absurd. Let me consider the matter in stages.

First, is it intolerant to enforce tolerance in behavior and prevent the intolerant from acting on their beliefs? Surely not. The rights of the persecuted demand this protection, and the demand to be tolerated cannot amount to a demand to do whatever one believes one must.

Second, is it intolerant to espouse tolerance as an official doctrine? We could put it on our coins: "In Tolerance We Trust." (Not a bad slogan, I think, although it would have to be pronounced carefully.) Is it intolerant to have tolerance taught in state schools and supported in state-sponsored advertising campaigns? Surely not, and again for the same reasons. The advocacy of tolerance denies no one their rightful place in society. It grants to each person and group as much standing as they can claim while granting the same to others.

Finally, is it contrary to tolerance to deny the intolerant the opportunities that others have to state their views? This would seem to deny them a standing that others have. Yet to demand that we tolerate the intolerant in even this way seems to demand an attitude that is almost unattainable. If a group maintains that I and people like me simply have no place in our society, that we must leave or be eliminated, how can I regard this as a point of view among others that is equally entitled to be heard and considered in our informal (or even formal) politics? To demand this attitude seems to be to demand too much.

If toleration is to make sense, then, we must distinguish between one's attitude toward what is advocated by one's opponents and one's attitude toward those opponents themselves: it is not that their *point of view* is entitled to be represented but that *they* (as fellow citizens, not as holders of that point of view) are entitled to be heard. So I have fought my way to the ringing statement attributed to Voltaire,[7] that is, to a platitude. But in the context of our discussion, I believe that this is not only a platitude but also the location of a difficulty, or several difficulties.

What Voltaire's statement reminds us is that the attitude toward others that tolerance requires must be understood in terms of specific rights and protections. He mentions the right to speak, but this is only one example. The vague recognition of others as equally entitled to contribute to informal politics, as well as to the more formal kind, can be made more definite by listing specific rights to speak, to set an example through one's conduct, to have one's way of life recognized through specific forms of official support. To this we need to add the specification of kinds of support that *no* way of life can demand, such as prohibiting conduct by others simply because one disapproves of it. These specifications give the attitude of tolerance

---

[7] He is said to have said, "I disapprove of what you say, but I will defend to the death your right to say it."

more definite content and make it more tenable. One *can* be asked (or so I believe) to recognize that others have these specific rights no matter how strongly one takes exception to what they say. This move reduces what I earlier called the vagueness of the attitude of tolerance, but leaves us with what I called the indeterminacy of more formal rights. This residual indeterminacy involves two problems.

The first is conceptual. Although some specification of rights and limits of exemplification and advocacy is required in order to give content to the idea of tolerance and make it tenable, the idea of tolerance can never be fully identified with any particular system of such rights and limits, such as the system of rights of free speech and association, rights of privacy, and rights to free exercise (but nonestablishment) of religion that are currently accepted in the United States. Many different systems of rights are acceptable; none is ideal. Each is therefore constantly open to challenge and revision. What I will call the spirit of tolerance is part of what leads us to accept such a system and guides us in revising it. It is difficult to say more exactly what this spirit is, but I would describe it in part as a spirit of accommodation, a desire to find a system of rights that others (all those within the broad reach of the relation "fellow citizen") could also be asked to accept. It is this spirit that I suspected might be lacking in my own attitudes regarding public prayer and the imprint on our coins. I need to ask myself the question of accommodation: is strict avoidance of any reference to religion indeed the only policy I could find acceptable, or is there some other compromise between secularism and the many varieties of religious conviction that I should be willing to consider?

The second, closely related problem is political. There is little incentive to ask this question of accommodation in actual politics, and there are usually much stronger reasons, both good and bad, not to do so. Because the boundaries of tolerance are indeterminate, and accepted ways of drawing them can be portrayed as conferring legitimacy on one's opponents, the charge of intolerance is a powerful political coin.

When anyone makes a claim that I see as a threat to the standing of my group, I am likely to feel a strong desire, perhaps even an obligation, not to let it go unanswered. As I have said, I feel such a desire even in relatively trivial cases. But often, especially in nontrivial cases, one particularly effective form of response (of "counterspeech") is to challenge the limits of the system of informal politics by claiming that one cannot be asked to accept a system that permits what others have done, and therefore demanding that the system be changed, in the name of toleration itself, so that it forbids such actions.

The pattern is a familiar one. For example, in the early 1970s, universities in the United States were disrupted by protesters demanding that speeches by IQ researchers, such as Richard Herrnstein and William Schockley, be canceled. The reason given was that allowing them to speak aided the spread of their ideas and thereby promoted the adoption of educational policies harmful to minority children. Taken at face value, this seemed irrational, because the protests themselves brought the speakers a much wider audience than they otherwise could have hoped for. But the controversy generated by these protests also gained a wider hearing for the opponents. Because "freedom of speech" was being challenged, civil libertarians, some of them otherwise friendly to the protesters' cause, others not so friendly, rushed into the fray. The result, played out on many campuses, was a dramatic and emotional event, provoking media coverage and anguished or indignant editorials in many newspapers. Whether the challenge to the prevailing rules of tolerance made any theoretical sense or not, it made a great deal of sense as a political strategy.

Much the same analysis seems to me to apply to more recent controversies, such as those generated by campus "hate-speech" rules and by the Indianapolis and Minneapolis antipornography statutes. I find it difficult to believe that adopting these regulations would do much to protect the groups in question. But *proposing them*, just because it challenges accepted and valued principles of free expression, has been a very effective way to bring issues of racism and sexism before the minds of the larger community (even if it has also had its costs, by giving its opponents a weapon in the form of complaints about "political correctness").

Challenging the accepted rules of tolerance is also an effective way of mobilizing support within the affected groups. As I have already said, victims of racist or anti-Semitic attacks cannot be expected to regard these as expressing "just another point of view" that deserves to be considered in the court of public opinion. Even in more trivial cases, in which one is in no way threatened, one often fails (as I have said of myself) to distinguish between opposition to a message and the belief that allowing it to be uttered is a form of partisanship on the part of the state. It is therefore natural for the victims of hate speech to take a willingness to ban such speech as a litmus test for the respect that they are due.[8] Even if this is an unreasonable demand, as I believe it often is, the indeterminacy and political sensitivity of standards of tolerance make it politically irresistible.

[8] See, for example, Mari Matsuda, "Public Response to Racist Speech: Considering the Victim's Story," *Michigan Law Review* 87 (1989). Matsuda emphasizes that legal prohibition is sought because it represents public denunciation of the racists' position.

Because of the indeterminacy of such standards – because it is always to some degree an open question just what our system of toleration should be – it will not seem out of the question, even to many supporters of toleration, to demand that one specific form of conduct be prohibited in order to protect a victimized group. This can be so even when the proposed modification is in fact unfeasible because a workable system of toleration cannot offer this form of support to every group. On the other hand, because of this same indeterminacy, a system of toleration will not work unless it is highly valued and carefully protected against erosion. This means that any proposed modification will be politically sensitive and will elicit strong opposition, hence valuable publicity for the group in question.

Moreover, once this protection has been demanded by those speaking for the group – once it has been made a litmus test of respect – it is very difficult for individual members of the group not to support that demand.[9] The result is a form of political gridlock in which the idea of tolerance is a powerful motivating force on both sides: on one side, in the form of a desire to protect potentially excluded groups; on the other, in the form of a desire to protect a workable system of tolerance. I do not have a solution to such problems. Indeed, part of my point is that the nature of tolerance makes them unavoidable. The strategy suggested by what I have said is to try, as far as possible, to prevent measures inimical to the system of tolerance from becoming "litmus tests" of respect. Civil libertarians like me, who rush to the defense of that system, should not merely shout "You can't do that!" but should also ask the question of accommodation: "Are there other ways, not damaging to the system of tolerance, in which respect for the threatened group could be demonstrated?"[10]

V. CONCLUSION

I began by considering the paradigm case of religious toleration, a doctrine that seemed at first to have little cost or risk when viewed from the perspective of a secular liberal with secure constitutional protection against the

---

[9] I am thinking here particularly of the Salman Rushdie case. The Ayatollah Khomeini's demand that *The Satanic Verses* be banned was unreasonable. On the other hand, many Muslims living in Britain felt they were treated with a lack of respect by their fellow citizens. Even if they could see that the Ayatollah's demand was unreasonable, it was difficult for them not to support it once it had been issued. Here the situation was further complicated (and the appeal to "unfeasibility" clouded) by the existence of a British blasphemy law that protected Christianity but not Islam. The result was gridlock of the kind described in the text.

[10] I do not mean to suggest that this is always called for. It depends on the case, and the group. But the difficult cases will be those in which tolerance speaks in favor of protecting the group as well as against the measure they have demanded.

"establishment" of a religion. I went on to explain why toleration in general, and religious toleration in particular, is a risky policy with high stakes, even within the framework of a stable constitutional democracy. The risks involved lie not so much in the formal politics of laws and constitutions (though there may be risks there as well) but rather in the informal politics through which the nature of a society is constantly redefined. I believe in tolerance despite its risks, because it seems to me that any alternative would put me in an antagonistic and alienated relation to my fellow citizens, friends as well as foes. The attitude of tolerance is nonetheless difficult to sustain. It can be given content only through some specification of the rights of citizens as participants in formal and informal politics. But any such system of rights will be conventional and indeterminate and is bound to be under frequent attack. To sustain and interpret such a system, we need a larger attitude of tolerance and accommodation, an attitude that is itself difficult to maintain.

11

The diversity of objections to inequality

I believe that equality is an important political goal. That is to say, virtually every society is marked by forms of inequality the elimination of which is a political objective of the first importance. But when I ask myself why I think it so important that these inequalities should be eliminated, I find that my reasons for favoring equality are in fact quite diverse, and that most of them can be traced back to fundamental values other than equality itself. The idea that equality is, in itself, a fundamental moral value turns out to play a surprisingly limited role in my reasons for thinking that many of the forms of inequality which we see around us should be eliminated.

When I say that the idea of equality plays surprisingly little role in my thinking here, I have in mind an idea of substantive equality – that it is morally important that people's lives or fates should be equal in some substantive way: equal in income, for example, or in overall welfare. This is in contrast to a merely formal notion of equal consideration, as stated for example in the principle that the comparable claims of each person deserve equal respect and should be given equal weight. This is an important principle. Its general acceptance represents an important moral advance, and it provides a fruitful – even essential – starting point for moral argument. But taken by itself it is too abstract to exercise much force in the direction of substantive equality. As Thomas Nagel and Amartya Sen have both pointed out,[1] even a rights theorist such as Robert Nozick, who would not normally be counted an egalitarian, could accept this principle, since he holds that everyone's rights deserve equal respect. My hypothesis is that the bare idea of equal consideration leads us to substantively egalitarian consequences only via other more specific values that I will enumerate, most of which are not essentially egalitarian.

[1] See Nagel, "Equality," in *Mortal Questions* (Cambridge: Cambridge University Press, 1979), and Sen, *Inequality Reexamined* (Cambridge, MA: Harvard University Press, 1992), p. 13.

In saying that I do not mean to attack equality or to "unmask" it as a false ideal. My aims, rather, are clarification and defense: clarification, because I believe that we can understand familiar arguments for equality better by seeing the diversity of the considerations on which they are based; defense, because I think that the case for pursuing particular forms of equality is strengthened when we see how many different considerations point in this direction. Opponents of equality seem most convincing when they can portray equality as a peculiarly abstract goal – conformity to a certain pattern – to which special moral value is attached.[2]

I will begin by distinguishing what seem to me to be the fundamental moral reasons lying behind our objections to various forms of inequality. I will then illustrate these ideas by showing how they figure in various ways in Rawls's views about distributive justice. Finally, I will return to examine one of these values – the one which seems the most purely egalitarian – in more detail. Let me turn, then, to an enumeration of our reasons for finding the pursuit of equality a compelling political goal.

I

In some cases our reason for favoring the elimination of inequalities is at base a humanitarian concern – a concern, for example, to alleviate suffering. If some people are living under terrible conditions, while others are very well off indeed, then a transfer of resources from the better to the worse off, if it can be accomplished without other bad effects, is desirable as a way of alleviating suffering without creating new hardships of comparable severity.

The impulse at work here is not essentially egalitarian. No intrinsic importance is attached to narrowing or eliminating the gap between rich and poor; this gap is important only because it provides an opportunity – a way of reducing the suffering of some without causing others to suffer a similar fate – and the strength of this reason for moving toward greater equality is a function of the urgency of the claims of those who are worse off, not of the magnitude of the gap which separates them from their more fortunate neighbors.[3]

---

[2] See, for example, Robert Nozick's objections in chapters 7 and 8 of *Anarchy, State and Utopia* (New York: Basic Books, 1974). I was led to the basic ideas of the lecture on which this essay is based in the course of working on a review of Nozick's book. Some of these ideas were briefly stated in that review, "Nozick on Rights, Liberty and Property," *Philosophy and Public Affairs* 6 (1976).

[3] A point made by Derek Parfit in his 1991 Lindley Lecture, "Equality or Priority?". Harry Frankfurt has gone further, suggesting that we replace concern for equality with concern for "sufficiency." He

In characterizing this first reason, I have spoken of "the alleviation of suffering" in order to present this reason in its strongest form, but its force may still be felt in cases where, although the term "suffering" would be inappropriate, those who are "worse off" are still living under conditions which we regard as seriously deficient. This force fades away, however, as we imagine the situation of both rich and "poor" to be greatly improved, while the difference between them is held constant (or even increased). We may still feel, even in this improved state, that the difference between richer and poorer ought to be reduced or eliminated. Our reason for thinking this will not, however, be the humanitarian concern I am presently concerned with, but some different reason, perhaps a more truly egalitarian one.

One possible reason for objecting to these differences would be the belief that it is an evil for people to be treated as inferior, or made to feel inferior. Social practices conferring privileges of rank or requiring expressions of deference are objectionable on this ground, for example. So also is the existence of prevailing attitudes of superiority (e.g. racial superiority) even when these are not expressed in or taken to justify economic advantage or special social privileges. Large differences in material well-being can be objectionable on the same ground: when the mode of life enjoyed by some people sets the norm for a society, those who are much worse off will feel inferiority and shame at the way they must live.

The egalitarian character of this objection is shown by the fact that it provides a reason specifically for the elimination of the difference in question rather than for the improvement of the lot of the worse off in some more general sense. This is obviously so where the differences are purely ones of status. But even where the basis of inferiority is a difference in material well-being, the aim of avoiding stigmatization can in principle provide a reason for eliminating the benefits of the better off (or for wishing that they had never been created) even if these cannot be transferred to the worse off. If simply eliminating these benefits seems wrong (perhaps even perverse), this judgment reflects a willingness to sacrifice the aim of equality (in the sense under consideration) for the sake of material benefit. This aim – the ideal of a society in which people all regard one another as equals – has played an important role in radical egalitarian thinking – a more important

writes, "What is important from the moral point of view is not that everyone should have *the same* but that each should have *enough*. If everyone had enough, it would be of no moral consequence whether some had more than others." See Frankfurt, "Equality as a Moral Ideal," in *The Importance of What We Care About* (Cambridge: Cambridge University Press, 1988), pp. 134–5. In the present essay I will be investigating whether, contrary to what Frankfurt says in this last sentence, there are further reasons for caring about equality beyond the one I have so far identified.

role than the idea of distributive justice which dominates much discussion of equality in our own time. This ideal may seem utopian, and there are interesting difficulties about how it should be understood. I will return to these matters below, after some other reasons for favoring equality have been considered.

A third reason for the elimination of inequalities is that they give some people an unacceptable degree of control over the lives of others. The most obvious example is economic power. Those who have vastly greater resources than anyone else not only enjoy greater leisure and higher levels of consumption but also can often determine what gets produced, what kinds of employment are offered, what the environment of a town or state is like, and what kind of life one can live there. In addition, economic advantage can be translated into greater political power – for example into the kind of power that the recent Campaign Financing Laws were intended to curb.

This example brings me to a fourth reason for pursuing equality, which overlaps with the one just mentioned but should be listed separately. Some forms of equality are essential preconditions for the fairness of certain processes, and the aim of making or keeping those processes fair may therefore give us a reason to oppose inequalities of these kinds, at least when they are very large. So, for example, in the case just mentioned, instead of speaking of unacceptable degrees of political power (thus appealing to the value of political liberty) we might have spoken instead of preserving the fairness of the political process. These two forms of argument overlap in this particular case, but they are in fact distinct. When inequality of starting points undermines the fairness of a process, domination of those who are placed at a disadvantage does not always result, since the process may confer no power but only honor or the opportunity for a more pleasant and rewarding life. Unfairness, however, remains, and can take several forms: some people can simply be excluded from competition, or background conditions such as inequalities in training and resources can render the competition unfair. So the idea of equality of opportunity – as expressed in the familiar metaphors of a "fair race" or "a level playing field" – provides a familiar example of this fourth reason for objecting to inequality: inequalities are objectionable when they undermine the fairness of important institutions.

As the common contrast between "equality of opportunity" and "equality of results" indicates, this idea is only weakly egalitarian, since it can be compatible with large inequalities provided that they result from a fair process and do not disrupt the fairness of on-going competition. But, as I will now argue, the idea of a fair procedure can also provide another kind of reason for insisting on equality of outcomes. (This is my fifth reason for objecting to inequalities.)

Suppose that the members of a group have equal claims to a certain form of benefit, such as the wealth produced by their combined efforts. If a distributive procedure is supposed to be responsive to these claims, then it will be unfair if (absent some special reason) it gives some of these people a higher level of benefit than others. This provides, in schematic form, an argument which leads us to a prima facie case for equality in a certain dimension of benefit. Its starting points include an idea of fairness together with substantive premises about the claims that the people in question have to this benefit and about the function of a particular procedure. To generate a particular egalitarian conclusion we need to fill in the relevant premises, and the force of this conclusion will depend on how plausible these premises are. We might, for example, begin with the idea that, other things equal, all individuals have equal claims to welfare. This sounds like quite a strong claim, but it might be a fairly weak one: much depends on how many things there are that might not be equal. A natural first step in specifying this would be to make explicit the fact that one class of relevant differences are differences in the choices people have made. This yields the principle that people ought to be equal in the levels of welfare they enjoy apart from differences in welfare resulting from their own free choices. I have not included an "other things equal" clause in the statement of this principle, but I assume that it is still only one moral idea among others, which might have to be sacrificed or balanced for the sake of other values.

These values enter in when we begin to specify the other premise mentioned above, that is, to ask what range of actions might be thought of as part of a "procedure" which is supposed to be responsive to these equal claims. It would not be very plausible, for example, to claim that all of our actions have this function (or must be thought of as part of a "procedure" with this aim). It does not seem that in general we are under even a "prima facie" duty to promote the equal welfare of all. A more plausible claim would be that the state, or in Rawls's phrase "the basic institutions of society," should be understood in this way, that is, as an institution whose function it is to respond to the (equal) claims to welfare of all of its subjects (equal, that is, apart from differences arising from individual choice). This is what might be called the "parental" conception of the state. I choose that term because it seems to me that the claim of unfairness to which this conception gives rise is similar to the one raised by a child who protests the fact that a sibling has received some benefit by saying "That's not fair!" The similarity rests in the fact that both claims are grounded in an idea that the agent to whom it is addressed is under an equal duty to promote the welfare of each of the parties in question.

As this description no doubt suggests, I do not myself find this conception of the state altogether compelling. A more plausible conception, and hence a more plausible case for equality, can be obtained if we view the citizens not merely as beneficiaries but rather as participants. It might be said, for example, that the basic institutions of a society should be seen as a cooperative enterprise producing certain benefits, and that citizens, as free and equal participants in this process, have (at least prima facie) equal claim to the benefits they collectively produce. (It is worth emphasizing that this premise does not lead to the conclusion that people should be equal in all respects, but only in their shares of these socially produced benefits. It therefore provides a plausible basis for some form of "equality of resources.")

This claim to equal outcomes is not indisputable. It might be maintained, for example, that insofar as social institutions are seen as cooperative undertakings for mutual benefit the claims of participants to their products are not equal but proportional to their contributions. My task here is not, however, to offer a full defense of the argument I have sketched, but rather to identify it as one among several sources of egalitarianism.

To summarize, I have identified five reasons for pursuing greater equality. The elimination of inequalities may be required in order to
(1) Relieve suffering or severe deprivation
(2) Prevent stigmatizing differences in status
(3) Avoid unacceptable forms of power or domination
(4) Preserve the equality of starting places which is required by procedural fairness.
In addition,
(5) Procedural fairness sometimes supports a case for equality of outcomes.

At least two of these reasons, (1) and (3), are based on powerful moral ideas that are not fundamentally egalitarian. The ideas behind (2), on the other hand, are clearly egalitarian, but while they are certainly important they do not seem to have as much moral force as the humanitarian ideals expressed in (1). Reason (4) is only weakly egalitarian, since the idea of procedural fairness which supports it is compatible with great inequalities of some kinds as long as these do not undermine the fairness of the continuing process. This leaves (5) and (2) as the clearest expressions of egalitarianism. Reasons of type (5) are at least as powerful as those to which (2) appeals, but these reasons come in a variety of forms, which vary in strength. The idea which they have in common is not that all men and women are created equal but rather that *if* all the members of a certain group have prima facie equal claim to benefit in a certain way then a fair procedure for distributing such benefits must (in the absence of special justification) result in equal benefits. I imagine that everyone would agree to the truth of this conditional statement, but its uncontroversial character is purchased by packing a great deal into its antecedent. The egalitarian thrust of (5) arises from the claim that this antecedent is true in an important range of cases – e.g. that participants in many cooperative ventures do have prima facie equal claims to the benefits produced, and, specifically, that this is so in the case of the basic institutions of a society.

Are there further reasons for favoring equality which I have omitted? The main possibility is a straightforward moral ideal of substantive equality, that is to say, the idea that a society in which people are equally well-off (as determined by some appropriate measure) is for that reason a morally better society. This is certainly an intelligible and even an appealing idea. But how much of a role does it actually play in our moral thinking? Reasons (1) through (5) discussed above are not, I think, derived from this idea. They are much more specific and have independent moral force. Once the distinctness of these reasons is recognized, how much force does the substantive ideal just mentioned retain? My own sense is that it may have the status of one appealing social ideal among others, but that it lacks the particular moral urgency which the idea of equality seems to have in ordinary political argument, a force which derives, I believe, from the other reasons I have listed.

II

To illustrate these five reasons for pursuing equality, I want now to consider how they figure in Rawls's theory of justice and account for much of the egalitarian content of his view. It may seem at first that Rawls's Difference Principle, which calls for us to maximize the expectations of the worst off, draws on the first of the reasons I mentioned: a humanitarian concern with the fate of the worst off. The argument for the use of the maximin rule, for example, seems to appeal to a first-person version of this concern insofar as it relies on the idea that there are certain outcomes "that one could hardly accept" and that it is rational, under the circumstances of the Original Position, to be primarily concerned with avoiding these outcomes, in comparison with which other gains are relatively insignificant.[4] Like

---

[4] *A Theory of Justice* (Cambridge, MA: Harvard University Press, 1971), p. 154.

the humanitarian case for equality mentioned above, this reason for the Difference Principle would diminish in force if the possible positions of the worst off were to become more and more bearable, holding constant the distance between these positions and those of the better off.

But the case for the Difference Principle is not primarily "humanitarian." That is to say, it is not primarily based in sympathy for the worst off. Rawls's central idea lies, rather, in his emphasis on seeing the basic structure of society as a fair system of cooperation, and on taking the question of justice to be that of how the benefits of such cooperation are to be shared. The case for the Difference Principle then rests on an appeal to reasons (4) and (5) above: the need for equality of starting points as a precondition of procedural fairness, and the appeal of equal outputs as a fair mode of distribution. Consider the latter first. This argument for the Difference Principle can be put in two steps. The first step is the prima facie case for equal shares as a fair way to distribute the fruits of cooperation among those who have participated in producing them. The second step is the idea that departures from equality which leave everyone better off cannot reasonably be objected to, as long as (a) the positions to which greater rewards are attached are "open to all under conditions of fair equality of opportunity" and (b) these inequalities do not give rise to unacceptable stigmatization of some members of the society as inferior.

Rider (a) incorporates the fourth idea mentioned above, that (at least a degree of) equality of starting places has to be preserved as a precondition for procedural fairness. At least it does so if, as is clearly Rawls's intent, "fair equality of opportunity" is understood to include more than the mere absence of legal restrictions and discriminatory practices.[5] The fact that this idea – of the importance of preserving at least approximate equality of starting positions – occurs only in a rider, as a constraint on permissible inequalities and a way of warding off possible objections, should not be allowed to obscure the central role it plays in the positive case *for* the Difference Principle. This centrality is shown in the fact that this idea is the basis of one of the main objections which Rawls levels against alternatives to his conception of distributive justice.[6] For example, his objection to the

---

[5] That this is Rawls's intent is made clear in *A Theory of Justice*, esp. pp. 83–9. It is natural to think of "equality of opportunity" solely in terms of the competition for economic advantage and positions of special status. In order for the considerations mentioned under (4) above to be fulfilled, however, it is essential to preserve the fairness of competition in the political realm. Rawls clearly believes and considers it important that this condition (what he calls "the fair value of political liberty") will be met when his Two Principles are satisfied (see *A Theory of Justice*, pp. 224–7), but he does not make this an explicit condition on the inequalities permitted by the Difference Principle.

[6] See *A Theory of Justice*, pp. 72–3.

laissez faire conception of justice that he calls "the system of natural liberty" is that the operation of this system over time can lead to great differences in family wealth with the result that individuals born into different positions in the society will have vastly different opportunities for education and for entry into economic life, as well as different dispositions to make use of the opportunities they do have. An important part of the case for Rawls's Two Principles is the fact that institutions which satisfy them will not be subject to this objection, and that, more generally, these principles guarantee the kind of background necessary for a system of pure procedural justice.

Alongside of this argument, and complementary to it, is the idea that the system of natural liberty should be rejected because it allows people's life prospects to be determined by factors, such as fortunate family circumstances, which are "arbitrary from a moral point of view." This might be understood as a restatement of the objection that I have just summarized: the system is unacceptable because it allows life prospects to be determined by competition under "arbitrary" conditions, rather than under conditions of "background fairness." But it can also be seen as an appeal to type (5) unfairness: a system of natural liberty is unfair because outcomes which are sensitive to the "accidents of birth" are not responsive to the equal claims of "free and equal cooperating members of society."

Because the distributive shares assigned to members of one generation are a large part of what determines the starting places of the next, considerations of these two kinds (equality of starting places and equality of distributive shares) tend to converge. Insofar as the focus is on fair sharing of what individuals *have produced* as free and equal members of a cooperative scheme, (5) seems to be particularly central; when the focus is on fairness to individuals born into certain social positions, their productive lives still lying ahead, (4) comes into play. Rawls certainly appeals at various points to reasons of both types. They are complementary but may differ in dialectical strength.

As I mentioned above, the force of the idea that fairness demands equal distributive shares depends on a prior claim that as participants in a cooperative scheme the individuals in question have equal claim to the fruits of their cooperation. This is an appealing moral idea, but a controversial one to take as *the starting point* for an argument in support of a particular conception of justice. By contrast, appeals to (4) rest, in the first instance, on the more broadly shared idea that the legitimacy of holdings is undermined when the process through which they are gained is unfair. The controversy in this case is over conditions of fairness: what kind of initial conditions must be provided in order for a process to be one whose outcomes cannot be complained of? There is certainly wide disagreement on this question,[7] but there may also be more scope for internal argument (about how best to extrapolate from shared examples, etc.).[8]

Let me return now to the idea of "stigmatization." I incorporated this idea as a rider on my restatement of Rawls's Difference Principle: economic inequalities are unjust if they give rise to unacceptable stigmatization of some as inferior. Rawls did not, of course, deal with this problem through a separate rider. Instead, his measure of what it is for the lot of the worst off to be improved includes, as one component, "the social bases of self-respect." His formulation thus allows, at least formally, for the possibility that loss in this dimension of well-being might be compensated for by other advantages. I do not believe that this difference in formulation will make much difference in practice, but I leave that question open.[9] What is important for present purposes is that Rawls took it to be an important feature of his conception of justice that it provided a more secure protection for individual self-respect than did alternative conceptions such as utilitarianism or the "system of natural liberty." He stresses that this protection is provided not only by the Difference Principle but also by his First Principle, which requires that the equal status of all citizens should be secured by their having equal civil and political rights and liberties.

The equality demanded by this principle is, on its face, rather formal: it demands that all citizens have the most extensive system of equal basic liberties. This is formal insofar as it deals only with what the laws and constitution specify. But Rawls also asserts, as an important advantage of his Difference Principle, that by assuring nearly equal economic shares it guarantees what he calls the "fair value" of these rights and liberties. The idea, then, is that the Difference Principle will be sufficiently egalitarian

---

[7] I defend the claim that this is the best way to understand the disagreement between Rawls and Nozick in Lecture 2 of "The Significance of Choice," in S. McMurrin, ed., *The Tanner Lectures on Human Values*, vol. 8 (Salt Lake City: University of Utah Press, 1988).

[8] The more controversial character of appeals to (5) may seem to reflect the fact, mentioned above, that (5) represents a stronger egalitarian idea, since (4) appears at first to be compatible with wide inequality of output. This apparent difference may turn out to be illusory, however, once it is noticed how the benefits assigned to members of one generation affect the starting places of the next. Rawls's version of (4) is not the familiar, weak idea of equal opportunity, and the degree of equality required to secure fairness of starting places seems likely to be very great indeed. But the degree to which this observation makes the egalitarian consequences of (4) more stringent is precisely the area of disagreement over the interpretation of "fair grounds of competition" which was mentioned above.

[9] Russ Shafer-Landau pointed out in the discussion following this lecture that Rawls's inclusion of the "social bases of self-respect" in the list of primary social goods (i.e. the measure of distributive shares) represents an integration of my (2) into (5). The result is a focus not on "stigmatization" in general but on equality in the distribution of those social indicators of status that it is the business of basic institutions to define and distribute.

to ensure the fairness of the political process (an instance of (4)) and thus to prevent some from exercising an unacceptable degree of power over others (3).

To conclude this brief discussion of Rawls: his argument for his Two Principles of justice, in particular for the second of these principles, appeals directly or indirectly to at least four of the grounds for equality mentioned above, namely numbers (2) through (5), and perhaps to (1) as well. But (4), or a combination of (4) and (5), appears to play the most central role. This emphasis on the claims of citizens qua participants in a fair procedure helps to explain the fact that the Difference Principle is concerned with individuals' shares of "primary social goods" (i.e. the fruits of their cooperation) rather than with their levels of overall welfare.

III

The second reason that I presented, in section I, for objecting to inequality was based on the idea that "it is an evil for people to be treated as inferior, or made to feel inferior." I want now to consider, at least in a preliminary way, some of the difficulties involved in determining more exactly how this objection is to be understood. My initial statement of this objection was cautiously ambivalent. It consisted of two parts, the first of which suggests that what is objectionable is a certain form of treatment (being *treated* as inferior, or not being "treated as an equal") and the second suggests that the evil is an experiential one (being made to *feel* inferior). More needs to be said both about how this "experiential" component is to be understood and about how it is supposed to be related to the underlying forms of treatment in order to give rise to the objection in question.

The experiential evil involved here can be characterized in several different ways – indeed, there are several different kinds of experience that one might have in mind. Let me distinguish two broad categories. The first, more "individualistic," characterization emphasizes what might be called damage to individuals' sense of self-worth: such things as feelings of inferiority and even shame resulting from the belief that one's life, abilities or accomplishments lack worth or are greatly inferior to those of others.[10] The second category emphasizes damage to the bonds between people: what might be called the loss of fraternity resulting from great differences in people's material circumstances, accomplishments and the social importance accorded to them. Unlike the first, this is a loss suffered by the

---

[10] See Rawls, *A Theory of Justice*, p. 440.

better off and worse off alike, and perhaps it is the more fully egalitarian of the two. Much more could be said by way of characterization of these two classes of experiential evils, but I will not pursue these questions here. My concern will instead be with the independence of these evils from other objections to inequality and with the particular difficulty of avoiding them. I will concentrate on evils of the first of the two kinds just distinguished, but I believe that the same points apply as well to evils of the second sort.

It is of course quite possible that someone might suffer from these forms of undesirable consciousness (such as a sense of inferiority and worthlessness) simply from psychological causes that have nothing to do with the actual facts of one's society. This would be a misfortune, but not the basis of an objection to social institutions. Such objections arise only when institutions *cause* people to have these undesirable feelings. Let me consider three ways that institutions might do this.

First, they might do it by depriving some people (but not others) of basic rights: denying them the right to move freely in public, the right to participate in politics, or the right to compete for other valued positions in the society. People treated in these ways would certainly not be treated "as equals." But the main objection in such a case would be to these forms of treatment themselves, not to their experiential consequences. So I will set this case aside.

Second, institutions which were not *otherwise* unjust might nonetheless treat some people in ways that could only be understood as intended to express the view that they were inferior. This might be done by, say, attaching special "dishonorific" titles to their names, or by requiring them to defer to members of other groups whenever they met in public. These signs of status are clearly objectionable, and our reasons for objecting to them depend on the fact that those subject to these forms of treatment could reasonably feel shamed and humiliated by them.

But the same objection would apply to institutional arrangements that, while they did not have the aim of *expressing* inferiority, nonetheless had the effect of giving rise to feelings of inferiority on the part of most reasonable citizens. This is my third case. The obvious examples are economic institutions which yield such great disparities of wealth and income that some people experience shame and humiliation because they must live in a way that is far below what most people in the society regard as minimally acceptable. There are also noneconomic examples, such as a society in which almost everyone places great value and importance on certain forms of accomplishment, forms that many, but not all, can attain, and in which it is regarded as a great misfortune not to be "successful" in these ways. These views imply that those whose accomplishments do not measure up are inferior in important ways. In this respect this case is like my second one; but it is not the *point* of these practices (as it was of those in the previous case) to mark some out as inferior. That is merely the side effect of the recognition of what is seen as valuable accomplishment and good fortune. While these two cases may be different, I will not make much of this difference here, but will suppose that both the second and the third cases I have just distinguished give rise to the objection to inequality that I earlier called "stigmatizing differences in status." My focus in the remainder of this essay will be on the question of whether and how these objections can be met or avoided.

Consider first a familiar example of objectionable inequality, the phenomena of racial and sexual discrimination in our societies. Women and African Americans have for many years been denied opportunities for forms of achievement which are most recognized and valued in society, including political leadership, positions of economic power and high status, positions recognizing accomplishment in academic, intellectual, and even many parts of artistic life. As in the first of the three cases I just considered, this denial is itself a form of unfairness: the process through which these positions and the rewards connected with them were awarded was unfair because women and blacks were not given the chance to compete. But this unfairness is not the only evil involved, and not the one I want to focus on. It is unfair, and wounding, to be denied important opportunities because of your race or gender. But one thing that makes this particularly wounding is the fact that race and gender are commonly taken to be signs of the lack of substantive qualification: stigmatization is added to unfairness when there is the (perhaps unstated) supposition that because you are not a white male you are less able to contribute to society and its culture in those ways that are regarded as particularly valuable and important.

Suppose now that all the underlying unfairness in this case were removed, and that everyone had a chance to compete on "equal terms." Assuming that the number of desired positions remained the same, and the number of competitors for them did not decrease, some people (a racially and sexually diverse group, let us suppose) would still be denied these rewards, and while they would not be excluded "from the start" by being ruled out of the competition they would, in an important sense, be denied rewards on the same grounds that women and blacks were: they would be judged to lack the relevant abilities and attainments. I will suppose that this meritocratic discrimination is not unfair: (1) it is not based on unfounded assumptions about differences in ability but on actual, demonstrated differences, and

(2) it is not unnecessary but serves important social goals. Nonetheless, as Thomas Nagel has pointed out,[11] the resulting differences in status and treatment are still to be regretted as objectionable inequalities. The evil involved is the one we have been considering: though not unfair, this meritocracy can be expected to deprive some people of a secure sense of self-worth – of the sense of their own value and the belief that their lives and accomplishments are worthwhile.

This evil, being deprived of important grounds for a sense of self- worth, is, as I have said, one of the important evils underlying the forms of discrimination with which we are familiar. In the case we are imagining these forms of discrimination have been removed, but the relevant experiential evil may remain and may even be aggravated in two respects. First, the inferiority would not be a matter of superstition, but will be documented by fair social practices. Second, if this fair meritocracy has been reached through a process of overcoming discrimination this history is likely to have the effect of dramatizing the value of the rewards and accomplishments in question and belittling the value of a life lived without them. In order to rouse the oppressed to battle and kindle sympathy and guilt in others, one would naturally emphasize not only the unfairness of discrimination but also the importance of the opportunities and forms of accomplishment and recognition in question, and the great value of a life with these things as compared to one without them. This has the effect of condemning the lives which victims of discrimination have had to lead, and hence also the lives which others will continue to lead once this discrimination is overcome. Overcoming it may represent a gain in fairness, but there may be no decrease, and perhaps even an increase, in objectionable consequences of inequality of the particular kind I am presently discussing.

I am not urging the fatalist thesis that people should "stay in their places" since inequality cannot be eliminated but only shifted around. I am all in favor of the elimination of discrimination and the reduction of inequality. My aim here is to understand the diversity of the evils which it involves. An egalitarianism which decries the evil I am characterizing may seem hopelessly utopian, because it may seem that the distinctions which give rise to it can never be avoided. Trying to eliminate them may seem to involve unacceptable costs not only in economic efficiency and the quality of the products of a culture but also in individual fulfillment. One thing

---

[11] In "Equal Treatment and Compensatory Discrimination," *Philosophy and Public Affairs* 2 (1973), reprinted as "The Policy of Preference," in *Mortal Questions*. My thought experiment also has obvious similarities to Michael Young's famous fable, *The Rise of the Meritocracy* (Harmondsworth: Penguin Books, 1963).

individuals naturally and reasonably want is to develop their talents and to exercise these realized abilities. Given an uneven distribution of talents, one result of this is that some will inevitably be distinguished from others in ways that generate the problem I have been discussing. Rousseau[12] can be read as suggesting that this is an inevitable and even tragic conflict. Even if one does not hold out much hope for eliminating this conflict, however, it is possible to conceive of some ways of at least reducing it.

The degree to which the accomplishment and rewards of some people undermine the grounds of other people's sense of self-worth depends upon the degree to which particular forms of ability and accomplishment are regarded as having preeminent importance. Even a highly differentiated meritocratic system of offices and rewards might not undermine the self-respect of those who are not successful in it if the attainments which it recognizes and rewards are regarded as less important indices of self-worth than good moral character, conscientiousness as a citizen, and devotion to the well-being of one's family and friends. A society which accorded these qualities their proper value might be able to enjoy the benefits of rewarding accomplishment without suffering the consequences which I am here decrying.[13]

A second strategy is diversification. If there are many different forms of accomplishment and distinction no one, or no few, of which dominate as *the* socially important measures of success in life, then the threat to people's sense of self-worth will be mitigated. This solution has been proposed, in different forms, by both Rawls and Michael Walzer. Walzer has suggested[14] that if there are many forms of inequality, each confined to its own "sphere," they will to some extent cancel each other out, and their effects will be acceptable – even appropriate and desirable. Rawls, on the other hand, has spoken of the partition of society into what he calls "noncomparing groups":

the plurality of associations in a well-ordered society, each with its own secure internal life, tends to reduce the visibility, or at least the painful visibility, of variations in men's prospects. For we tend to compare our circumstances with others in the same or in a similar group as ourselves, or in positions that we regard

---

[12] In his *First and Second Discourses*. But it seems likely that his concern was more with what might be called a loss of fraternity than with what I have here termed a blow to individual self-respect.

[13] It might be countered (as Richard De George pointed out in the discussion following this lecture) that since people are bound to be unequal in these "moral attainments," a society which gave them preeminent place would be just another form of meritocracy, admirable in some respects, perhaps, but just as damaging (maybe even more damaging) to the self-respect of those whom it condemns. The reply, I suppose, is that these feelings of loss of self-respect, if deserved, would not be objectionable.

[14] In his book, *Spheres of Justice* (New York: Basic Books, 1983).

as relevant to our aspirations. The various associations in society tend to divide it into so many noncomparing groups, the discrepancies between these divisions not attracting the kind of attention which unsettles the lives of those less well placed.[15]

Each of these proposals may seem unsatisfactory when understood as a general response to inequality; but there is much to be said for them when they are seen, in a more limited way, as a response merely to the aspect of inequality which I am presently discussing. Walzer, for example, advocates "complex equality" as a general solution to the problem of inequality. He argues that inequalities in wealth, power, fame, and other goods are acceptable as long as each good is distributed on the grounds appropriate to it, and no one good is allowed to "dominate" the others as, for example, when wealth is used to buy power, fame, medical care, and so on. In addition, he couples this view with a denial that there are general standards of justice which every society must satisfy. Both of these doctrines – his doctrine of "spheres" and his relativistic thesis – have been widely criticized. But the idea of complex equality is more appealing if we view it merely as a way of mitigating the conflict between the protection of self-worth and the necessity of recognizing differences in ability and accomplishment. There is some plausibility to the claim that this problem is best approached not by trying to minimize differences but rather by fostering a healthy multiplicity of distinctions and by trying to ensure that no one (or no few) of these "dominates" the others by becoming established as *the* form of distinction that really matters.

Similarly, Rawls's idea of noncomparing groups has been criticized because it has been seen as a way of making unacceptable inequalities seem acceptable by hiding them. But Rawls is supposing that the inequalities in question already satisfy principles of justice: they are justified in the way that the Difference Principle requires, and conditions of fair equality of opportunity are assumed to obtain. The point could be put by saying that people are owed more than fairness in the distribution of concrete goods: they are also owed a concern for the maintenance of their sense of self-worth (in his terms, self-respect) and this is, as I argued above, importantly a matter of the character of their experience. Whether they reasonably feel a loss of self-worth is a function not only of the inequalities which they know exist but of the way in which those inequalities figure in their lives. As far as this concern goes, then, the device of noncomparing groups may be a perfectly appropriate one.

---

[15] *A Theory of Justice*, pp. 536–7.

I suggested earlier that the particular egalitarian concern which I have been discussing in this section – the problem of stigmatizing differences in status – is a source of strong motives for opposing inequality and a source which is more purely egalitarian than most of the others I have enumerated. About its motivational strength there seems to me to be no doubt. The instinct to preserve the grounds of one's self-esteem and to oppose what threatens it is a powerful force in the world today, supporting not only struggles for greater equality but also, I would argue, forms of nationalism and nativism, religious fundamentalism, and racial and religious bigotry. It is commonly said, for example, that many white males see doctrines of racial and gender equality as a threat to their sense of standing and self-worth.

What has to be claimed is that these reactions, however real they may be, are not reasonable and therefore do not support objections of the kind I have been discussing. In other cases, reasonable feelings of loss of self-esteem may be deserved, hence again not objectionable.[16] What should be claimed, then, is that a regime of equality would be one that protected its members adequately against *reasonable* and undeserved feelings of loss of self-esteem.

To conclude: relief of suffering, avoidance of stigmatizing differences in status, prevention of domination of some by others, and the preservation of conditions of procedural fairness are basic and important moral values. Within the framework of the principle of equal consideration they provide strong reasons for the elimination of various inequalities. Taken together these values account for at least a large part of the importance that equality has in our political thinking. They may account for all of this importance, or there may be an important role to be played by a further moral idea of substantive equality. But it remains unclear exactly what that idea would be.

[16] See footnote 13 above.

12

Punishment and the rule of law

This essay will consider how some central issues that Carlos Nino discussed in his writings on the philosophical theory of punishment are relevant to the difficult empirical and political problem of building a legal order that preserves the rule of law and provides remedies for victims of past human rights abuses. Carlos Nino was remarkable in combining philosophical scholarship with important and courageous contributions to this difficult political problem. My first contact with him came when he submitted his article "A Consensual Theory of Punishment" to the journal *Philosophy and Public Affairs*, of which I was then an associate editor. This article attempts to provide a justification for criminal penalties that avoids retributivism but also explains why a system of penalties cannot be justified solely on the basis of its deterrent effects. It was, for me, an exciting paper to read. I very much agreed with the main line of Nino's theory, although I thought that there were certain rather subtle ways in which it went astray. We had a brief but stimulating correspondence about these issues. In retrospect it is striking – indeed, to someone like me who has spent his adult life in the sheltered academy it is truly amazing – that the seemingly academic issues discussed in Nino's article, including the rather subtle point on which we disagreed, turned out later to be of very considerable practical importance.

Philosophical reflection on the problem of punishment has focused on two general questions: the justification for punishment and the limits on its legitimate application. Theoretical reflection of this kind bears on the practical problems we are discussing in at least four ways:

1. It bears on the grounds and interpretation of the prohibition against retroactive punishment.
2. It bears more generally on the state of mind required in an offender as a precondition of legal guilt.
3. It bears on the permissibility of selective punishment. Nino stated, for example, in his response to Diane Orentlicher in the *Yale Law Journal* that only a retributivist theory of punishment requires punishing *all* of

those believed guilty of a given offense.[1] All other views, he argued, leave open the possibility that even where punishment is merited, it may be omitted for other reasons, including reasons of political necessity.

4. Finally, theoretical reflection on the problem of punishment bears on the interpretation and legitimacy of the demands of victims for legal response to the wrongs done them.

Let me begin my consideration of philosophical theories by distinguishing four moral ideas that are often cited in arguments about punishment. We will need to bear in mind the degree to which each of them figures in a rationale for having a *system* of punishment or in a rationale for carrying out punishment in an individual case.

The first idea is *retribution.* I will identify retributivism as an account of the rationale for legal punishment, with the view that, first, it is a good thing morally that those who have committed certain moral wrongs should themselves suffer some loss as a result and, second, that bringing about this coincidence between welfare and desert is a central part of the justification for legal institutions of punishment. On such a view there are good moral reasons to bring about losses to those who are guilty of wrongdoing, and the force of these reasons is sufficient to justify not only the suffering of the guilty parties but also the costs to others involved in bringing this about. Both the guilt in question here and the reason for repaying it with loss are to be understood in an extra-institutional (that is to say a moral, not a legal) sense. So understood, retributivism is to be distinguished from the view that because the institution of the criminal law is justified on other grounds, there is reason that those who are *legally* guilty should suffer the penalties that are *legally* prescribed.

Nino was firm in rejecting retributivism as a justification for punishment, and in this he was in agreement with the majority of contemporary philosophical and legal thought. The reason for this widespread rejection is not skepticism about the ideas of moral guilt or moral justification but one or both of two further ideas. The first is rejection of the notion of moral desert, at least in the form of the thesis that it is a good thing, morally, that those who are guilty of moral wrongs should suffer. The second is the idea that even if this thesis is accepted it is not a proper basis for the justification of a political institution. An institutional practice of depriving some citizens of their rights and inflicting other losses on them cannot be justified simply on the ground that this brings their fate more nearly in line with moral

---

[1] Nino, "The Duty to Punish Past Abuses of Human Rights Put into Context," *Yale Law Journal* 100 (1991), 2619–40, p. 2620, replying to Diane Orentlicher, "Settling Accounts: The Duty to Prosecute Human Rights Violations of a Prior Regime," *Yale Law Journal* 100 (1991), 2537–615.

desert. I myself accept both of these ideas, and therefore agree with Nino in rejecting retributivism.[2] The central thesis of retributivism struck both of us as, in Herbert Hart's words, "a mysterious piece of moral alchemy, in which the two evils of moral wickedness and suffering are transmuted into good."[3]

But something *like* retributivism is not so easy to avoid. In the Argentine context, retributivism was appealing to many because it seemed to support what they thought of as the correct answers to the four questions I listed: it explained why retroactive punishment was justified; it identified what it was about the torturers and kidnappers that called for punishment: the evil of their actions; it provided a basis for insisting that all such criminals must be punished; and it thereby accounted for the legitimacy of the demands of the victims' families for a response to what had been done to them and their loved ones.

The main alternative to retributivism as a rationale for punishment has, of course, been *deterrence*. This is in the first instance a rationale for having a *system* of punishment, and it provides a rationale for punishing in individual cases only indirectly: punishment should be carried out in an individual case because that is required by an institution that is (in light of its deterrence effects and perhaps other considerations) justified.[4] Thus, while punishment is addressed to a past crime, its rationale is addressed to future possible crimes which, one hopes, may not occur. So, in cases of the kind I am concerned with in this essay, the deterrence account appeals to the need, first, for a general practice of punishing human rights offenders even if their actions were allowed by the legal and political order in place at the time they were committed, and then, second, to the justifiability of punishment in particular cases as something that must be required by any such system.

This future orientation makes pure deterrence theory seem deficient from the perspective of another moral idea, which I will call *affirmation* of the victims' sense of having been wronged. This idea is not often discussed in philosophical theories of punishment, but nonetheless plays an important part in our thinking about the subject.[5] It is, I am afraid, a rather vague

---

[2] This rejection, on grounds close to those just mentioned, is spelled out in chapter 4 of Carlos Nino, *Radical Evil on Trial* (New Haven: Yale University Press, 1996).

[3] H. L. A. Hart, *Punishment and Responsibility* (New York: Oxford University Press, 1968), pp. 234–5.

[4] Deterrence theorists may disagree as to whether the need for deterrence can be taken into account in adjusting the penalty in an individual case, some holding, perhaps, that this is required in any efficient system, while others see it as introducing an unacceptable form of arbitrary inequality.

[5] It is recognized by Joel Feinberg in "The Expressive Function of Punishment," in his collection of essays, *Doing and Deserving* (Princeton: Princeton University Press, 1970).

idea. I will try to clarify it as I go along, but part of my point is simply to call attention to the importance of examining the various ways in which this idea might be understood and incorporated into a larger theory of punishment.

This importance is particularly clear in the Argentine case, in which one crucial political element was the pressure of victims' groups such as the Madres de la Plaza de Mayo, who demanded retribution. In fact, as Carlos Nino points out in *Radical Evil on Trial*, insistence on a retributivist view of punishment was something that the Madres and the members of the juntas had in common, although they of course used it to draw opposite conclusions.[6] The Madres argued that everyone who took part in the dirty war was guilty and therefore must be punished; the generals maintained that none of them should be punished, since what they had done was morally justified. This agreement between opposites is not surprising. Both are drawn to retributivism because each is looking for a standard safely beyond law: in the case of the generals, in order to argue that whatever the law may be now, their acts were *morally* justifiable and hence unpunishable; in the case of the Madres, in order to argue that whatever the law may have been *then*, these acts were morally evil and hence deserve punishment. This common strategy suggests that in its emphasis on an extralegal standard, the rationale of retributive theory is in some tension with the idea of the rule of law.

Despite this tension, if retributivism is the only theory of punishment that adequately incorporates the idea of affirmation, this may seem to count in favor of its claim to moral adequacy. Even more likely, this will give retributivism real political force, especially in a dramatic context like that of Argentina in the 1980s but also in the somewhat cooler debates about crime in the United States.

So it is worth asking whether demands like those of the Madres de la Plaza de Mayo might be recognized as legitimate (but in a more tractable form) outside of a retributive theory. This illustrates a more general suggestion that philosophical theory can contribute to actual politics by helping to distinguish various ways in which popular demands can be understood.

Another intuition that is sometimes cited as supporting retributivism is the widespread sense that there is something seriously amiss when those who have committed terrible crimes are allowed to go on living as normal citizens as if nothing had happened. In the Argentine case, for example, many expressed outrage that the officers who had ordered and carried

---

[6] Nino, *Radical Evil on Trial*, ch. 4.

out the kidnapping, torture, and murder of thousands of citizens should be allowed to go on living as respected members of Argentine society. I share this intuition, but I do not believe that what it supports is properly called retributivism. It is important that terrible wrongs be recognized by an appropriate response, and the victims of such wrongs are demeaned when the victimizers are treated as respected citizens with no mention of their crimes. But what makes it appropriate to recognize these wrongs is not that this involves suffering or loss on the part of the wrongdoers. It is rather that the absence of such recognition reflects indifference on the part of society toward the wrongs and those who suffered them. What is crucial is recognition, not suffering. Ideally, of course, one wants the perpetrators themselves to acknowledge these wrongs and express contrition for them. This will be painful, but it is not the pain that makes it desirable.

Like retribution, affirmation is an aim that responds to the past and is addressed in the first instance to each particular case. But it also provides a reason for having a system in which particular claims to be wronged can be recognized and given a form in which they can be publicly expressed and responded to.[7] Having such a system is also relevant to the aim of deterrence, understood in a general sense of discouraging future crime, rather than the narrower sense of doing this by threatening retaliation.[8] People whose sense of being wronged is not recognized and affirmed by the law have less respect for and less investment in it. Lack of affirmation, then, supports what Nino calls anomie, the cynical lack of respect for law which he identified as a main problem of Argentine society. The right response to the demand for affirmation may undermine this dangerous tendency, thereby building the rule of law. As Nino emphasized in his writings on deliberative democracy, the public character of the proceedings within a trial, and the public discussion surrounding it, can play a crucial positive role of this kind. One can hope that occasions like the dramatic trials of the members of the juntas in the Federal Court of Buenos Aires will lead to greater public commitment to the rule of law. Surely they are one of our best hopes.

I have mentioned affirmation as a value and suggested that it is something citizens may reasonably demand of a system of law. It does not seem likely that a system of law that fails, in general, to respond to such demands is likely to survive. I am not suggesting, however, that victims have a right

---

[7] The idea that one of the crucial functions of a system of criminal law is to give definite form to the sense of being wronged was emphasized by Nietzsche. See *The Genealogy of Morals*, second essay, sections 10–15.

[8] Nino calls this more general view "preventionism." See *Radical Evil on Trial*, ch 4.

that those who have wronged them be punished. A defensible legal order must, in general, define and defend citizens' rights, but this does not require that every offender be punished. In the case of the crimes of the dirty war, for example, prosecution of those in decision-making positions, and those who went beyond orders to commit private wrongs (i.e. those in Alfonsín's first two categories)[9] could be held to represent adequate recognition of every sufferer's wrong, even though not every wrongdoer was called to account. There is also the possibility, which I will not be able to explore here, that legitimate demands for affirmation of wrongs may be met through means other than punishment – for example, through some form of public authoritative recognition and declaration.[10]

Finally, let me mention a fourth value, or category of values, which I will label *fairness*. Considerations of fairness do not provide a justification for having a system of criminal punishment, but constitute a class of reasons for insisting that this system be of a certain kind. In principle, fairness might provide a reason for insisting on punishment in a particular case insofar as refraining from punishment is seen as unfair or arbitrary, in view of the fact that others were punished for similar crimes.

In this respect, fairness may seem to be allied with retributivism, and perhaps even to presuppose some form of it. It may seem to presuppose retributivism insofar as the idea of fairness appealed to is that punishment should go equally to those who are equally *deserving* of it. But this need not be retributivist in the hard sense I am discussing, since fairness need not appeal to a pre-institutional sense of moral desert as the relevant standard. Still, fairness may seem allied with retributivism in the answer it implies to my third question, about the permissibility of punishing some offenders but not others, for political reasons.

Carlos Nino believed that selective punishment could be defended as a political necessity. As I have mentioned, he said that only a retributivist theory of punishment would require punishing *all* of those believed guilty of a given offense. All other views, he argued, leave open the possibility that even where punishment is merited, it may be omitted for other reasons, such as political necessity. Against this, it might be claimed that considerations of fairness, which need not have a retributivist basis, at least *normally* speak

---

[9] Nino describes these categories, which he says were first outlined by Alfonsín in a lecture at the Argentine Federation of Lawyers' Colleges in August 1983, as follows: "(a) those who planned the repression and gave the accompanying orders; (b) those who acted beyond orders, moved by cruelty, perversity, or greed; (c) those who strictly complied with the orders." *Radical Evil on Trial*, p. 63.

[10] As argued, with reference to the case of Chile, by Jorge Correa Sutil, in "Dealing with Past Human Rights Violations," *Notre Dame Law Review* 67 (1993), 1455–94.

against selective punishment. There is room for argument, however, that unequal punishment for reasons of political necessity would not be unfair (even though differential penalties for political reasons of other sorts would be). I will not pursue this argument here. My point is just that this is another case where a consideration whose moral significance might seem to rest on (and hence to support) retributivism can in fact be explained on other grounds.

I have suggested in passing that one important step in building respect for the rule of law lies in ensuring that people have the right sense of what they can demand from a legal system and that they see the legal order as valuable because it provides these benefits. Looking at the various possible rationales for punishment from this point of view, we can ask what answers they suggest to the question, what can citizens reasonably demand from a system of criminal law?

I have suggested that it is not appropriate for them to demand retribution. What they can demand of a system of law is:

1. That it be effective in deterring private wrongdoers.
2. That it affirm their rights and provide a hearing for their sense of having been wronged.
3. That it be fair.
4. That it be safe.

The creation of a coercive apparatus of punishment to enforce the criminal law is the creation of a potentially dangerous instrument of force and violence. Even though this may be necessary as a protection against private wrong, law-abiding citizens can reasonably demand assurance that it will not attack them as well.

This question of safety brings me to the second side of the philosophical theory of punishment: from the justification for punishment to the limits on its application. The safety just mentioned was that of law-abiding citizens, but the theoretical question is why the safety of law-breakers should be any less important. Why is it permissible to inflict losses on those who break the law, in order to deter future crime, when it is not permissible to "use" others in this way? The aim of deterrence itself provides no answer, since sweeping a wider net that inflicts losses on guilty and innocent alike may have an even greater deterrent effect, and may be claimed to make everyone safer in the end. Justifications of this kind were actually offered for the "dirty war against subversion," and they are a chilling reminder that this argument is not just a stale academic warhorse. This point was particularly important for the Alfonsín administration: because one of the things they most wanted to overcome was the crude expediency of the juntas' justification of their policies, they needed a principled basis for deciding who could be punished for the crimes of that period. Merely to appeal to the importance of deterring such acts in future would just be more expediency.

Retributivists have an answer to this question: it is all right to punish law-breakers insofar as they are morally guilty and hence deserve to suffer. And retributivists might go on to add that the problem I am now addressing is just the natural result of replacing retribution, the proper moral aim of punishment, with the mere expediency of deterrence.

Nonetheless, Nino and many others (myself included) reject retributivism, so we need some other answer. Nino's answer is provided by his consensual theory of punishment. According to this theory, those who commit crimes thereby consent to the normative consequences of their actions. This consent provides the crucial element in "licensing" punishment, even though it does not justify or require it. I want to examine this theory in more detail.

Following Herbert Hart, Nino pointed out that there is a wide range of cases, not restricted to punishment, in which acts implying consent have a licensing effect – that is, they make permissible other actions to which there would otherwise be serious objections.[11] He mentions in particular two such cases. The first is that of legal contracts, in which the consent implied by entering into a contract licenses the state in enforcing it, thereby depriving the party of a liberty he or she would have otherwise enjoyed. The second example is the assumption of risk in tort cases, in which the fact that a person voluntarily undertook some risky behavior licenses the denial of a remedy when injury results. In order for an act to "imply consent" in a way that has this licensing effect, Nino says, an act must be voluntary and the agent must know what the legal consequences of his or her action are – know, for example, that he or she is giving up certain legal claims or immunities.[12]

The idea of consent (or of an action implying consent) fits the case of contract much better than it does cases of assumption of risk. The condition of knowledge that Nino mentions seems out of place in the latter context: surely a person need not be aware of tort law in order to "assume a risk" in a legally significant way. Even in the case of contracts, the requirement that an agent know the legal consequences of his or her act may seem too strong

---

[11] Carlos Nino, "A Consensual Theory of Punishment," *Philosophy and Public Affairs* 12 (1983), 295–6. See the essays in Hart's *Punishment and Responsibility*, especially "Prolegomenon to the Principles of Punishment" and "Legal Responsibility and Excuses."

[12] Nino, "A Consensual Theory," p. 296.

when understood literally. But it does seem that a party to a contract must intend, and hence believe, that he or she is laying down some legal right (whether or not he or she must know exactly what that right is). This makes it appropriate to speak of consent. In the case of assumed risk, however, it is a stretch to speak even of implied consent to a *legal* consequence. In both cases we may say that some right is laid down, or some possible future claim stopped, but in saying this are we merely reiterating the *legal* consequence or saying something more?

If these examples are to point toward an answer to the question that puzzled us in the case of punishment, rather than merely being further examples which raise that same question, they must suggest some explanation of why defensible legal institutions must take a particular form – why they must, for example, make the loss of certain legal immunities dependent on actions that imply consent (or something like it). To provide this explanation we need to appeal to some extra-institutional value, like the extra-institutional idea of desert on which retributivism is founded. To what value should we appeal?

One possibility is the idea that, *morally speaking*, consent has a licensing effect. This may be what Nino had in mind. He wrote, "Another way of describing the situation is to say that the consent to certain *legal* normative consequences involves *moral* normative consequences. The individual who, for instance, consents to undertake some legal obligation is, in principle, morally obligated to do the act which is the object of that obligation."[13] What is appealed to here is not an idea of desert, but a deontological idea about how people's actions affect what they are (morally) entitled to, hence what they can (morally speaking) demand of their legal institutions. But insofar as this idea involves a full-bodied notion of consent it is, as I have said, more clearly applicable to the case of contracts than to torts or punishment.

An alternative would be to appeal not to deontological ideas of consent and entitlement but rather to the value that people reasonably place on having certain forms of control over what happens to them. Because we have reason to value these forms of control, they are factors that must be taken into account in assessing legal institutions. Such factors play somewhat different roles in the two cases Nino mentions.

In the case of contracts, the value of control figures both positively and negatively. Positively, it is a central aim of the law of contracts to give effect to the wills of the parties. In order to do this, it must make the

---

[13] Ibid.

legal normative consequences of an act dependent on the beliefs and intentions of the agent. Negatively, this dependence greatly weakens the case of a person who complains about the enforcement of a contract knowingly and voluntarily undertaken: if he or she wished not to be bound, he or she could simply have refrained from consenting. In offering this way out, the law gives us a crucial form of protection against unwanted obligations.

The law of torts has a different aim: compensating people for loss and injury. The positive part of the case just made thus has no application in the case of torts, but an analogue of the negative part still applies. The law of torts is supposed to protect us against injury and loss, but there are limits to the protection we can demand. By having the opportunity to avoid loss simply by avoiding behavior that can be seen to be very risky, we already have an important form of protection against that loss. Indeed, it can be argued that this is as much protection as can reasonably be asked.

This account explains why Nino's strong requirement of knowledge of the legal normative consequences of one's action makes more sense in the case of contracts than in that of assumed risk. In the first case, creating legal normative consequences that reflect the parties' intentions is a central aim of the law. (This was the "positive" appeal to the value of control.) So knowledge, or something like it, has a natural relevance.[14] Where only the negative value of control is at issue, however, an agent's state of mind is less relevant. Since the question is whether the person had the protection provided by an opportunity to avoid the loss, what is relevant is not what the person knew about the normative consequences of his or her act but what he or she could have known, by exercising a reasonable level of care, about its likely consequences, and about the availability of alternative courses of action.

With all this as background, then, let me turn to the case of punishment. In Nino's view, the consent-implying character of a criminal's act licenses punishment but does not justify it. That is to say, the inclusion in a system of law of the requirement that punishment can be inflicted only on those who have voluntarily (and perhaps knowingly) violated it is a necessary but not sufficient condition for that system's being morally justifiable, and the occurrence of a consent-implying act is a necessary but not necessarily sufficient condition for punishment to be justifiably applied in a particular case. The idea of consent thus fills the "gap" discussed above in the justification

---

[14] Even here, it may be too strong a requirement, but I will not go into the details. As I have said, it does seem that the party to a contract must at least intend and believe that he or she is performing an act with normative legal consequences.

of punishment. The fuller account of that justification is summarized by Nino as follows:

If the punishment is attached to a justifiable obligation, if the authorities involved are legitimate, if the punishment deprives the individual of goods he can alienate, and if it is a necessary and effective means of protecting the community against greater harms, then the fact that the individual has freely consented to make himself liable to that punishment (by performing a voluntary act with the knowledge that the relinquishment of his immunity is a necessary consequence of it) provides a prima facie moral justification for exercising the correlative legal power of punishing him.

The principle of distribution, which that moral justification presupposes, is the same as that which justifies the distribution of advantages and burdens ensuing from contracts and the distribution achieved in the law of torts when the burdens that follow from a tort are placed on the consenting injured party. This justification of course presupposes that several conditions have been satisfied. First, the person punished must have been capable of preventing the act to which the liability is attached (this excludes the rare case of punishing an innocent person that pure social protection might allow). Second, the individual must have performed the act with knowledge of its relevant factual properties. Third, he must have known that the undertaking of a liability to suffer punishment was a necessary consequence of such an act. This obviously implies that one must have knowledge of the law, and it also proscribes the imposition of retroactive criminal laws.[15]

There is much in this account that I agree with. In particular, the idea of using something *like* consent to fill the logical gap left by the removal of desert is very appealing. I want, however, to raise two related questions. The first is whether the knowledge requirement entailed by Nino's notion of consent is too strong. The second is whether the underlying moral idea, which explains, among other things, the permissibility of retroactive criminal laws, is best understood in terms of consent or in some other way.

The question of knowledge is well raised by the problems faced by successor governments in punishing human rights violations under prior regimes. A coup d'état, we may suppose, is a heady affair. Might not those who carry it out be convinced by the rhetoric of their own decrees and believe that previous law had been swept away giving them full legal power to do what they thought necessary to put the society in order? If they did believe this, and hence did not *know* that their acts had the normative consequence of leaving them legally liable to punishment, would this provide a defense against later charges?

I am not in a position to say what the facts were in this regard in the cases of the members of the Argentine juntas. They sounded as if they

---

[15] Nino, "A Consensual Theory," p. 299.

were convinced that what they did was *morally* justifiable. Perhaps they also thought it was legally permitted; perhaps not. Perhaps they simply did not give much thought to matters of legality, at least not until the end when thoughts about what the next government might do led them to enact the "self-amnesty" law. The question I am concerned with, however, is whether their liability to punishment depended on this question about their state of mind.

Whatever the facts may have been in that case, this general question remains, and is raised by more humdrum examples. Consider, for example, the overconfident law graduate who is firmly convinced that he or she has found a way, without being guilty of murder or even manslaughter, to do away with the now burdensome spouse, who worked at a dull job to pay the law school fees. This state of mind does not seem to constitute a defense.

What is relevant in all these cases is not what the agent knew about the legal normative consequences of his or her action, but rather what the agent could, through the exercise of due care, have reasonable grounds for believing about these consequences. This suggests that the underlying value in these cases is not the deontological licensing power of consent but rather the value of having a fair opportunity to avoid falling afoul of the law – analogous to the "negative" appeal to the value of control which I discussed above. Both the overconfident law graduate and the members of real and imaginary juntas have this opportunity.[16]

What I would like to do, then, is to follow Carlos Nino's strategy for filling the "gap" in a nonretributivist account of punishment, but to de-emphasize his literal appeal to *consent*.[17] This strategy runs the risk of minimizing, in an implausible way, the difference between civil and criminal law. The moral idea of consent, as Nino invoked it, was not an idea of desert. Nonetheless, insofar as it was a matter of the actual state of mind of the agent, it retained a link with that aspect of the criminal to which the criminal law and punishment are appropriately addressed: a state of mind that separates the criminal from the law-abiding citizen. In moving from consent to fair opportunity to avoid a sanction, we move away from the agent's state of mind to a mere benefit that the criminal has enjoyed, by virtue of which he cannot object to being punished. The result may seem a

---

[16] One way to make it particularly clear that violations of human rights incur legal liability would be to eliminate constitutional provisions licensing suspension of basic liberties by declaration of a "state of siege." This suggestion may be thought unrealistic, but such provisions (in addition to offering an air of legality to acts that do not merit it) invite a kind of cynicism by suggesting that even the law itself recognizes that civil liberties are something that can be enjoyed only in "good times."

[17] I have presented a view of this kind in "The Significance of Choice," in S. McMurrin, ed., *The Tanner Lectures on Human Values*, vol. 8 (Salt Lake City: University of Utah Press, 1988), pp. 151–216.

passionless and rather apologetic account of the mental element in criminal law, the sort of thing that is taken in some quarters to give "liberals" like me a bad name.

Newspaper editorialists and talk-show hosts would say that this view of punishment is so concerned with the rights of criminals that it pays no attention to the claims of victims. I can give this objection a more theoretical form by repeating that, as I said earlier, one thing citizens may reasonably demand of a system of law is that it affirm their rights and, in particular, their sense of having been wronged. To this I would add that a system that affirms a victim's sense of being wronged must condemn the agent who inflicted the wrong, and the mental element that makes this appropriate must go beyond merely having had the opportunity to avoid this sanction.

Here it is important to bear in mind the diverse elements that must go together to make punishment justified in Nino's view or mine, and to recognize the different contributions that these elements make to that justification.

The idea that justifiable punishment must be for something that is properly condemned figures in a theory of punishment in at least two ways. First, a defensible criminal law must defend something that the victim is entitled to have defended *and that the perpetrator cannot object to being excluded from.* (Otherwise that law would be an unacceptable deprivation of liberty.) Second, the fact that actions of a certain type are in this sense unjustifiable intrusions against their victims is a necessary condition for making these actions the object of a law with condemnatory force. A "mental element," in the form of specific intent or reckless disregard for the likely consequences of one's actions is important here: harms do not constitute unjustifiable intrusions if they were unavoidable.

The fact that an action is an unjustifiable intrusion (in the sense just described) is a necessary condition for condemning it, and usually also a sufficient condition for doing so. But it is not (on a nonretributive view) a sufficient condition for depriving the agent of liberty or inflicting other forms of harsh treatment on him. For such harsh treatment, some further justification is required beyond the desirability of expressing our judgments. This is where we must appeal to the utility of deterrence as a way of providing a kind of protection that we need and are entitled to, and to the fact that everyone will have a fair opportunity to avoid liability to the penalties involved.

This account enables us to put what I have been calling "affirmation" in its proper place. I said above that this notion has seemed puzzling because the expression of condemnation seems to be importantly connected with justifiable punishment, yet does not seem weighty enough to provide that justification. The central function of criminal law is to protect rights whose violation makes condemnation appropriate. So punishment will not be justifiable except where condemnation, and hence the affirmation of victims' rights, is appropriate, and just punishment will constitute such affirmation. In addition, as I pointed out in the case of Argentina, authoritative condemnation of certain acts as criminal can play an important role in building respect for the rule of law, and hence in a strategy of deterrence broadly understood.

The "mental element" in the definition of a crime plays two roles in the account I have just given. It occurs once as part of what makes an action an unjustifiable intrusion, which is justifiably condemned. It occurs again, in the form of "fair opportunity to avoid," as part of the account of why it is permissible not only to condemn certain actions but also to attach severe penalties to them as a mechanism of deterrence.

The mistake (as I see it) of retributive theories is that they lump together these two roles for the "mental element" in criminal punishment: its role as a condition for the appropriateness of condemnation and its role as a condition for the permissibility of inflicting loss. The weakness of non-retributive theories is that they may seem unsatisfactory because they separate these elements too widely and concentrate too much on the second (the permissibility of inflicting loss on the criminal) because the question it raises is seen as theoretically more challenging.

What philosophers do, of course, is to work hard at identifying the differences between theories of this kind and then try to decide which of them offers the most satisfactory account of "our" settled convictions. Reaching agreement about such matters is not easy, even when the "we" in question is just the group of people around a seminar table, or even when it is the single person in front of the computer screen.

The real-world political problems to which this inquiry is addressed involve building at least a partial consensus among a large and varied group of people on such issues as what the rule of law is, why it is to be valued, and what the preconditions are for just punishment. Some of us may think, after years of philosophical reflection, that we have answers to these questions. It would be hopeless to think that others will take our word for these conclusions, or even that everyone will agree with them. What we can do, however, is to try to call the alternatives we have distinguished to the attention of our fellow citizens, so that they can decide, for example, whether their view of punishment is actually retributivist or just seemed to be so because they had not noticed what the alternatives were.

Even imagining this role for philosophy in public discourse may seem optimistic, particularly given the abysmal level of recent debates in the United States. But this is the hopeful model that Carlos Nino's idea of deliberative democracy seems to suggest. More remarkably, it is the model he put into practice in his life, in ways which made him an inspiration to us all.

13

Promises and contracts

I. INTRODUCTION

The similarity between a promise and a contract is so obvious that it is natural to suppose that there is much to be learned about one of these notions by studying the other, or even that the legal notion of a contract can be understood by seeing it as based on the moral idea of a promise.[1] This essay will examine some of the similarities between these two notions. These similarities are due to the fact that contract and promise arise in response to, and are consequently shaped by, some of the same underlying values. They are in this respect parallel ideas. But they respond to these values in different ways and are independent notions, neither of which is properly seen as based on the other.

The law of contracts is clearly a social institution, backed by the coercive power of the state and subject to modification through judicial decisions and legislative enactments. Promising is also often seen as a social institution of a more informal kind, defined by certain rules which are not enacted but rather backed by moral argument and enforced through the informal sanction of moral disapproval. Many have argued that the wrong involved in breaking a promise depends essentially on the existence of a social practice of this kind. Hume,[2] for example, maintains that fidelity to promises is "an artificial virtue," dependent on the existence of a convention of keeping

A draft of this paper was presented at the third Drum Moir conference on philosophy of law. I am grateful to participants in the conference for their many helpful suggestions, and especially to Jody Kraus, for his comments at that session and for subsequent correspondence and discussion, which has been extremely valuable. I also am indebted to Richard Craswell for extensive comments, and to Peter Benson for help at many stages in the process.

[1] As suggested by Charles Fried in *Contract as Promise: A Theory of Contractual Obligation* (Cambridge, MA: Harvard University Press, 1981).

[2] In D. Hume, *A Treatise of Human Nature*, ed. L. A. Selby-Bigge (Oxford: Clarendon Press, 1960), book III, part II, ch. v.

agreements, and other accounts of this kind have been advanced in our own day by Rawls[3] and others.

These analyses do not seem to me to be convincing. I do not doubt that there is such a thing as a social practice of promising, which consists in the fact that people accept certain norms, which they often invoke by using the words "I promise." I do not believe, however, that either the obligation generated by a promise or the wrong involved in breaking one depends on the existence of this practice. I will argue that the wrong of breaking a promise and the wrong of making a lying promise are instances of a more general family of moral wrongs which are not concerned with social practices but rather with what we owe to other people when we have led them to form expectations about our future conduct.[4] Social practices of agreement making, when they exist, may provide the means for creating such expectations, and hence for committing such wrongs. But I will argue that these practices play no essential role in explaining why these actions are wrongs.

In section ii, I will present some examples of one class of wrongs that I have in mind, formulate principles that would explain why they are wrongs, and argue for the validity of these principles within the contractualist account of right and wrong that I have defended elsewhere.[5] These principles

---

[3] See J. Rawls, *A Theory of Justice* (Cambridge, MA: Harvard University Press, 1971), pp. 344–50.

[4] Neil MacCormick expressed similar misgivings in "Voluntary Obligations and Normative Powers i," *Proceedings of the Aristotelian Society*, 46 (Supp. vol.) (1972), 59. He goes on to offer an account based on a general obligation not to disappoint the expectations of others whom we have knowingly induced to rely upon us (ibid., p. 68). I will set out the moral foundations of a similar account that I hope will avoid objections such as those raised by Joseph Raz in his contribution to that same symposium ("Voluntary Obligations and Normative Powers ii, " p. 79) and in J. Raz, "Promises and Obligations," in P. M. S. Hacker and J. Raz, eds., *Law, Morality and Society: Essays in Honour of H. L. A. Hart* (Oxford: Oxford University Press, 1977), p. 210. In the latter article, Raz distinguishes between the "intention" conception of promises, according to which the essence of a promise lies in the communication, under the proper circumstances, of a firm intention to act in a certain way, and the "obligation" conception, according to which the essence of a promise lies in the intention to undertake, by that very act of communication, an obligation to perform a certain action. In my view, which lies in the common ground between MacCormick's account and Raz's, the elements of intention and obligation are interdependent: promises are distinguished by the fact that the intention expressed is supposed to be made credible by appeal to shared conception of obligation, but the grounds of this obligation lie in a principle very close to the one which MacCormick states. Judith Thomson presents an account of promises that is similar to mine in *The Realm of Rights* (Cambridge, MA: Harvard University Press, 1990), ch. 12.

[5] In "Contractualism and Utilitarianism" (1982) in this volume, essay 7 pp. 124–50, and in *What We Owe to Each Other* (Cambridge, MA: Harvard University Press, 1998). This account is commonly called "contractualist" because of its appeal to the idea of people trying to reach agreement on standards of conduct. But since it does not rely on the idea that there is an obligation to keep the agreements one has entered into, it does not presuppose a notion of contract that would make it viciously circular for present purposes.

all deal, in one way or another, with one's responsibility for harms that others suffer as a result of relying on expectations one has led them to form about one's future conduct. The task of section III is to extend these principles to one that explains the obligation to keep a promise. In section IV, I will take up the question of the moral permissibility of laws that enforce obligations of the kind that these principles describe. The two main questions to be addressed here are, first, the relation between the existence of a moral obligation and the moral justifiability of laws that require those who violate this obligation to compensate those to whom it was owed, and, second, the justifiability of requiring those who violate a contract to pay "expectation damages." Finally, in section V, I will consider how the requirement that a valid promise or contract must be voluntary arises and is justified within the moral framework I am employing.

II. MANIPULATION AND REGARD FOR EXPECTATIONS[6]

As a first step toward understanding the morality of promising let me consider the wrong of making a "lying promise" – a promise that one has no intention of fulfilling. I maintain that this is an instance of a more general class of wrongs that do not depend on the existence of a social institution of promising and need not involve the making of a promise at all. Consider the following examples.

Suppose that you and I are farmers who own adjacent pieces of land, and that I would like to get you to help me build up the banks of the stream that runs through my property in order to prevent it from overflowing each spring. I could get you to help me by leading you to believe that if you help me then I will help you build up the banks of *your* stream. There are several ways I might do this. First, I might persuade you that if my stream is kept within its banks, then it will be worth my while to see to it that yours is too, because the runoff from the flooding of your field will then be the only obstacle to profitable planting of mine. If my stream were contained, then, simply as *homo economicus*, I would have sufficient reason to help you build up the banks of your stream. Alternatively, I might lead you to believe that I am a very sentimental person and that I would be so touched by your neighborly willingness to help me that I would be eager to respond in kind, both out of gratitude and out of a desire to keep alive that wonderful spirit of neighborly solidarity. A third alternative would be to persuade you that

---

[6] Most of what I say in this section and the next is taken, with a few significant changes, from T. Scanlon, "Promises and Practices," *Philosophy and Public Affairs* 19 (1990), 199.

I am a devoted member of the Sacred Brotherhood of Reindeer, and then say, "I swear to you on my honor as a Reindeer that if you help me with my stream I will help you with yours." (It is assumed here that you are not yourself a Reindeer, and it is left open whether I am or not and whether the Sacred Brotherhood of Reindeer even exists.) Fourth, and finally, having led you to believe that I am a stern Kantian moralist, I might offer you a solemn promise that if you help me, I will help you in return.

Assume for the moment that in all of these cases my intentions are purely cynical. My only concern is how to get you to help me, and I have no intention of helping you in return. Given this assumption, it seems to me that these four cases involve exactly the same wrong, which I will refer to as "unjustified manipulation." The principle forbidding it might be stated as follows.

Principle M: In the absence of special justification, it is not permissible for one person, A, in order to get another person, B, to do some act, X (which A wants B to do and which B is morally free to do or not do but would otherwise not do), to lead B to expect that if he or she does X then A will do Y (which B wants but believes that A will otherwise not do) when in fact A has no intention of doing Y if B does X, and A can reasonably foresee that B will suffer significant loss if he or she does X and A does not reciprocate by doing Y.

I take this to be a valid moral principle; that is to say, a correct statement about which acts are wrong. Let me take a moment to explain what I mean by this and why I think it is so. In my view, an action is wrong if any principle that permitted it would be one that, for that reason, someone could reasonably reject even if that person were moved to find principles for the general regulation of behavior that others, similarly motivated, also could not reasonably reject.[7] This general account applies to the present case in the following way. Potential victims of manipulation have strong reason to want to be able to direct their efforts and resources toward aims that they have chosen, and not to have their planning coopted in the way Principle M forbids whenever this suits someone else's purposes. So they have strong prima facie reason to reject a principle offering any less protection against manipulation than M would provide. Whether it would be reasonable in the sense in question for them to reject such principles depends on the strength of the reasons that others have to want the opportunities that these principles would provide. The perfectly general reasons that people may have for wanting to be able to manipulate others whenever it would be convenient to do so are not strong enough to make it unreasonable to insist

---

[7] I elaborate and defend this account of wrongness in the works cited in footnote 5 above.

on the protection that M provides. These general reasons are weaker than the reasons people have to want to avoid being manipulated in part because manipulation would undermine expectations about others' behavior that it would be very difficult to avoid relying on. By contrast, we generally have many means other than manipulation of the kind M rules out to pursue the ends it might be used for.

Of course, there are special situations in which one has particularly strong reasons for manipulating someone (and no alternative to doing so) or in which the normally strong reasons for rejecting a principle that would permit manipulation are weakened (because manipulation would not be contrary to the interests of the person who is manipulated). The existence of such situations is recognized by the limiting clause, "in the absence of special justification," and it would be reasonable to reject a principle that did not include such a clause. Situations covered by this clause include at least the following: (1) *emergency cases*, in which A, or someone else, is in danger and A cannot communicate with B directly but can make it appear that it would be in B's interest to do something that will help the endangered person (or will bring B closer so that A can ask for help); (2) *threat cases*, such as when A (or someone else) has been kidnapped by B and A needs to mislead B in order for the victim to have a chance to escape: (3) *paternalistic cases*, such as when B's capacities for rational choice are significantly diminished and misleading B is the least intrusive way to prevent him or her from suffering serious loss or harm; (4) *permission cases*, such as when A and B have entered, by mutual consent, into a game or other activity which involves the kind of deception that is in question.

It would be misleading to say that these are cases in which special justifications "override" or "outweigh" the obligation specified by Principle M. Rather, they are cases in which M does not apply because the reasons that support it in normal cases are modified in important respects. A stricter version of M, which did not recognize these exceptions, could therefore reasonably be rejected. In emergency cases, for example, A's legitimate reasons for needing to mislead B are much stronger than normal. In threat cases, these reasons are also particularly strong and, in addition, the force of B's reasons for objecting to being manipulated is undermined by the fact that the course of action that he is pursuing is itself wrong – any principle that permitted it would be one that A could reasonably reject. In paternalistic cases and permission cases, B's reasons for objecting to manipulation are also weakened, but for different reasons. In paternalistic cases it is because incapacities undermine the value for B of being able to make his or her own choices. In permission cases it is because being vulnerable to certain restricted forms of manipulation is an essential part of practices that we have good reason to want to engage in.

Principle *M* clearly does not depend on the existence of a social practice of agreement making. When such a practice exists, it provides one way of committing the wrong of unjustified manipulation, because it provides one kind of basis for a person's expectation that another person will respond to his or her action in a certain way. But, as the above examples show, these expectations can have other bases, and manipulating others by creating such an expectation is open to the same moral objection whatever the basis of the expectation may be.

The examples I have described all involve wrongful deception, but this similarity should not be allowed to obscure other respects in which these examples are morally different from one another. I have in mind here, in particular, differences in the degree and nature of the obligation to fulfill the expectation one has created, and differences in the degree to which the person who forms the expectation can be said to have a "right to rely" on it. So let me change the examples I have given by assuming that when I set out to make you expect reciprocal help I have every intention of fulfilling this expectation. Why would it be wrong for me to change my mind and fail to perform once you had done your part? To answer this question we need to appeal to a richer set of underlying moral principles.

Principle *M* states one moral constraint governing the creation of expectations about one's behavior. There are other principles of this kind, one of which is what I will call the principle of Due Care.

Principle D: One must exercise due care not to lead others to form reasonable but false expectations about what one will do when there is reason to believe that they would suffer significant loss as a result of relying on these expectations.

This principle is more demanding than Principle *M* since it requires a degree of vigilance beyond mere avoidance of intentional manipulation. In contrast to *M*, which prohibits a specific class of actions, *D* does not state explicitly what actions it requires. Its validity consists just in the fact that one can reasonably refuse to grant others license to ignore the costs of the expectations they lead one to form, though there is no obvious way to specify the exact nature and extent of the "due care" that is required. The following principle of Loss Prevention is slightly more specific, and extends beyond mere care in the creation of expectations.

Principle L: If one has intentionally or negligently (that is to say, in violation of Principle *D*) led someone to expect that one is going to follow a certain course of action *X*, and one has reason to believe that that person will suffer significant loss as a result of this expectation if one does not follow *X*, then one must take reasonable steps to prevent that loss.

The idea of "reasonable steps" incorporates a notion of proportionality between the steps taken and the magnitude of the threatened loss, as well as sensitivity to the degree of negligence involved in creating the expectation. I take Principle *L* to be valid on the same grounds as *M* and *D*: it is reasonable to refuse to grant others the freedom to ignore significant losses caused by the expectations they intentionally or negligently lead one to form.

Principle *L* does not require one always to prevent others from suffering loss in such cases, and even when it does require this, the choice of means is left open. One way of satisfying *L* would obviously be to fulfill the expectation once one realized that the other person was relying on it. But this is not required. *L* can also be satisfied by warning the other person before he or she has taken any action based on this expectation.

If no such warning has been given, and the expectation has not been fulfilled, Principle *L* can still be satisfied by compensating the person who was misled. What level of compensation is required? It would obviously be *sufficient* for *A* to compensate *B* for any loss suffered as a result of relying on this expectation. Given that all *A* has done is to create an expectation in *B* that *A* will do a certain thing, it would be reasonable for someone in *A*'s position to reject a principle requiring him or her to do more than restore *B* to as good a position as he or she would have been in if the expectation had never been created. But this may not always be required. In many cases, the benefits *B* would have reaped if his or her expectations about *A*'s conduct had been fulfilled would have been greater than the costs to *B* of relying on this expectation. But this is not always the case. Suppose, for example, that *B* had highly unrealistic plans about how he or she might benefit if *A* did *X*, and that *B* has expended great sums either in furtherance of this plan or in anticipation of its benefits. Most of these funds would have been lost even if *A* had acted as *B* expected. It would be reasonable for *A* to reject a principle that required *A* to make *B* as well off as he or she would have been if none of this had occurred, that is to say, to bear the cost, no matter how great, of *B*'s schemes, no matter how foolish they may have been. It would be reasonable to reject a principle that required *A*, in such a situation, to do more than make *B* as well off as *B* would have been if *A* had done *X*, as *B* expected him to.

As I have said, *A* can satisfy the requirements of Principle *L* just as fully by giving *B* a timely warning that *A* is not going to do *X* as by fulfilling this expectation. But the obligation to fulfill a promise is not neutral in this way between warning and fulfillment. Suppose, for example, that I promise to drive you to work if you will mow my lawn, and that you accept this arrangement. Then, a day or so later (but before the time has come for either of us to begin fulfilling the bargain) I think better of the deal and want to back out. On most people's understanding of promising, I am not free to do this. I am obligated to drive you to work unless you "release" me, even if I warn you before you have undertaken any action based on our arrangement. If I am not going to drive you to work then it is better to warn you than not to do so, but even if I do this I am breaking a promise.

The same can be said of compensation. If one fails to fulfill a promise, one should compensate the promisee if one can, but the obligation one undertakes when one makes a promise is an obligation to do the thing promised, not simply to do it or compensate the promisee accordingly. The difference between fulfillment and compensation is made particularly salient by the fact that in personal life, as opposed to the commercial transactions with which the law of contracts is centrally concerned, our main interest is likely to be in the actual performance of actions that have no obvious monetary or other equivalents, and by the fact that in the domain of informal personal morality (in contrast to the domain of law) there is no designated third party, presumed to be impartial, who is assigned the authority to make judgments of equivalence. The central concern of the morality of promises is therefore with the obligation to perform; the idea of compensation is of at most secondary interest.

Moreover, when compensation is in order for failure to fulfill a promise, the considerations bearing on the level of compensation that is required are different than in the case of *L*. When a person has failed to keep a promise, and not merely disappointed an expectation, it is plausible to say that the appropriate compensation must take the form of making the promisee as well off as he or she would have been had the promise been kept, even if doing this is more costly than compensating the promisee for reliance losses.

So in order to explain the obligations arising from promises it will be necessary to move beyond Principle *L* to a principle stating a duty specifically to fulfill the expectations one has created under certain conditions. How might such a principle be formulated and defended?

III. FIDELITY AND THE VALUE OF ASSURANCE

The difficulty can be stated as follows. The arguments I offered for Principles M, D, and L appealed to the reasons individuals have to want to avoid losses that they would incur by acting on other people's false or misleading representations about what they will do. The problem is how to extend these arguments to support a principle that requires agents to do what they have promised even when (as in the car and lawn example above) no "reliance loss" would result from one's failure to do so, since the promisee has not yet made any decision relying on the assurance given. The key to the problem lies in noticing the narrowness of the idea of reliance that I have just used in stating it. The reliance losses that are normally thought of in this context (and those that I invoked in arguing for Principles M, D, and L) are of two kinds: first, time, energy, and resources that have been expended and are wasted or lost because the other party fails to perform as expected; and, second, opportunities to make or look for alternative arrangements that are passed up because of this expectation. Considerations of these two kinds do provide reason to reject principles that would permit others to act in the ways that M, D, and L forbid. But they do not exhaust the reasons we have for wanting to be able to make stable agreements with others about what they will do. There are good reasons for wanting to have reliable assurance about what others will do that do not concern the consequences of acting on these assurances.

Suppose, for example, that George has, quite accidentally, come into possession of information about you, or about your firm, which would be damaging if revealed. (I will assume that it is not information that he is under any obligation to reveal, such as evidence of a crime, or of a danger that people need to be warned against, and that he would violate no duty to you by revealing it.) In such a case you might well ask him to promise not to tell anyone what he has learned. If there is nothing else you could do to prevent George from revealing this information, and nothing you can do to mitigate the effects of his doing so, then your reasons for rejecting a principle that would permit him to reveal the information after promising not to cannot depend on reliance losses of the two kinds I have mentioned.

As described, this is a unilateral "executory" promise, but the same point could be made by an example of bilateral exchange. If it would be advantageous for George to use this information in a way that would reveal it to others, you might make a reciprocal promise to reward him in some way after five years if he has kept his promise by not revealing the secret.

Your willingness to make this promise indicates the interest you have in his keeping the one he makes, but the reason you would have for rejecting a principle permitting him to break his promise remains the same as before: your interest in being able to make it the case that he will not reveal the information. Reliance losses of the two kinds mentioned above are still not an issue, since if he breaks his promise, and reveals the information, you will be under no obligation to reward him. This may seem to be a special case, but I believe that it illustrates a general point: one reason we have for wanting to be able to rely on what others tell us about what they will do is in order to avoid losses resulting from decisions that we may take on the basis of this information, but this is not our only reason.[8] I will call this more general reason the value of assurance.

In the examples I have just discussed, your reason for wanting the other person not to behave in a certain way is that this would make you worse off than you would have been in the absence of any interaction with that person at all (although he or she is under no duty not to injure you in this way). The value of assurance is equally well illustrated, however, in cases involving benefits rather than injury.[9] Suppose, for example, that you want to buy my horse, and that no other horse is as desirable to you. You make me an offer, and I promise to sell it to you at the end of the season. In this case there is no threat of your being made worse off than you were before I came along, but the crucial elements of the value of assurance are nonetheless present: you have reason to want me to do a certain thing; I am free to do this and would violate no duty by not doing it; and you thus have reason to want to make an arrangement with me that provides assurance that I will act in the way in question. Unless you had some reason to want me to do this thing you would have no interest in having this assurance. But since, despite this reason, I am morally free to do it or not, an analysis

---

[8] Dennis Patterson has suggested that my argument mixes ideas of expectation and reliance that are in fact incompatible. See D. Patterson, "The Value of a Promise," *Law and Philosophy* 11 (1992), 400. I do not believe this to be the case, but some confusion may result from the fact that I employ these notions in a different way than is common in the legal literature. "Expectation" and "reliance" can refer to incompatible standards of remedy for breach of promise, and to incompatible criteria for determining whether a promise is binding (is it binding if it leads someone to form an expectation or only if it has been relied on?). But as I am using these terms here they are not incompatible. The question I am addressing is the reasons people have for accepting or rejecting principles of conduct regarding the expectations we lead others to form about what we will do. The most general reason is that we want to be able to form expectations about what others will do so that we can be confident are correct. One important special case of this reason is that we may need to rely on these expectations in action, and we want to avoid losses from so acting. So our interest in reliance is one reason for caring about the expectations others lead us to form. But it is not, as I have just argued, the only such reason.

[9] I am indebted to Peter Benson for prompting me to clarify this point.

that bases promissory obligation on the value of assurance does not reduce promise breaking to some independently explainable wrong.

In their influential discussion of why the law of contracts should be concerned with what they call "the expectation interest" – that is, with making promisees as well-off as they would have been had the promise or contract been fulfilled – rather than merely with compensating promisees for losses suffered as a result of reliance on a promise or contract that was broken, Fuller and Perdue consider, as "perhaps the most obvious answer," one which they label as "psychological."[10] They refer here to promisees' "sense of injury," to their "degree of resentment," and to "the impulse to assuage disappointment."[11]

The value that I am calling the value of assurance is intended to answer a moral analog of the question Fuller and Perdue are addressing: to explain why morality should be concerned with "the expectation interest." (Although what I am presently concerned with is why our moral obligations should reflect this interest, not with whether it should figure in determining compensation that is owed when those obligations are breached.) The value of assurance, as I have described it, might be called "psychological," since one thing the people I describe have a reason to want is a certain confident state of mind about what is going to happen. But the value I have in mind is not *merely* psychological. What you have reason to want is not merely the peace of mind of believing that someone will not reveal damaging information about you, or that I will sell you my horse; you have reason to want these things actually to be the case. What I am calling the value of assurance reflects reasons of both of these kinds, but it is the latter that are primary.

Given the reasons that potential promisees have for wanting assurance about what others will do, potential promisors have reason to want to be able to provide this assurance.[12] In a situation in which both parties know that they have these reasons, promisors may seek to provide assurance by saying that they will do the thing in question unless the other person gives them permission not to. From the point of view of both potential promisees and potential promisors, then, there is reason to reject any principle that would permit a person who has given such assurance to fail to perform in the way in question (in the absence of special justification for not doing so).

---

[10] L. L. Fuller and W. R. Perdue Jr., "The Reliance Interest in Contract Damages," *Yale Law Journal* 46 (1936), 52.

[11] Ibid., pp. 57, 58.

[12] The importance of promisors' interests in being able to bind themselves is pointed out by Joseph Raz. See J. Raz, *The Morality of Freedom* (Oxford: Clarendon Press, 1986), p. 173.

If it would be reasonable to reject any such principle, then the acts that they would permit are wrong. This result is summed up in the following Principle of Fidelity:

Principle F: If (1) in the absence of objectionable constraint, and with adequate understanding (or the ability to acquire such understanding) of his or her situation, *A* intentionally leads *B* to expect that *A* will do *X* unless *B* consents to *A*'s not doing so; (2) *A* knows that *B* wants to be assured of this; (3) *A* acts with the aim of providing this assurance, and has good reason to believe that he or she has done so; (4) *B* knows that *A* has the beliefs and intentions just described; (5) *A* intends for *B* to know this, and knows that *B* does know it; and (6) *B* knows that *A* has this knowledge and intent; then, in the absence of special justification, *A* must do *X* unless *B* consents to *X*'s not being done.

This is a principle of the kind we have been seeking: one that goes beyond Principle *L* in requiring performance rather than compensation or warning. The reasons that potential promisees and promisors have to reject principles that would permit the actions that Principle *F* rules out are sufficient to make it reasonable to reject these principles, and hence to establish Principle *F* as correct, unless it would be reasonable to object to this principle because of the burden it would impose on those who create expectations in others. So we need to consider what these burdens might be and whether they could easily be avoided. One could, of course, avoid bearing any burden at all simply by refraining from voluntarily and intentionally creating any expectations about one's future conduct. But the availability of this option would not, by itself, be enough to rule out reasonable objections. A principle according to which the only way to avoid obligations that are as binding as those specified by Principle *F* is to avoid voluntarily creating any expectations at all about one's future conduct would be too limiting. It would mean, for example, that we could never tell people what we intend to do without being bound to seek their permission before taking a different course of action.

Principle *F* does not have this effect, however, since it applies only when *A* has acted with the aim of assuring *B* that *A* will do *X* unless *B* consents to *A*'s not doing so, when *A* knows that *B* wants this assurance, and when this and other features of the situation are mutual knowledge.[13] No

---

[13] In the absence of these conditions, *A* might still have some obligations to *B*, including at least obligations of the weaker kinds specified by Principles *D* and *L*. Since my aim is to show how full-fledged promises can be accounted for on a noninstitutional basis, I leave aside the question of whether *F* might be supplemented by a principle specifying that *A* has a stronger obligation of the kind provided by *F* if *A* has unintentionally given *B* good reason to believe that conditions of *F* are fulfilled.

one could reasonably object to a principle that, when these conditions are fulfilled, imposes a duty to provide a warning at the time of creating the expectation if one does not intend to be bound – to say, "This is my present intention, but of course I may change my mind," or to make this clear in some other way if it is not already clear in the context. Since the burden of such a duty to warn is so slight, and the advantages of being able to enter into binding obligations are significant, one can hardly complain if failure to give such a warning under these conditions leaves one open to the more stringent duty to perform or seek permission not to. But this is just the duty stated by Principle F, since condition (1) of that principle entails that no such warning has been given.[14] Indeed, quite the opposite has occurred, since A has acted with the aim of providing assurance that he or she will do X that is not hedged in this way in a situation in which he or she knows that the difference between an expectation qualified by such a warning and one without that qualification is important to B.

I conclude that when the conditions of Principle F are fulfilled it would be wrong, in the absence of special justification, for the party in A's position not to do X. As in the case of Principle M, this justification need not take the form of considerations that *override* the obligation specified by Principle F. But there are cases in which this term may seem more appropriate than in the four examples I listed in discussing manipulation. For example, if it turns out that the thing one has promised to do would be improper or wrong because of the harm it would cause to third parties, then one should not do it despite having promised to do so.[15] In such cases there might remain an obligation, of the kind specified by Principle L, to warn the promisee that one will not perform or, if he has performed first, to compensate by repaying the cost of that performance.

---

[14] It entails this since A has led B to believe that he or she will do X *unless* B *consents to* A's *not doing* X. This is the assurance that A is said to know that B wants and that A intends to provide. But A would not have provided this assurance if A added the rider, "But of course I may change my mind and reserve the right to do so."

[15] A principle that did not recognize such a limitation would be one that third parties could reasonably reject. Under the form of contractualist moral argument that I am employing, however, these objections are to be considered one by one, not as an aggregate. That is, the question is whether any particular third party could reasonably reject the principle in question. At least in the first instance, then, only the harms to each individual are weighed, not the sum of such harms. This individualistic character is a significant difference between the moral framework I am employing and the ideas of efficiency typically employed in law and economics approaches. See, for example, the discussion of incentives in Richard Craswell, "Two Economic Theories of Enforcing Promises," in Peter Benson, ed., *The Theory of Contract Law* (Cambridge: Cambridge University Press, 2001), pp. 19–44. The question of how aggregative harms or benefits can become morally significant is discussed in *What We Owe to Each Other*, ch. 5 sec. 9.

When the conditions of F are fulfilled, in addition to its being wrong for the person in A's position not to do X, the party in B's position has "a right to rely" on this performance: that is to say, the second party has grounds for insisting that the first party fulfill the expectation he or she has created. This right differentiates the case of promising (though not only that case) from some of the other examples of expectation-creation that I have been discussing. For example, in the first version of the story about the farmers, I spoke of one farmer persuading the other that if the first farmer's stream were contained then it would be in that farmer's economic interest to help contain the neighbor's stream as well. We could imagine this persuasion taking place in a face-to-face encounter, although it is not necessary to suppose that the encounter culminates in anything one would call an agreement. Alternatively – and this is the possibility I want to focus on – we might suppose that when the first farmer sets out to get the second farmer to believe that he or she will reciprocate, this is done without ever speaking to the second farmer directly. (The first farmer might drop broad hints at the feed store about the problem of the stream, and give the loquacious county agent a detailed version of the story the neighbor is supposed to hear.) In this case it would be wrong of the first farmer to fail to perform after the second had done so but all right to fail to perform after warning the neighbor before any reliance had occurred. We would not say in this case that the second farmer had any right to rely on his neighbor's reciprocation. In performing first, he or she "goes out on a limb" morally speaking. But in order for this not to be the case – in order for the second farmer to have "the right to rely" – it is not necessary for the first farmer to have used the words "I promise." It is enough that the conditions of intention and mutual knowledge specified in Principle F be fulfilled.

Principle F is not just the social institution of promising under another name. To begin with, the principle is not itself a social institution – its validity does not depend on its being generally recognized or adhered to. The moral force of undertakings of the kind described by Principle F depends only on the expectations, intentions, and knowledge of the parties involved, and these can be created *ad hoc*, without the help of standing background expectations of the kind that would constitute an institution. Second, the conditions of expectation and knowledge that Principle F specifies can be fulfilled in many ways other than by making a promise. As the examples of the farmers indicate, this can be done without invoking a social institution (or by invoking a fictitious one). Promising is a special case, distinguished in part by the kind of reason that the promisee has for believing that the promisor will perform.

An established social practice or "convention" can play either of two roles in the creation of obligations of the kind described by Principle F, but neither of these is essential. First, a linguistic convention governing the use of the words "I promise" can provide an easy way for speakers to indicate their understanding that they are in a situation of the kind described in F and that they intend to be offering the kind of assurance described there. But this can be conveyed in other ways, without using these words, such as by saying "You can count on me to do it." Second, where a social practice of promising exists and promise-breakers are subject to social sanctions, this can provide the promisee with reason to believe that the promisor will behave as promised. But this incentive is not necessary. In what I take to be the central cases of promising, saying "I promise" expresses the speaker's intention to offer assurance of the kind described in Principle F and indicates that he or she is aware of and takes seriously the fact that if this assurance is accepted then it would be wrong to fail to do the thing promised.[16] So understood, promissory obligations are instances of Principle F in which the first party's awareness of that principle itself is invoked as the source of motivation that gives the second party reason to believe that the assurance offered can be relied upon. Not every instance of Principle F operates in this way, however. Some may appeal to other sources of motivation such as those mentioned above in my examples of the two farmers.

The idea that a social practice of promising involves certain rules that are conventionally established suggests another function that such a practice might serve but I believe does not. It might be that when we are deciding whether a given promise is binding or whether, for example, certain factors excuse the promisor from his obligation, what we are doing is trying to determine what the rules of our social practice are. But it seems clear to me at least that this is not what we are doing: whether a promise binds and what it requires are determined entirely by the combination of general moral requirements (such as the principles I have stated) and the content of the particular promise in question. Facts about particular social practices

---

[16] Insofar as it holds that saying "I promise" involves this acknowledgment that one is in a situation in which offering assurance involves undertaking an obligation, my account resembles P. S. Atiyah's view that a promise is an admission that an obligation exists. See P. S. Atiyah, *Promises, Morals, and Law* (Oxford: Clarendon Press, 1981), ch. 7, esp. pp. 192–3 (hereinafter *Promises*). But I would not say, as Atiyah does, that the obligation in question is independent of the promise and that the function of the promise is thus primarily evidentiary. In my view, by saying "I promise" one can simultaneously create a new obligation and acknowledge that one is doing so. Indeed, one can do the former in part by doing the latter.

are relevant only insofar as they are made relevant by considerations of these primary kinds (that is to say, only insofar as they are part of the content of the promise, or are morally relevant because, say, they affect the costs or the significance of performance, or nonperformance, for the parties in question).

IV. CONTRACTS AND ENFORCEABILITY

Even if, as I said at the outset, there are obvious similarities between the idea of a promise and that of a legal contract, important differences between the two notions are also apparent. While promises do not, I have argued, presuppose a social institution of agreement making, the law of contracts obviously is such an institution. Moreover, it is an institution backed by the coercive power of the state, and one that, unlike the morality of promises, is centrally concerned with what is to be done when contracts have not been fulfilled. In this section I will shift my attention from promises to legal contracts, and will therefore take up both of these questions: the question of enforceability and the question of remedy. I will also address the question of how the moral permissibility of using the power of the state to enforce contracts (or to require those who break them to pay compensation) depends on, or is related to, moral conclusions of the kind discussed above about what individuals should do.

This dependence might be thought to be quite direct: because individuals are morally required to keep their promises (Principle F), and are morally required to compensate promisees if they do not (Principle L), the power of the state can be legitimately used to force them to do these things. But the fact that some action is morally required is not, in general, a sufficient justification for legal intervention to force people to do it; and the rationale for the law of contracts does not seem to be, as this account would make it, an instance of the legal enforcement of morality.[17] There is, I believe, a connection between the morality of promises and the legitimacy of the law of contracts, but it is not this direct.

A second account of the enforceability of promises would appeal to the idea that while the power of the state is not legitimately used to enforce just any moral requirement, it is properly used to enforce individuals' rights, and it is legitimately used when individuals have consented to its use. The enforcement of compensation for breach of contract might then be justified

---

[17] As Joseph Raz points out in "Promises in Morality and Law," *Harvard Law Review* 95 (1982), 917, p. 937.

on the grounds that promisees have a right to compensation, and promisors, by entering into legal contracts, have consented to their enforcement.[18]

I will take a different approach. Rather than beginning with specific moral elements, such as rights and consent, I will apply the general moral framework that I have employed above. On this view, the use of state power to enforce contracts, or to require compensation when they are breached, is morally permissible if a principle licensing this use is one that no one, suitably motivated, could reasonably reject.

I will consider first the permissibility of enforcing the compensation portion of Principle *L*. That principle specified that one must take reasonable steps to prevent others from suffering significant losses as a result of relying on expectations that one has intentionally or negligently led them to form about what one is going to do. These reasonable steps could take the form of a timely warning, or performance as expected, or compensation for the loss that the person incurred as a result of one's failure to act as expected. Now consider a principle that says that if a person has led another to form expectations in the way *L* describes, and has neither warned this person nor performed as expected, and the person has suffered significant loss as a result of relying on the expected performance, then the coercive power of the state may be used to force him or her to compensate the other person for this loss, provided that a law authorizing this is established and applied in a system of law that is tolerably fair and efficient. Call this Principle *EL* (since it concerns the enforceability of *L*). As I mentioned above, what Principle *L* normally requires is compensation for the person's reliance loss – as measured by the degree to which his or her situation has worsened as a result of relying on the expectation in question. This constitutes an upper bound on what *L* can require but, as I pointed out above, the limit of compensation is even lower than this in some cases. I will understand *EL*, in the light of this earlier discussion, as licensing the legal enforcement of compensation up to but not exceeding that required by *L*.

The argument for *EL* has two stages. The task of the first stage is to identify the reasons for having such a principle (or, alternatively, the reasons for rejecting a principle which prohibited state enforcement of compensation in such cases). The second task is to consider whether, despite these reasons in favor of it, *EL* could nonetheless reasonably be rejected. The prima facie reasons for accepting *EL* are clear. They consist of our need to rely on others' representations about what they are going to do, and the reasons

---

[18] For an account of this kind, see R. E. Barnett, "A Consent Theory of Contract," *Columbia Law Review* 86 (1986), 269.

we have for wanting to avoid significant losses that can result when these representations prove false. These constitute reasons for *EL* because most of us would be more likely to have to bear such costs if we were denied legal recourse of the kind that *EL* would permit.

The next question is whether this principle could reasonably be rejected from the point of view of those whom such laws would require to pay compensation. If the law were perfectly administered, and unjustified suits for damages were never brought, then laws of the kind licensed by *EL* would not impinge on anyone who complied with the noncompensation parts of Principle *L*: that is to say, on people who, whenever they had reason to believe that others would suffer significant losses as a result of relying on expectations about their behavior that they had intentionally or negligently created, either fulfilled these expectations or gave timely warning that they were not going to do so. One cost of laws of the kind *EL* would permit (I will call it the compliance cost) would thus be the cost of constraining one's behavior in this way. Since legal systems are imperfect, however, and unjustified suits are bound to occur, even a person who complied with the noncompensation parts of *L* would still be vulnerable to the risk of bearing the cost of defending himself against unjustified suits and perhaps paying the damages required by mistaken verdicts. Call these the error costs of *EL*.

If the law is administered with reasonable efficiency, these error costs will be much lower than the cost of being left defenseless against losses imposed on one by violators of Principle *L*, as one would be in the absence of laws of the kind described in *EL*. Error costs therefore do not provide grounds for reasonably rejecting *EL*. What then of the claim that compliance costs alone make it reasonable to reject *EL*, even given the reasons in its favor? I argued above that the costs of complying with *L* do not provide grounds for reasonably rejecting that principle, given the burdens that its violations impose on others. The compliance costs of *EL* are like those of *L*, with the slight modification that what one will be forced to comply with, under threat of legal sanctions, will be an interpretation of *L* that is the outcome of some legislative and judicial process. Given the need people have for the protection that can only be provided through such a process, this additonal cost does not make *EL* reasonably rejectable.

This argument for Principle *EL* has elements in common with the two arguments mentioned at the beginning of this section, the argument involving the legal enforcement of morality and the argument appealing to rights and consent. But it does not coincide with either of these. The argument just given relies on the conclusion of the argument for Principle *L* – that is to say, the conclusion that the loss of the opportunities that *L* rules out does not constitute sufficient grounds for reasonably rejecting L given the reasons people have to want the protection it offers. But it does not rely on the conclusion that actions violating L are morally wrong (nor on the idea that because these actions are wrong it is permissible to make them illegal, or to legally require people who commit them to compensate their victims). So the case for EL is not an instance of the legal enforcement of morality.

But even if the argument for EL does not depend on the general thesis that if an action is immoral then it can be made illegal, it may seem to imply this thesis. If the fact that actions of a certain type are immoral means that the compliance costs of a principle, P, forbidding these actions do not provide grounds for reasonably rejecting such a principle, then, just as the argument for L led to a defense of EL, it might seem to follow that the costs of complying with a principle EP that permitted the legal prohibition of these acts would not provide grounds for rejecting such a principle.

This argument is mistaken on at least two counts. First, it cannot be reasonable to reject a principle permitting actions of a certain kind unless there are individuals on whom these actions would impose burdens, and these burdens must be appealed to in order to make even a prima facie case for the permissibility of legally prohibiting a class of actions. But the notion of wrongness that is characterized by this idea of reasonable rejection does not capture the full range of actions commonly called immoral, since this term is commonly applied to actions, such as certain forms of sexual behavior, that have no victims.[19] Objections to the legal enforcement of morality are strongest in just such cases, in which it is plausible to say that because there are no victims with claims to be protected, there is no need to have a mechanism for collectively defining these forms of immorality and enforcing legal prohibitions against them. Second, even when actions do impose costs on certain individuals, these costs may not be great enough to justify having such a mechanism. So the argument I have offered for EL does not entail a general conclusion about the legal enforcement of morality.

The argument for EL depends on the assumption that people have good reason to want to avoid uncompensated reliance losses, and that such losses are in this sense a morally relevant consideration. But it does not presuppose the idea of a *right* to compensation. Not every morally significant interest is a right. My argument also takes into account the fact that (errors aside)

---

[19] I discuss this distinction between broader and narrower notions of morality in *What We Owe to Each Other*, ch. 5.

people can avoid the costs of *EL* by making the appropriate choices, and it considers the costs to them of so choosing. But it does not rely on the idea of consent as part of the justification for legally enforced compensation. (I will consider the difference between these two forms of argument in more detail in section v.)

Like *L*, Principle *EL* applies to cases in which no promise or contract is involved. It would, for example, support the decision in *Hoffman* v. *Red Owl Stores*,[20] in which Red Owl was required to compensate Hoffman for losses resulting from actions that they knew he was taking in the expectation, which they knew to be unrealistic, that he was going to get a Red Owl franchise. Principle *EL* explains why compensation can be required in such cases without appealing to the idea of an "imputed contract."[21] But it also explains why appeal to the idea of contract might seem appropriate: Even when they do not involve contracts, situations falling under *EL* are *like* breaches of contract in involving responsibility for the expectations one has led others to form about one's future conduct.

EL also allows for legal remedies in most cases of breach of contract. If recovery for breach of contract were confined to compensation for reliance losses, and hence also to cases in which reliance has occurred, the moral permissibility of contract law would be fully accounted for by *EL*. But there seem to be at least some cases in which legal enforcement of compensation for breach of contract is permissible even though no reliance has occurred, and other cases in which it is permissible to require specific performance or compensation for expectation damages that go beyond reliance losses. So I want to consider whether there is a stronger principle, analogous to Principle *F*, that provides for these remedies. Identifying the moral basis for such a principle will put us in a better position to respond to doubts about expectation-based remedies (and distinctively contractual forms of liability) such as those expressed by Fuller and Perdue and by Patrick Atiyah, among others.[22]

The principle in question would be one that, under certain conditions, permitted the use of state power to enforce contracts by such means as requiring specific performance or the payment of expectation damages even when these go beyond losses incurred in reliance. As in the case of *EL*, I will

[20] 133 N.W. 2d 267, 26 Wis. 2d 683 (1965).

[21] Principles *L* and *EL* thus account for the phenomena Atiyah describes when he writes, "whenever promises are implied from conduct, it is often, perhaps always, the case that the conduct itself justifies the creation of the obligation." *Promises*, p. 174.

[22] Fuller and Perdue, "The Reliance Interest in Contract Damages"; P. S. Atiyah, *The Rise and Fall of Freedom of Contract* (Oxford: Clarendon Press, 1979) (hereinafter *Freedom of Contract*), and other writings.

proceed by first identifying the reasons for having such a principle and then considering possible grounds for objecting to it. Considering these grounds will help us to formulate the principle by identifying the conditions that it must contain in order not to be reasonably rejectable.

The situations the principle would deal with are ones like those described in Principle F, in which one person, A, offers another, B, assurance that A will do X unless B consents to A's not doing it, where A has reason to believe that B wants such assurance. As I pointed out in discussing the argument for Principle F, the reasons that people in B's position have for wanting assurance include the interests they have in avoiding reliance loss but are not limited to these interests. A's promise can provide assurance insofar as B believes that A will be moved to do X either by a sense of obligation or by a desire to avoid social sanctions such as loss of reputation and the withdrawal of future cooperation. Since these motives may prove inadequate, however, people in B's position may have reason to want to have them supplemented by legal remedies, and when this is so A may thus have reason to want to offer additional assurance of this kind.

On the other hand, people have good reason to want to be able to make promises, even about things that matter a great deal to them, without making legally binding agreements, and it would therefore be reasonable to reject a principle that permitted a legal system to make every significant promise legally enforceable in the ways we are now discussing. The principle I propose will avoid this objection by requiring that A must indicate that he understands himself to be undertaking a legal obligation to do X.[23]

This is part of the more general requirement, which any nonrejectable principle must include, that a person in A's position must have adequate opportunity to avoid legal liability of the kind being discussed. This means, first, that A's understanding of his situation must not be unacceptably restricted. Obviously, perfect knowledge is not required: a certain amount of uncertainty is an unavoidable fact of life and an essential aspect of many situations in which contracts are made. But it would be reasonable to reject a principle that allowed the law to enforce contracts that were entered

---

[23] Since my present aim is just to establish a conclusion about the possible legal enforceability of contracts, I leave aside the question of whether this might be replaced by the weaker requirement that A do something which he knows or should know will create a legal obligation unless he disclaims this intent, and A does not issue such a disclaimer. For similar reasons, I will not explore the extension of the principle I am formulating to cover cases in which one party negligently gives the other good reason to believe that a contract is being entered into. Even in cases that do not fall under this principle or its extensions, however, recovery for reliance losses may be allowed by Principle *EL*. (compare note 13 above). I am grateful to Richard Craswell and Jody Kraus for calling these issues to my attention.

into only because of trickery or because information that *A* was entitled to have was withheld. Second, a nonrejectable principle must require that *A*'s alternatives not be unacceptably constrained. Again, ideal conditions cannot be required: the point of making a contract may well be to obtain the means for extricating oneself from a situation one would rather not be in. But an acceptable principle must not allow the force of law to be brought to bear to enforce agreements obtained through coercion. I will say more in the next section about how this condition is to be understood. In stating these requirements I have used explicitly normative terms – "adequate opportunity to avoid," "not unacceptably restricted," and "not unacceptably constrained" – the application of which requires moral judgment. For reasons I will discuss more fully in the next section, I believe that this is unavoidable. (In particular, it cannot be avoided by saying that enforceable agreements must be "voluntary.")

The requirement that *A* indicate the intention to be undertaking a legal obligation to do *X* leaves it quite open what *A* takes this to involve, but *A* can hardly be said to have had adequate opportunity to avoid legal penalties for breach of contract if *A* could not fairly easily have found out what these penalties are likely to be. *B* also must be able to find this out: someone in *B*'s position could reasonably object to a law that provided a remedy that was much lower than the one he or she had reason to expect and on which *B*'s willingness to accept the terms *A* offered was predicated.

Finally, the remedies for breach of contract that a nonrejectable principle allows must not be excessive. "Excessive" is, again, an undeniably moral notion. It cannot be eliminated, but the contractualist framework provides a structure that guides us in interpreting it. The general idea is that a penalty is excessive if it is one that contracting parties do not have good reason to want to have available given the costs of having it. The requirement that contracting parties have adequate opportunity to avoid being bound, and thus to avoid whatever remedy is prescribed, provides a significant degree of protection against this cost. But this protection is not absolute. People need to make contracts, and they may fail to keep them. We are all prone to errors in judgment, some of us more than others, and even given "adequate opportunity" to avoid the penalties for breach of contract, people will sometimes have to pay these penalties. A remedy is excessive if it is grossly out of proportion to the costs and benefits that are at stake in the contract itself. (Imprisonment for defaulting on small debts would be a case in point.) This disproportion means that the penalties are much greater than what is likely to be needed to overcome the conflicting motivations that the contracts give rise to. Any advantages in assurance that they bring are therefore slight, and not sufficient to justify the cost of incurring them: if the threat of a serious harm can be avoided altogether at slight cost, then arranging that it will befall only those who choose badly does not constitute adequate protection against it.

Bringing these considerations together, the principle we are looking for might be formulated as follows:

Principle EF: It is permissible legally to enforce remedies for breach of contract that go beyond compensation for reliance losses, provided that these remedies are not excessive and that they apply only in cases in which the following conditions hold: (1) A, the party against whom the remedy is enforced, has, in the absence of objectionable constraint and with adequate understanding (or the ability to acquire such understanding) of his or her situation, intentionally led B to expect that A would do X unless B consented to A's not doing so; (2) A had reason to believe that B wanted to be assured of this; (3) A acted with the aim of providing this assurance, by indicating to B that he or she was undertaking a legal obligation to do X; (4) B indicated that he or she understood A to have undertaken such an obligation; (5) A and B knew, or could easily determine, what kind of remedy B would be legally entitled to if A breached this obligation; and (6) A failed to do X without being released from this obligation by B, and without special justification for doing so.

EF supports the permissibility of remedies such as specific performance and the payment of expectation damages (if these damages could reasonably have been foreseen at the time the contract was made) as long as these remedies are not "excessive" in the sense just discussed. (And they will in general not be excessive since they are, by definition, not disproportionate to the costs and benefits dealt with in the contract in question.) Like EL, however, EF is a principle about what it is morally permissible for a legal system to do, not a claim about what such a system must do or a claim about how the law of any particular system should be understood. There may, for example, be good reasons of policy for taking expectation as the measure of damages in some kinds of cases and reliance losses as the standard in others. The point of considering EF is to establish that the former is at least permissible in some cases in which the expectation value of a contract exceeds any reliance loss.

EF allows for the legal enforcement of merely executory contracts, but it avoids a common objection to such contracts because it is restricted to cases in which A has indicated the intention to undertake a legal obligation. It does not seem appropriate for the law to enforce every personal promise, such as a parent's promise to a child, even when the amount involved is significant. But the objection to such enforcement is undermined when the promisor has specifically indicated the intent to be making a legally binding commitment, and something important is gained by allowing parties to make such a commitment when they wish to do so.

Principle *EF* does not include any requirement of consideration: it does not require that *B* have given *A* anything or made any reciprocal promise in return for *A*'s undertaking an obligation to do *X*. My account does, however, identify several functions that consideration might be taken to serve. Consideration might, like a seal, serve to signal the parties' understanding that *A* is making a legal contract, not merely a promise. For this purpose, however, what *B* gives *A* need not be anything of value. A peppercorn would suffice. Alternatively, *B*'s giving *A* something (even a token) in return for his promise might be a way of indicating that the conditions of *EF* (or for that matter the corresponding conditions of *F*) are fulfilled: that *B* does want assurance that *A* will do *X* and takes *A* to be providing it by undertaking a legal obligation. Requiring consideration for this reason would be a way of making certain that "threat-promises" and other forms of unwanted assurance are excluded from the realm of enforceable contracts. Third, consideration might be a sign that the matters at stake in a given agreement are of sufficient importance to the parties to warrant the law's attention. For this purpose, if not for the first two, what *B* gives *A* in return for his or her undertaking to do *X* would have to be something of significant value.

These are three functions that consideration *could* serve, but each could also be served in other ways. It can be perfectly clear in a given context, even without any consideration being given, that parties understood themselves to be making a legal contract, that the assurance offered was in fact desired, and that the subject matter of the agreement should not be dismissed as trivial. So, although the account I have offered explains why consideration might sometimes be relevant, it provides no moral basis for the idea that it is always required.

Principle *EF* requires that *A* indicate an intent to be undertaking a legal obligation, and that both parties know, or can easily find out, what remedies for breach this entails. In addition to having fair notice of the remedies they are leaving themselves open to or relying upon, however, parties to a contract may have reason to want to be able to choose what these remedies will be. This flexibility can be provided in at least two ways. If the remedy that the law provides is the enforcement of specific performance where this is possible or, failing that, expectation damages, then the parties can achieve the effect of *A* having different remedy *R* if *A*, instead of contracting to do *X*, contracts to provide *R* if he does not do *X*.

Alternatively, the law might allow parties to specify, within certain limits, what the penalty for breach will be, perhaps by setting a "default" remedy which parties can modify (within these limits) if they wish to.[24] In this case then, whether it is the default remedy or some alternative that applies in a given case, this will apply only because the parties have chosen it, or at least have failed to object to it, given adequate notice that it will apply.[25]

Given this fact, it is tempting to say that in such a system the remedy is also based on a contract: that in addition to their primary contract the parties make a second "remedy contract" specifying what is to happen if A fails to fulfill this primary agreement. In my view, however, this is not a satisfactory description of the situation. First, if the remedy contract is just another contract then the question arises what is to be done in the event that it, in turn, is breached. (Specific performance seems to be presupposed.) Second, while a second contract could specify additional penalties that are to apply if the first contract is breached, it is not clear how such a contract could lower the remedy that would be appropriate in this event. To do this the parties would have to exercise some legal power other than merely making another contract.

I turn now to the argument for EF. Principle F itself provides no direct support for EF, since F deals only with what individuals should morally do, and says nothing either about enforcement or about remedy. But, as in the case of L and EL, an argument for a principle authorizing the enforcement of expectation damages may be constructed by both tracking and relying on the argument for F.

As explained in that argument, people have good reason to want to be able to make agreements that they can rely on even when they have taken no action in reliance on these agreements (perhaps because there is no way for them to do so). This is what I called above the value of assurance. Given that promisees have reason to want assurance of the kind I have described, promisors have reason to want to be able to provide it. Since the moral motives on which promises rely often fail to move people to keep promises they have made, both promisors and promisees have good reason to want

---

[24] For an example of this approach, and a discussion of such remedies, see R. Craswell, "Contract Law, Default Rules, and the Philosophy of Promising," *Michigan Law Review* 88 (1989), 489.

[25] It might seem that there is a difference here between default and nondefault remedies, since the latter must be consciously chosen while the former may hold even though one or both of the parties has failed to consider what the remedy will be. But on the view I am presenting there is in principle no difference here. Just as default remedies may (or may not) be arrived at by conscious choice and deliberation, even when a nondefault remedy is specified in a written agreement, one party may have failed to notice this. Just as in the default case, conscious choice is not required: It is enough that both parties had fair notice that this remedy would apply. For helpful discussion of this point, see J. Coleman, *Risks and Wrongs* (Cambridge: Cambridge University Press, 1992), pp. 166–73.

to be able to make legally binding agreements that are enforced in some way that provides this kind of assurance, and there is thus good prima facie reason to permit the state to do this. The question, then, is whether this use of state power is something that those against whom it may be used could reasonably object to.

As in the case of *EL*, the costs of *EF* are of two kinds: error costs and compliance costs. Error costs, the costs of wrongful accusation and wrongful judgment, will be lower than in the case of *EL*, since the line between making and not making an agreement of the kind described *EF* is clearer than the line drawn by Principle *EL*. So if *EF* can reasonably be rejected it would seem to be on the basis of compliance costs.

If the law is correctly applied, would-be contractors can avoid having state power used against them in the way that Principle *EF* would allow by taking either of two courses of action: they can refrain from offering the particular kind of assurance that the principle describes, or they can fulfill the assurances they offer. What *EF* allows a state to do is to deprive them of the opportunity to offer such assurances and then not fulfill them, even in the absence of special justification, without fear of legal intervention.

People in *A*'s position may have reasons for regretting a contract and wishing to be free of it. They may simply decide that they made a bad deal, or they may have discovered a better one. But *EF* cannot be reasonably rejected on such grounds. First, the main point of making a contract in the first place, both from the point of view of the promisee and that of the promisor, is to provide assurance against this kind of reconsideration, so a principle that recognized these conditions as justifying nonfulfillment would undermine the main purpose of contracts. Second, parties in *A*'s position are adequately protected against the cost of being bound in this way by the fact that they know, or have access to, the facts of their situation and the agreement they are making, and can if they choose refuse to enter into this agreement. (One of the justifications for nonfulfillment that an acceptable principle must recognize is that special features of *A*'s situation may deprive *A* of this protection.)

A number of writers have expressed doubts about the basis for legal enforcement of expectation damages that go beyond reliance losses and, in particular, doubts about the rationale for enforcing any remedy in cases in which there has been no reliance. Fuller and Perdue, in their classic article, maintain that what they call "the expectation interest" is much weaker than "the reliance interest" as a basis for contractual liability and that this interest in turn is weaker than "the restitution interest." They go on to ask the not merely rhetorical question, "Why should the law ever protect the expectation interest?"[26] In a similar vein, Atiyah observes that the grounds for the imposition of promise-based obligations "are, by the standards of modern values, very weak compared with the grounds for the creation of benefit-based and reliance-based obligations."[27]

The view I have been presenting responds to these doubts in two ways. First, the distinction between principles *EL* and *EF* acknowledges that there are different bases for legal remedy in breach-of-contract cases, and offers a characterization of this difference. The argument for *EL* provides a basis for reliance damages in breach-of-contract cases that is continuous with the grounds for similar recovery in cases in which there is no contract (and even no promise). It expresses what might be called the underlying tort-like

---

[26] Fuller and Perdue, "The Reliance Interest in Contract Damages," pp. 56–7. Although they regard the restitution interest as a stronger ground for remedy than the reliance interest, they observe that the two "coincide" in many cases. They write, "If, as we shall assume, the gain involved in the restitution interest results from and is identical with the plaintiff's loss through reliance, then the restitution interest is merely a special case of the reliance interest . . ." (ibid., p. 54). This involves a non sequitur. It may be true that the cases in which the restitution interest supports recovery will be a subset of those in which the reliance interest does so, and the form of damages they recommend in those cases may coincide. But this does not make the restitution interest a special case of the reliance interest, since the two interests provide different rationales for recovery even when they recommend the same thing.

The restitution interest applies in cases in which the defendant has received something as advance payment for goods or services he has contracted to provide but then fails to deliver. The rationale for recovery which this interest picks out is the idea that the defendant's claim to the payment received is undermined by his breach of contract, or, alternatively, the idea that it is not a good thing for people to be allowed to keep goods they have obtained unjustly, and better that they should be forced to return them to their rightful owners. The former interpretation seems to me a stronger one, but, whichever way the underlying rationale for state action supported by the restitution interest is understood, this rationale depends crucially on the rightfulness or wrongfulness of the defendant's gain. The aim of restitution may be like the reliance interest in being concerned to "make the plaintiff whole," but the reliance interest is concerned exclusively with this aim and is quite independent of the rightfulness of the defendant's claim to any benefits he has received or even to whether he has received any benefit at all. This explains why the range of cases covered by the reliance interest is broader, but also indicates that where the two both apply they stem from different reasons. This also may explain why Fuller and Perdue believe that the restitution interest gives rise to a stronger claim for judicial intervention (ibid., p. 56). In cases in which the reliance interest alone applies, the defendant is to be asked to give up goods to which he otherwise has a perfectly valid claim. So there is something that needs to be overcome by a reason for compensating the plaintiff's loss. In restitution cases, however, the defendant's claim to possession is itself invalid, and the goods in question in fact already belong to the plaintiff. This is what makes the name "restitution" appropriate: the judge acts with the aim of restoring to plaintiffs what is already rightfully theirs. For this reason, it is misleading to use the term "compensation" to cover what is done when acting in service of all three of these interests. The reliance interest is an interest in compensating plaintiffs for the losses they have suffered. This is true as well in expectancy cases where what is required is not specific performance but "compensation" for the failure to provide what was promised. Specific performance, however, is fulfillment of a promise rather than compensation for not fulfilling it, and restitution is, as I have said, a matter of giving back what rightfully belongs to plaintiffs rather than compensating for the loss of it.

[27] *Freedom of Contract*, p. 4. By benefit-based obligations, he means ones arising from some benefit received.

basis for such damages. By contrast, *EF* provides a ground for recovery that is unique to contracts and could fairly be called "promise-based."

Second, the argument for *EF* responds to doubts about this form of liability by providing it with a rationale, based on the value of assurance. As I argued in section III, our reasons for caring about assurance are related to our reasons for wanting to avoid reliance losses, but are not reducible to these reasons. Assurance is something that people have reason to care about, quite independent of what the law may be, but it is also something that legal institutions can support and protect. As I pointed out earlier, assurance is not merely a "psychological" notion. What people have reason to want is not only a certain state of mind – confident belief that certain things will happen – they also want to make it more likely that these things will in fact occur.

Laws of the kind licensed by *EF* help to provide assurance partly because the threat of legal enforcement of specific performance or expectation damages provides people with an incentive to fulfill the contracts they make. This rationale for these remedies thus has what Fuller and Perdue call a "quasi-criminal aspect." They go on to say that this makes a policy of enforcing expectation damages analogous to "an ordinance that fines a man for driving through a stop light when no other vehicle is in sight."[28] But this analogy will seem apt only if one supposes that the only interest in assurance is the interest in avoiding loss due to actions taken in reliance. As I have argued in section III, this does not seem to me to be the case.[29] The rationale that the idea of assurance provides for requiring specific performance or expectation damages is not merely "quasi-criminal," since these remedies do not merely serve to deter promisors from breaching contracts but also, in each of the cases in which they are applied, give promisees what they have wanted to be assured of (or come as close to doing this as is practically possible).

One reason that Atiyah cites for resisting the idea of purely promissory liability is that he sees it as an expression of the emphasis on freedom of choice that is part of the classical *laissez faire* moral and political outlook. Part of this outlook, as he understands it, is the idea that there is liability for another person's reliance loss only where the agent has chosen to accept

---

[28] Fuller and Perdue, "The Reliance Interest in Contract Damages," p. 61. See also Atiyah, *Freedom of Contract*, p. 3.

[29] Atiyah (ibid.) says, in regard to the idea that a promisee whose expectations are disappointed is thereby made worse off, that "Psychologically this may be true; but in a pecuniary sense, it is not." The assumption, which I am contesting, is that if the promisee is not worse off "in a pecuniary sense" then any reason he may have for objecting to what has happened must be a matter of psychology.

responsibility for this loss by giving a promise and that "if I have given no promise, you act at your peril, not mine."[30] On this point, the view I have offered represents an intermediate position between Atiyah's view (very nearly rejecting purely promissory liability) and the view he takes himself to be attacking (nearly limiting liability to cases where it has been consented to). On the one hand, Principle *EL* authorizes legal liability in cases where there is no contract, or even promise. On the other, Principle *EF* recognizes an independent basis of purely contractual obligation.

A second ground for Atiyah's concern about promissory liability is that the classical *laissez faire* view that he associates with it takes an exaggerated and absolutist view of the value of freedom of choice. This view, as he understands it, fails to recognize the case for paternalistic restrictions and ignores the fact that, due to "material resources, skill, foresight, or temperament," some people are more able than others to take advantage of freedom of choice.[31] I believe that my account of promissory liability avoids these difficulties. In order to see why, we need to consider in more detail how ideas of voluntariness and choice figure in the arguments I have offered. This is the task of the next section.

V. VOLUNTARINESS

It is generally agreed that promises and contracts are binding only if they are entered into voluntarily. Principles *F* and *EF* endorse this truism, since the obligations they support and allow to be enforced must be entered into intentionally, with adequate understanding, and without objectionable constraint. Taken together, these conditions amount to what would ordinarily be called a requirement of voluntariness. In this section I want to examine in more detail how this requirement arises, and what it involves.

There are a number of different ways of classifying actions as voluntary or involuntary, and these classifications have different kinds of moral significance and involve different conditions. According to one familiar conception of voluntariness, an action is voluntary if it is a reflection of the agent's will, that is, of his or her judgment about what to do in the situation in question. It is this notion of voluntariness (or something close to it) that is the most basic precondition for the applicability of moral praise and blame.[32] But this idea of voluntariness is considerably weaker than one that

---

[30] P. S. Atiyah, Book Review of *Contract as Promise* by C. Fried, *Harvard Law Review* 95 (1981), 509, p. 521.

[31] Ibid., p. 526.   [32] I discuss this claim in *What We Owe to Each Other*, ch. 6.

is commonly invoked when we say, for example, that a coerced promise was not made voluntarily. Even a coerced promise can be voluntary in this basic sense. Moreover, it can be true that people acted voluntarily in this sense (true that what they did can be attributed to them in the sense relevant to moral praise and blame) even though much of what they believed about their actions and circumstances was mistaken. What matters for the moral assessment of agents is how they understood their situation and what they took to be a sufficient reason for acting in a certain way in that situation as they understood it.

A different way of assessing the conditions under which an agent acts is involved in the idea that individuals are likely to be the best judges of their own welfare, and that a person's choices, as long as they are informed and not constrained, are therefore likely to be a good indication of the outcomes that are best from that person's point of view. It follows from this idea that if efficiency is a morally significant goal, then it will matter morally whether agents' choices are voluntary in this stronger sense – that is to say, informed and unconstrained – since it will be a good thing morally speaking to let individuals make their own choices when these conditions are fulfilled, but not necessarily a good thing (at least not for this reason) when they are not.[33]

It is obvious why it should matter, from this efficiency-based point of view, whether an agent is well-informed. People are likely to make better choices among outcomes if they have the relevant information about these outcomes. Duress, however, is another matter. The requirement that there be no duress means that no penalties can be attached to choosing any of the alternatives. Since attaching such penalties amounts to changing what the alternative outcomes are, the assumption that agents are the best judges of their own welfare would indicate that they would also be the best judges of these changed alternatives. But the latter choice, insofar as it was affected by these penalties, might not be a good indication as to which of the original alternatives was best for the agent. So the reason for ruling out duress comes down to the idea that in order for an agent's choice to indicate which, among a given set of alternative outcomes, is best for him, it must be a choice among *those* alternatives, not some altered set.

The account that I am offering of the moral significance of choice and voluntariness is similar to this efficiency-based rationale but differs from it in starting from the point of view of the agent. The basic idea of my account is what I call the value of choice: that is to say, the value for an

---

[33] This idea is invoked in Craswell, "Two Economic Theories of Enforcing Promises," pp. 24, 37–9.

agent of having what happens (including what obligations are incurred) depend on how he or she responds when presented with a set of alternatives under certain conditions.[34] Many different factors go into determining this value. These include, but are not limited to, the values of the alternatives the agent can choose and the significance of having these outcomes occur by virtue of his or her having chosen them. The value of a choice also depends on whether, under the conditions in question, the agent would be able to think clearly, and would have, or know how to get easily, the information necessary to make a reliable choice. Usually, but not invariably, the value of a choice is enhanced by the addition of alternatives, provided that they are ones that the agent might want to realize. Often, the value of having a certain choice is decreased by having alternatives removed, or by duress (that is, by the addition of penalties that make certain alternatives less attractive). But this is not always so: given that we are imperfect choosers, we may have good reason to prefer choosing in a situation in which certain alternatives with long-range bad consequences have been made unavailable, or more immediately unattractive. Thus, when paternalism is justified – when it is legitimate to restrict choices "for the agent's own good" or to treat choices as lacking their usual moral significance – this is so because in these cases unconstrained choices lack their normal value for the agent rather than simply because this value is overridden by other considerations.

The value of choice is not a conception of voluntariness. Nor have I appealed to the notion of voluntariness to explain what makes a choice more or less valuable from an agent's point of view. Rather, I have appealed to such things as the value and significance of the alternatives and the influence of various conditions on the choice one is likely to make. Since these are factors that play a role in various ideas of voluntariness, a moral argument based on them may reach the same conclusion that would be reached by appealing to one of these notions. But, as I will now explain, it need not proceed by way of any such appeal.

So far, I have not described the value of choice in moral terms, but rather in terms of what an individual has reasons to want. But these reasons take on moral significance within the kind of moral argument I have been presenting because they figure in determining the strength of the reasons

---

[34] I develop this account in more detail in "The Significance of Choice," in S. McMurrin, ed., *The Tanner Lectures on Human Values*, vol. 8 (Salt Lake City: University of Utah Press, 1988), and in *What We Owe to Each Other*, ch. 6. The strategy I follow was laid out in H. L. A. Hart, "Legal Responsibility and Excuses," in *Punishment and Responsibility: Essays in the Philosophy of Law by H. L. A. Hart* (Oxford: Oxford University Press, 1968).

that various individuals may have for rejecting or not rejecting principles of the kinds I have listed above. This happens in two ways.

First, because people have reason to want certain alternatives to be available to them (under the right conditions) they have prima facie reason to favor principles that provide these alternatives (as Principle *F* does, for example), and prima facie reason to reject principles that would deny them the opportunity to make these choices or would permit others to interfere with this opportunity. Recognizing the value of choice in this way does not involve singling out "freedom of choice," or "freedom of contract" as a paramount value that is never, or almost never, to be interfered with. The value of choice as I understand it is highly variable, depending on the choice in question and the alternatives under which it is to be made. (Some choices have negative value.) Moreover, this value is only one kind of reason among the many that figure in determining whether a principle can reasonably be rejected.

Second, the value of choice as a protection against unwanted outcomes can reduce the force of individuals' reasons to reject a principle. If a person has good reason not to want a certain thing to occur, and a given principle would allow others to behave in ways that would bring that thing about, then this gives that person prima facie reason to reject that principle. But if the outcome in question is one that the person could easily avoid by choosing appropriately (or if the principle would license others to bring it about only if that person chose, under favorable conditions, to permit them to do so), then the force of this objection may be reduced or even eliminated.[35] It is generally worse to be faced with having an unwanted outcome occur whatever one does than to be faced with having it occur only if one does not choose to prevent it.

The value of choice figured in both of these ways in the arguments I gave above for Principles *F* and *EF*. On the one hand, positively, potential promisors and promisees have reason to favor these principles because they provide opportunities to choose to give and receive assurance that they have reason to want. On the other hand, potential promisors' objections to being bound in ways they would not like are greatly weakened by the fact that they will be bound only if they choose to be so under the appropriate conditions. The value of choice also figured in this second way in the arguments for

---

[35] I say "may be," since it depends on the choice in question and the conditions under which it would be made. As we saw above in discussing "excessive" penalties for breach of contract, the fact that an agent could avoid a certain outcome by choosing appropriately does not necessarily eliminate his objection to a principle that makes it available. Given the imperfections of choice, one may have good reason to prefer that an outcome not be available at all.

Principles *L* and *EL*, since it was an important part of those arguments that individuals could avoid being obligated to compensate others by taking due care about the expectations they create or by giving timely warnings. Thus, in one important way, the idea of choice plays the same role in the case for the "tort-like" principle *EL* and the case for the "promissory" principle *EF*. In this respect, the difference between the arguments for the two principles is a matter of degree rather than a sharp difference in kind, although the value of choice does also play a second, "positive" role in the case for *EF*.

As I said at the beginning of this section, this line of argument supports the familiar conclusion that promises are binding, and can be enforced, only if they are entered into voluntarily. But if we ask what "voluntariness" amounts to here, it turns out that a choice is voluntary in the relevant sense just in case the circumstances under which it was made are ones such that no one could reasonably reject a principle that took choices made under those conditions to create binding (or enforceable) obligations. The relevant notion of voluntariness is thus given its shape by the argument for the principle in question rather than being an independently specifiable notion that is appealed to in that argument. What is appealed to in the argument, and shapes its conclusion, is not voluntariness but the value of choice.

An alternative approach would begin with a conception of when a choice is voluntary – for example, with the idea that a choice is voluntary if it expresses the agent's genuine will – and with the moral principle that if a choice is voluntary in that sense then it confers moral legitimacy on its outcome. We might say, for example, that a choice is voluntary in the relevant sense if it is voluntary in the basic sense required for moral responsibility and is made under conditions in which the agent has, and is aware of, acceptable alternatives to so choosing. But this runs into familiar difficulties. If we say that a promise to pay a robber is not voluntary, because the only alternative to making it was immediate, painful death, what are we to say about a promise to pay a surgeon for an operation, the only alternative to which is equally grim?[36] (A similar question might be raised about a treaty entered into at the end of a war by the defeated nation.)

On the view I am proposing, we address these questions by asking, for example, whether it would be reasonable to reject a principle requiring one to keep a promise to a robber, made under threat of death. The idea of the value of choice enters into the answers to these questions in two ways. First,

---

[36] The example given by Hume, *A Treatise on Human Nature*, book III, part II, sec. v., esp. p. 525.

part of the case for the nonrejectability of Principle *F*, for example, lay in the fact that the obligations it imposes on promisors are ones that they can avoid by refusing to promise. In this case, the robber's threat makes that option much less attractive, so a principle requring one to keep the promise to the robber would in this respect be more open to objection. But second, such a principle, by making it possible to enter into a binding commitment under such conditions, also makes available an option one might very much want to have (or might want not to have, since it gives robbers incentive to ask for such promises). It may be unclear how these considerations balance out.[37] In the case of the promise to the surgeon, however, the result is clear: one has reason to want to be able to make such a promise, and to have it be binding, even though when one makes it one will "have no other choice."

But the reasonableness (from the point of view of the promisor) of rejecting a principle that would require one to keep eiher of these promises also depends on whether potential promisees have forceful objections to the alternative principle, which would permit these promises to be broken. Here a clear difference between the two cases emerges. The robber has no reasonable objection to such a principle. Since his threat violates other valid principles, he cannot object to a principle that prevents him from gaining by making it. The surgeon, on the other hand, could object to such a principle (at least if the fee in question is something the surgeon is entitled to demand).

There are, then, at least three considerations at work in these cases: the interest of promisors in being able to avoid an obligation by having an acceptable alternative course of action; the interest of promisors in being able to make binding commitments in some cases even when they lack such alternatives; and the varying strength of the interests of promisees in being able to rely on assurances they are given. The first two considerations may cancel each other out in some cases. Whether or not they do this in the cases we have been considering, these cases are distinguished by a decisive difference of the third kind.[38]

---

[37] Deciding how they balance out is a matter of assessing the relative strength of reasons for wanting to have certain options available. It is not a question about the "will" or preferences of any particular promisor: whether I am or am not bound by such a promise does not depend on whether I in particular would prefer to be able to make it or not.

[38] On the account I am proposing, the "voluntariness" of an action under given conditions depends on whether it would be reasonable to reject a principle that attached certain moral consequences to a choice under those circumstances, and this depends in turn on the claims of others as well as those of the agent in question. I am thus in general agreement with the view proposed by Anthony

If this analysis is correct, then it is not mistaken but nonetheless somewhat misleading to say that what we should ask in such cases is whether the promise was or was not made voluntarily. Because this same term is also used to denote the basic condition of moral attributability, its use in this context suggests that what is at issue here is simply whether the promisor's action reflected his or her will, and whether this will was or was not constrained by lack of knowledge or absence of acceptable alternatives. But if voluntariness were a matter of the agent's will and the degree to which it is constrained by the unavailability of alternatives then we would have to say either that the promise to the robber and the promise to the surgeon are both voluntary (although the first may be invalid for other reasons) or that neither is voluntary (but the second is valid nonetheless). But "voluntariness" is commonly used to distinguish between such cases: a promise is called voluntary if and only if the circumstances under which it was made do not constitute a decisive objection to taking it to be binding. I have no objection to this way of speaking as long as it is understood that when "voluntary" is used in this way an action is voluntary just in case it was made under conditions such that a person could not reasonably reject a principle according to which actions made under those conditions have moral consequences of the kind in question.

This is why, in stating principles F and EF, I have specified that A acts intentionally, in the absence of objectionable constraint, and with adequate understanding of his situation (or the ability to acquire such understanding) rather than saying that what A does is voluntary. As the examples I have just discussed indicate, there is no simple way to spell out which limits of an agent's options are objectionable. Similar difficulties prevent us from specifying, in non-normative terms, what constitutes "adequate" access to information about one's situation. Thus, in order to defend a particular law of contracts as legitimate under EF, one must argue that the exceptions it recognizes ensure that the contracts it would hold to be binding would not include ones made under objectionable constraint or ones in which a person's lack of information or impaired capacity to deliberate was being taken advantage of in unacceptable ways. This illustrates how the idea of the value of choice can explain the positive value and moral significance of having a choice in a way that does not lead to absolutist conclusions of the kind that Atiyah rightly objects to.

Kronman in "Contract Law and Distributive Justice," *Yale Law Journal* 89 (1980), 472. I would not say, however, that assessing whether an action is "voluntary" in this sense (e.g. whether it can be taken to create a binding or enforceable commitment) is in general a question of distributive justice.

VI. CONCLUSION

In this essay I have tried to do the following things. I have presented a series of principles governing our behavior toward others whom we have led to form expectations about what we are going to do, and have argued for the validity of these principles within a contractualist conception of right and wrong. The principles I argued for explain how promises can be morally binding, and show that promissory obligations do not require the existence of a social practice of agreement making. I then went on to argue, within this same framework, for the validity of principles permitting the legal enforcement of promises and other related obligations. Finally, I tried to explain how the requirement that promises and contracts must be voluntary in order to be binding arises, within the contractualist framework I have been presupposing, from what I have called the value of choice. The idea of choice is often given special moral status – both in the form of the licensing power of consent, which is often taken as a basic moral axiom, and in the form of the idea of freedom of contract, which is taken as a value deserving special protection. I have tried to show how the value of choice can account for the moral significance that these notions actually have without giving them the special status often claimed for them.

Index